AMERICAN

HOSTAGE

A Memoir of a

Journalist Kidnapped in Iraq

and the Remarkable Battle

to Win His Release

MICAH GAREN and
MARIE-HÉLÈNE CARLETON

SIMON & SCHUSTER

New York • London • Toronto • Sydney

SIMON & SCHUSTER
Rockefeller Center
1230 Avenue of the Americas
New York, NY 10020

The names of some individuals have been changed.
All dialogue with the kidnappers takes place in Arabic
unless otherwise noted.

SIMON & SCHUSTER and colophon are
registered trademarks of Simon & Schuster, Inc.

For information about special discounts for bulk purchases,
please contact Simon & Schuster Special Sales at
1-800-456-6798 or business@simonandschuster.com.

Designed by Dana Sloan

Manufactured in the United States of America

10 9 8 7 6 5 4 3 2 1

Library of Congress Cataloging-in-Publication Data

Garen, Micah.
    American hostage / Micah Garen and Marie-Hélène Carleton.
        p.   cm.
      1. Garen, Micah—Captivity, 2004.   2. Carleton, Marie-Hélène Carleton.
    3. Iraq War, 2003—Personal narratives, American.   4. Hostages—Iraq—Biography.
    5. Hostages—United States—Biography.   6. Journalists—United States—Biography.
    I. Title.

    DS79.76.G37 2005
    956.7044'37—dc22
    [B]   2005050041

ISBN: 1-4165-8631-8
ISBN 13: 978-1-4165-8631-9

This book is dedicated to our families,
the journalist community,
and the sisterhood

Eva and Chantal

And if you gaze for long into an abyss, the abyss gazes also into you.

—FRIEDRICH NIETZSCHE

You only understand the meaning of life when you stand at the edge of the volcano.

—AMIR DOSHI (ATTRIBUTED TO NIETZSCHE)

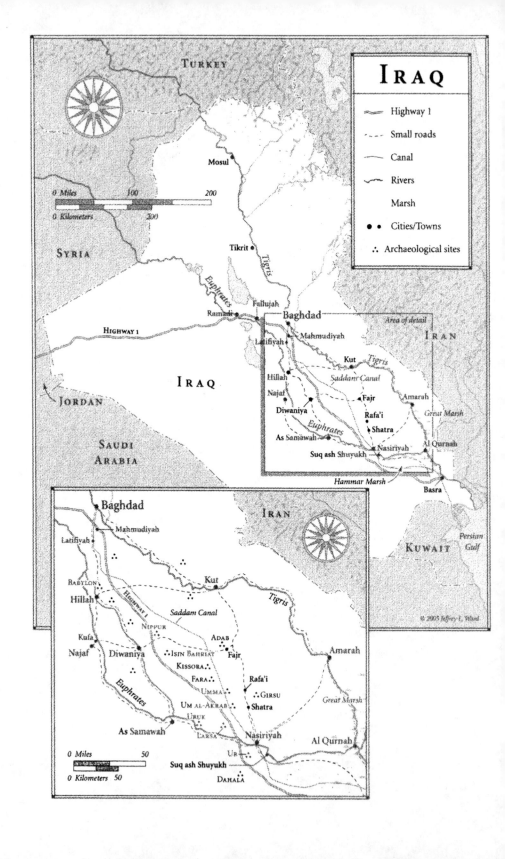

AMERICAN HOSTAGE

INTRODUCTION

In the summer of 2004, Iraq was descending into chaos. The U.S.-led Coalition was fighting a war on two fronts: the predominantly Sunni insurgency in the north, and the Shi'ite uprising in the south led by the religious leader Muqtada al-Sadr, and the militia loyal to him, the Mahdi Army.

There was a conspicuous vacuum of authority after the transition from U.S.-led Coalition control of the country on June 28, 2004. Iraq was officially sovereign and the reconstituted Iraqi security and police forces were expected to lead security operations for the country, but they lacked the training, weapons, and numbers to be effective. The Coalition had stepped back just far enough to create a void that insurgents moved quickly to fill, and many parts of Iraq fell under the control of fundamentalists or outlaw gangs.

Kidnapping and killing of Iraqis had been a problem throughout the country following the war, but videotaped executions of kidnapped foreigners, like those of Nick Berg and Kim Sun-il, had become the weapon of choice among insurgents trying to terrorize and influence policy among Coalition member countries.

We had come to Iraq in spring 2004 to make a documentary film about the rampant looting of archaeological sites and the tragic ongoing loss of world history due to the deteriorating security. It was my third trip to Iraq, Marie-Hélène's first.

Our journey took us back and forth from Baghdad to Nasiriyah all summer, where we would drive for hours and never see Coalition troops or Iraqi forces. Following the violent uprising of Iraqi insurgents and the Mahdi Army, security seemed to melt away in the heat, leaving us at the mercy of the roads.

As the summer progressed, the situation in Iraq grew steadily worse. In July, Muqtada al-Sadr's Mahdi Army took over the Shrine of Imam Ali in Najaf, one of Shi'a Islam's holiest sites. The interim Iraqi government and the American forces were determined to bring an end to the fighting and drive the Mahdi Army from the shrine. On August 5, the Coalition began what they hoped would be a final offensive against the Mahdi Army in Najaf.

Our film project was coming to a close as well. After three months of grueling work, Marie-Hélène left on July 30. I stayed for another two weeks, a total of five months, to finish a few interviews and film the first day of the new civil guards working to protect Umma, a heavily looted Sumerian site two hours north of Nasiriyah.

In the early morning of Friday, August 13, as the fighting escalated in Najaf, I drove from Baghdad to Nasiriyah with Amir, our friend and translator, for a final weekend of filming.

PROLOGUE

Micah, Amir, and I drove quickly along the airport road as it cut through a landscape, razed and desolate. We slowed to a crawl at a military checkpoint where a handpainted sign threatened lethal force if a car did not stop, then waited an hour in the sun for the only bus that drove from the checkpoint to Civilian Terminal C at Baghdad International Airport. I was heading home, and Micah and Amir had come to see me off. We sat near the front of the bus, framed by shattered windows. The driver tapped his foot to the tinny music on the radio and shouted at the few passengers over the clattering rhythm of the bus, "We were shot at last week. Let's see what happens today."

The previous three months had been some of the happiest of my life as I'd traveled between Baghdad and Nasiriyah, taking photos, shooting video, interviewing. Now my work on our documentary film was complete, and I was heading to Europe for a long-awaited vacation with my mother and sister.

We arrived safely at the terminal, but only Micah could accompany me through the metal detectors to the gate. I turned to say good-bye to Amir. He looked down and kicked his right foot back and forth.

"Amir, you have been wonderful. We couldn't have done this without you. You're a great friend." He continued looking down, holding in his emotion. "Promise me you will look after Micah?"

He squeezed my hand, so tightly it hurt.

"I promise, Mary-Helen, I promise."

Moving to the Royal Jordanian counter, I looked back once more. Amir waved, then turned away.

"It won't be the same," Micah told me, despondent, as we waited for my luggage check. There were only seven other passengers and one dog,

1

named AK by the contractor bringing him home to his daughters. "I wish I could come with you."

Micah had insisted on staying in Iraq for two more weeks to film some final scenes. I wanted him to leave with me, too, but didn't want to dampen the last couple of weeks of work with my concern. I had waved him off to Baghdad and welcomed him home before. Soon, I'd be picking him up at JFK.

"It's only a few more days of filming," I told him. "Don't stay longer. And don't do anything I wouldn't do."

Hugging him as long as I could before the loudspeaker announcement called me to the plane, I whispered, "I love you, I love you." It was the one thing I wanted him to remember over the next two weeks.

He stood and watched me, a hand to his heart, as I walked to the gate.

"See you in New York," I called out.

When I turned around a last time, he was gone.

The four-hour drive south from Baghdad to Nasiriyah was quiet. I kept my eyes down as we passed a Mahdi Army checkpoint on the main road just outside the town of Fajr, the center for Iraq's illicit antiquities trade. One hundred yards farther was a modest Iraqi police checkpoint. The twin checkpoints signaled an uneasy truce that had been struck in the Dhi Qar province, while just a few hours east in Najaf fighting raged between the Mahdi Army and Coalition forces. We drove past the two checkpoints without slowing down. They were a token show of force by both sides, a delicate balance. Stopping cars might upset the balance.

We arrived in Nasiriyah at ten A.M. and stopped outside Amir's small translation office in the center of town. Amir got out of the car, looked both ways to see that everything was okay; then I quickly followed him up the stairs with my bags. I didn't know where I would stay that night. I was no longer welcome at the Italian base and had not heard back from my request earlier in the week to stay at the American base. The local hotel for foreigners, the Al-Janoub, was too dangerous. That left the Nasiriyah Museum, Amir's office, or possibly his house, none of which were good options.

Amir told me to wait, saying he had good news, and went out, padlocking the door behind him for my safety. I sat on his old sofa thumbing through a worn copy of the *Norton Anthology of Modern Poetry*, one of many books that lay scattered around his cluttered office, the walls papered with pictures of Don Quixote, French philosophers, and works by local artists.

Amir returned a half hour later, smiling, holding my small digital camera. The camera was the smallest of the half dozen we carried, a pocket digital that could shoot a few minutes of grainy video, allowing us to film or photograph without drawing much attention or suspicion. It had been stolen two days before by one of the guards at the Nasiriyah Museum. Mr. Hamdani, an archaeologist and antiquities inspector for the Dhi Qar province, who looked after the museum, had managed to apply enough pressure and, in Amir's words, "the situation was resolved."

"Which guard was it?" I asked.

"Don't worry," Amir said, "your camera is back."

"But which one?" I insisted.

"The one who helped you look for it." That was the way things were done. It mattered less who was responsible than that the camera had been returned safely.

Since we had an hour to kill before a meeting with Mr. Hamdani at the Nasiriyah Museum, with my camera back we decided to film the market.

We headed first to a nearby Internet center so I could check messages. Public places were not safe for foreigners, but I blended in so well by now that no one noticed me unless I spoke: Iraqi haircut, the sort of beige plaid polyester shirt that almost every Iraqi man owned, and, most importantly, a bushy mustache. Amir sat me down at a computer and whispered to me not to say a word, then disappeared to run an errand.

Internet centers had sprung up all over Iraq shortly after the war, and were full most days with young men chatting by Internet phone or instant messenger with relatives and friends all over the world. Use of personal computers and Internet communication with the outside world was heavily restricted during the time of Saddam, so most Iraqis typed awkwardly, with two fingers. I sat quietly and checked for an email from Marie-Hélène. Nothing. She was traveling and it would be difficult for her to get her email, but the empty inbox was a disappointment. It had been over a week since her last message. Traveling in Iraq had always been dangerous while we were together, but in the two weeks since she'd left things seemed to be getting considerably worse. I wanted to keep her updated on my whereabouts, but since she had not yet replied to my last email, I decided to wait.

I sent an email to John Burns, the *New York Times* bureau chief in Baghdad, with an update on the road to Nasiriyah. We'd eaten lunch together the day before to discuss a follow-up article I would write about the looting. He'd been surprised when I'd told him that the Mahdi Army, a Shi'ite militia loyal to the powerful cleric Muqtada al-Sadr, had set up checkpoints along the road in plain view of Iraqi police checkpoints. It meant the Iraqi forces were clearly not in control. I also sent one to my mother in which I confessed,

```
to tell you the truth, i have to drive through
mahdi army checkpoints and sometime battles every
```

other day. . . . anyway, back early next week. i am
down in nasiriyah, where the mahdi army work hand-
in-hand with the local police. they are just kids,
and generally they are not aggressive towards foreigners, but it's good to keep a low profile.

This was the first time in six months I had told her anything about the
dangers I faced—perhaps because this was my last trip down to
Nasiriyah, perhaps because I was growing confident that I had made it
through my five-month journey safely.

Amir returned and we set out to visit the market. The civil guards
hired to protect the archaeological sites often carried their own guns,
purchased at places like the market. I wanted a few minutes of video
footage of gun sellers for our documentary about the looting of archaeological sites and the efforts to protect them. Nothing fancy, just some
solid background shots of a gun market.

I carried carefully chosen items, nothing that would make me stand
out as a foreigner, and nothing that would identify me as an American if
I was stopped. My glasses were hidden in my shirt pocket—you don't
wear them if you don't want to look Western—and I brought only the
essentials: my press card, watch, wallet, and the small camera. My wallet
held only cash, American dollars, as common as Iraqi dinar.

The market in Nasiriyah, just east of the main square adorned with a
statue of Habubi, a poet and religious leader who fought for freedom
against the British in 1915, was a few minutes by car from Amir's office.
Rows of stalls, shops, and street vendors' carts overflowed with com-
merce. You could buy almost anything there: posters of Shi'ite religious
leaders, video CDs of Friday prayers and recent fighting filmed by the
Madhi Army, secondhand books, Quranic texts, plastic sandals, vegeta-
bles, furniture, televisions, and satellite dishes. The part of the market
where guns were sold was a short, dusty road lined on both sides with
shops, easily missed if one wasn't looking closely. We parked and got out
of the car. Hatem, our seventeen-year-old driver, waited patiently in the
driver's seat.

The gun sellers discreetly displayed their wares on old wooden boxes
or cloths laid on the ground. We approached the first man. Trying to gain
his trust, I bent down to admire his pistols, about five of them, neatly laid
out on a box. Then, checking with Amir first, who nodded his head okay,
I cautiously pulled out the small camera and began filming. The gun

seller saw my camera and asked Amir if we could take a picture of him and a friend. I felt uncomfortable that they had noticed the camera. Was Amir nervous? He smiled and played along. The two put their arms around each other and smiled. I snapped a picture and showed them the digital image on the back. "Good," one said with a thumbs-up, to which I nodded my head and smiled. It was like swimming with sharks: unpredictable, they could turn on me at any time.

Farther down the narrow road, we passed a man standing next to a stool on top of which was a long, thick, black-metal tube with large holes running lengthwise. Genuinely curious about this monstrous piece of machinery, I walked over to look at it up close. It was some sort of machine gun with a bullet clip lying next to it that loaded from the side. I smiled at the man and turned to walk away. Amir suggested it was okay to photograph the man and his machine gun. Against my gut, I snapped a picture. The man suddenly became agitated. Only later would we learn that he had spent ten years in an Iranian prison and was mentally disturbed.

Amir immediately called me over to delete the image, which I did, turning the camera to show the man that there was no image in the screen. It made no difference. He wanted the roll of film, but my camera was digital. His face reddened, his body stiffened, and he began shouting. A crowd gathered.

Amir tried to reason with him, but the man grabbed the machine gun off the stool and loaded the clip. As Amir spoke he squeezed the trigger, firing a short burst at Amir's feet, the bullets absorbed by the ground in small clouds of dust.

"Take it, take it," Amir pleaded, trying to give the man the camera, but the man was fixated on me.

"Go back to the car," Amir urged me in a grim whisper.

Nervously scanning the road, I began walking, making it about five feet before I heard another gunshot, so loud my shoulders flinched and my ears rang. I turned to see the angry face of a man who had just fired his pistol in the dirt a few steps behind me, a clear warning that I should not leave. Amir was doing his best to calm the enraged man with the machine gun. With frantic motions—arms furiously working to control the growing storm of anger—he tried pushing the camera into the gun seller's hands. "Take it! Take it!" he implored, while yelling and waving at me to go back to the car.

The enraged man held the machine gun at waist level, pointing it at my stomach. I looked at him for a second as he stared back at me, still shouting, his hands shaking with fury. I was amazed that he did not fire the gun. How easy it would have been to shoot me at that moment.

Determined to get back to the car, I quickly turned and walked away, pretending I had nothing to do with the chaos. Young men were fast filling the street, drawn by the commotion. As I walked past the first gun seller, the one whose picture I had taken with his friend, he turned and asked in Arabic, "What happened?"

Afraid that ignoring his question would raise suspicion, I shrugged my shoulders and said *"Ma ba'raf,"* which means "I don't know" in Arabic. Egyptian Arabic.

I wanted to grab the words as they left my mouth, the look on his face confirming my mistake. The moment hung like dust clouds from the feet of children rushing into the fracas, then fell as he seized on my words, his face erupting in rage and excitement. Jabbing his finger in the air at me, he began shouting, "FOREIGNER!"

A spark had been lit and the market exploded. A deep vein—a history of oppression, tension, distrust, and hatred of the West—had ruptured, and emotions flooded the marketplace in an uncontrollable stream. Immediately there were men everywhere, fingers . . . faces . . . hands grabbing at me. A small child thrust his full hand into my back pocket until he managed to wrestle out my wallet. I saw his little face light up as he ran off looking at the cash inside. My glasses—I didn't see them go. A large knife appeared, held in the left hand of a man whose right hand gripped my collar. He looked over his shoulder toward the man with the machine gun for some indication of whether he should use it.

I was just a few feet from the car now, but the car was empty, the driver's door wide open. Hope fled, faster than Hatem. I thought of running, but I would have to break free from this man with the knife. The others had guns. I wouldn't make it a block. And what about Amir?

The crowd that had swarmed Amir caught up, and the two crowds became one teeming mob. I managed to push my back up against a wall, holding up my press card, shouting, "JOURNALIST, FRENCH, *FRANÇAIS,* FRENCH, *SADIQI, SADIQI,"* which means "friend." If I said I was an American I was dead.

"French?" a man asked. He was well dressed and seemed thoughtful, duly considering the commotion.

"NAM, FRANÇAIS, SADIQI." Yes, French, friend, I yelled, trying to reason with him.

"French, no *sadiqi*," he replied firmly, correcting me.

I thought, *Yes, yes sadiqi,* but his tone was so final and so full of anger, I realized it hardly mattered. My words dropped lifelessly from my mouth, my spirit with them. If the French, well regarded throughout Iraq, weren't their friends, who were?

Out of the madness Amir appeared, still shouting in Arabic, and next to him was the enraged man, still holding the machine gun. Pushing through the crowd, he came straight up to me with deep concentrated anger and said in staccato English, "I have an issue with you!"

Pleading with him, I remembered a phrase I had never used before: *Ana bisharbic,* which literally means "I am in your mustache." It was an Iraqi tribal saying that I had been taught by Munawar, our driver, translator, and friend in Baghdad, meant for just this occasion, when you are without options and you have to beg for protection. In Iraqi tribal tradition, if someone asks for your protection, it is shameful to refuse. To my astonishment, it worked. The man suddenly calmed down. He looked bothered that I knew the phrase, and so I repeated it again, advancing toward him, trying to convey sincerity, trying to communicate a simple message: *I meant no harm, it was a misunderstanding.* He moved away, absorbed by the crowd, and that was the last I saw of him.

But the crowd was out of control and he no longer mattered. They continued to press madly, tearing at our clothes and tugging us in different directions, like a giant rugby scrum, with no sense of direction or purpose. Amir and I managed to force our way to an appliance shop across the street, and I pushed myself into a seat facing the door. Amir tried desperately to get the owner to close the metal gate as the crowd streamed in. "What will happen to my shop?" the owner protested, afraid to help.

"Call the police, call the police!" Amir begged as he hung from the gate, trying to pull it down himself.

At least one person, possibly the man with the knife, had stayed close to me and was perched to my left with his hand on my shoulder. He seemed more focused than the others, cleanly dressed with short hair. Another man stuck a hand in my right front pocket, shouting at me as he tried to take my journal. We locked in a tug-of-war as I desperately held on to it and my seat, but he tore it from my hands, opening it violently, certain he would find something incriminating. There were two business cards from friends in the Italian army tucked in the pages, and I was sure he would seize on them. All that was left was my press pass and my watch.

The well-dressed man who had shadowed me said in English, "Come with me" and pulled me out of the chair by my shirt, a gun grasped firmly in his other hand. The crowd parted as he led Amir and me out. In front of the shop, a small four-door car was waiting in the dirt road. Two men with pistols pushed Amir and me into the back seat, the man with Amir getting in on his side. With the three of us, the back seat was almost full. My shadow tried to get in, but I kept my elbow out so he couldn't manage it. The car was not going to move until he got in and shut the door. The driver looked around to see what the problem was. After a few seconds, I realized there was nowhere to go with this idea and relented. My shadow forced his way in, half on my lap holding himself up by the plastic hand strap from the roof, slammed the door, and the car started off.

In the front passenger seat, a man with one deeply reddened eye was shouting furiously in Arabic and waving his pistol in the air, intermittently looking back and pointing the pistol at me.

"Amir, where are they taking us?" I asked in a hushed voice between the man's outbursts.

"I don't know. Be quiet."

I stared at the man's reddened eye as it flashed back at me in brief spasms of fury, unable to think of much but that eye—an infection he was fighting, rage against foreign bodies, and a grotesque symbol of the impoverishment and lack of health care in that part of the country.

After five months in Iraq, I was supposed to leave in just a few days. Instead, a new journey, not of my choosing, had begun.

Italy

Breakfast in the Italian villa was quiet, and Aunt Sophia's breakfast breads were carefully arranged on a cloth. I kissed my mom on the head, wishing her a happy birthday.

"You cannot tell your Aunt Sophia you have been to Iraq," my mother said. This was her birthday, and that was her wish. Nothing about Iraq is simple, she would explain. You may think it is about your personal experience there, or about culture. In the end, you can't get away from politics.

In my family, keeping things quiet is part of an old code of conduct that is perhaps unusual today. Identity does not come from public conversation but from private reflection. Family is strongly present, and the bonds tight-knit. Since our father's death, my mother had become the protector of our small family, always encouraging her two daughters to strive yet at the same time, trying to keep us safe.

"If you go, you could get shot or blown up," she'd say, a refrain whose echo continued long after it was spoken, reverberating off cameras and bags of film and the bulletproof vest, women's size, that filled my apartment as I prepared for my trip.

Once, but only once, my mother had told me about another reason. She was thirty-eight, married, living in Beirut, working at the United Nations, and had seen a tall, beautiful, blond woman in the souk, the market. Initially drawn to the woman as a vision of her unborn daughter, she has spent the next thirty-one years haunted by the memory. The woman was missing a leg. Do not ride a motorcycle. Do not go mountain climbing. Do not go to Iraq. You might lose your leg. Or worse.

Losing part or all of a child is unnatural to a mother, and I understood her desire to protect me.

I chose a different protection, the *hijab* of heavy, black polyester, a covering worn by women in Iraq. In southern Iraq, the temperature in summer can rise to 150 degrees. Merely blinking in the *hijab* causes beads of sweat to roll down your face, to be caught at the chin by the tightly bound headscarf pinned with the special silver safety pin concealed in modern, made-in-China plastic covers. It is a playful accessory, the *hijab*'s one nod to femininity. Any movement might make the *hijab* slip, and a stray lock of hair, if not tightly pinned, might suddenly appear and be noticed. Noticed as indelicate and wrong. And, by me, as a security breach.

In the south, Iraqi women, usually older, would take me for Iranian from the lighter skin tone of my face. They would often come up to me and grasp my hands, and say, "My regards to the shrine in Isfahan." This is how I knew that my *hijab* and the *abaya* that covered me all the way down to my ankles, legs hidden in thick, dark stockings, were working. My *hijab* and my *abaya* were my protection not only because they made me blend in but because they showed my desire to understand and respect Iraq's religious traditions.

Shi'ite Muslims are a small minority in Islam, but they make up almost the whole of Iran's, and 60 percent of Iraq's, population, living primarily in the south. They form a human crescent from Karbala, in Iraq, to Zahedan, in Iran, sharing the same holy sites and history of martyrdom and oppression. Iranian and Iraqi Shi'ites each year pilgrimage together to the Imam Hussein shrine that marks the site of his murder in the holy city of Karbala, and to the Shrine of Imam Ali in Najaf, where Mohammed's murdered son-in-law, and the successor to the Prophet, is buried.

A wisp of blond hair peeking out while taking a picture, or filming, would place me far from Isfahan—with the Americans besieging the holy cities, or the French, who ban headscarves in schools. The *hijab* and the *abaya* also gave me something else. I could work in Iraq, and travel between Baghdad and the south with them. They gave me freedom.

Is love protection or freedom? Out of love, I sometimes forgo things that are personally important so as not to hurt or worry those who love me. Sometimes, out of love, I act because I must and because it is important and meaningful, even if it is difficult.

The car pulled up alongside a building on the bank of the Euphrates River. The men, still holding their pistols, led us quickly through the gate and into a single-story white building. Amir and I removed our shoes at the open door. Young men were milling around, looking curiously at the two odd creatures being led in.

"Where are we?" I whispered to Amir.

"Sadr's office."

For a moment, I felt relief; the situation might be under control. Although American forces had been locked in a bitter conflict with the Mahdi Army that erupted in frequent battles throughout cities in southern Iraq, the Mahdi Army generally respected journalists' neutrality, understanding how good relations benefited their side of the story. The Mahdi Army office in Sadr City, on the outskirts of Baghdad, even issued press credentials to journalists who wanted to cover events there. While many Western journalists had been detained by Mahdi militants, including John Burns of *The New York Times,* as far as I knew, none had been killed. Besides, I had not told anyone in the market I was an American.

Marie-Hélène and I had carefully avoided the Mahdi Army. We were following the story of the looting of archaeological sites, not the ongoing conflict with insurgents. But the trail of looting in the south began to point more and more in the direction of militants aligned with the Mahdi Army. In May, during a Mahdi uprising, the Nasiriyah Museum had been looted and burned. Sumerian-inspired sculptures around the city of Nasiriyah had been smashed, particularly those of women with their legs exposed. The cities of Rafa'i and Fajr, hotbeds of Mahdi militants and Sadr sympathizers, were centers of looting. Anti-Coalition graffiti appeared, scrawled across the destroyed guard towers at looted archaeological sites. Recently we had heard that a hidden fatwa, a religious decree from an Imam, had been issued. Based on the third pillar of Islam, *zakat,* the purification of money, the hidden fatwa cleansed money from the sale of looted objects if the money was used to buy arms to fight the Coalition. There were even rumors that the treasures of the Shrine of

Imam Ali had been plundered while under control of the Mahdi Army. Publicly, though, everyone condemned looting.

We passed through the front door and were led into a room to the left. A thin man in a black robe and white turban sat on the ground at the far end, talking quietly on an old rotary phone with a cord that trailed off into the wall. We were instructed to kneel beside him. A young man leaned over and whispered in his ear. The man with the turban seemed preoccupied and paid no attention to us, never lifting his eyes. After a short time several young men lifted Amir and me by our arms and led us out past the door we had come in, and into another empty room. I moved to the back wall and knelt down on my heels, ready to spring to my feet, while Amir sat in the far corner.

A short, heavyset man in slacks and a button-down shirt entered. He walked with a pronounced limp and held a dark wooden cane in his right hand. Amir began speaking quickly in Arabic, imploring on my behalf.

"My name is Amir Doshi. We are journalists. I am a translator. Everyone knows me in Nasiriyah. Ask my friend Adnan al-Sharifi, the deputy governor."

"We are at war with the government!" the man with the cane shouted, cutting Amir off. Venomous anger coursed through his face. He punctuated his words by pounding his cane on the floor. Looking me over, he demanded Amir's wallet, which Amir pulled from his back pocket, his hands shaking. The stout man flipped through it violently, then turned toward me, asking Amir where I was from.

"America, America," Amir answered, in a placating tone.

"France, France!" I interjected, giving Amir a hard stare. I was dumbfounded. What possible reason could he have for telling them I was an American? Was Amir trying to save himself? I quickly drew my Paris-based *International Herald Tribune* press card from my pocket and held it out with my head slightly bowed.

The man grabbed the press card and examined it closely.

"Ana sahafi, ana sadiqi," I am a journalist, a friend. I said slowly and earnestly.

Amir began to speak again, more rapidly this time, repeating what he had said before. "We are journalists. You can ask my friend Salah al-Shimary on the governing council. I am a translator. Everyone knows me in Nasiriyah—"

The man thundered back in a voice one would expect to hear echoing from the loudspeakers of a minaret, not from this short man with the burning red face. The tone was brutal, an admonishment so severe that the meaning, without translation, seemed entirely clear.

When he finished, I turned my head in Amir's direction and spoke softly: "Amir, what's he saying?"

"He says America is the enemy," Amir translated.

Amir persisted. "We are journalists. We are working on the story of archaeology. Ask Mr. Hamdani at the Directorate of Archaeology. I work at the Directorate of Archaeology. Ask Deputy Governor Adnan al-Sharifi, ask Governor Rumaiath." Salah Rumaiath was the recently appointed governor of Nasiriyah; at one time he had worked for Mr. Hamdani as a civil guard at the archaeological sites.

Sitting on his heels now with his hands raised in front of him in an imploring gesture, almost as if in prayer, Amir continued to plead our case.

"We are journalists," he repeated. "We are working on the story of the looting of archaeology. Ask Mr. Hamdani at the Directorate of Archaeology. I work at the Directorate of Archaeology—"

The stout man's anger grew with every word. Amir continued speaking, more rapidly, but I could sense that he was crossing some invisible boundary. His words were noxious to this man. Outrage blossomed on the man's face, and I felt what was coming. He had to silence Amir, put an end to the lies churning from the mouth of this infidel. *Stop talking, Amir,* I thought to myself. The stout man walked toward Amir, shouting in Arabic, "Don't defend him, defend yourself!" With a backhanded swing of his cane, he struck Amir squarely on the jaw. The blow landed with a sickening crack. He had either broken Amir's jaw or split his skull. Amir crumpled in the corner, holding his right jaw with both hands, moaning. With my press card tight in his hand, the stout man left the room.

Children, fingers gripping the concrete, pulled themselves up to peer in through the small rectangular window openings high on the wall. "What's going on?" I heard one ask in Arabic. "Amerekee," another replied. "Ahhhhhh."

"*Nishrab damkoum!*" a child's voice shouted from behind the wall. We will drink your blood!

"Amir, are you all right?" I asked.

"I don't know. I'm in pain—I think he broke my jaw," Amir said, as he slowly righted himself.

That blow was meant for me. Amir had not tried to defend himself, willingly absorbing the venom and anger of the moment, and accepted the punishment to help me. It would be weeks before the selflessness of that act fully sank in. At that moment, I was fixated on elemental concerns: freedom or captivity, life or death.

I looked back at the window above Amir where the children had been spying. Could I fit through there? It must lead to an alleyway. Maybe I could run and get help.

Trying desperately to think of a way out, I remembered the words of James Longley, a friend and documentary filmmaker who had worked for several months in Nasiriyah: "If you ever have trouble with Sadr's group in Nasiriyah, tell Sheik Aws al-Khafaji that you are a friend of mine." Journalists often spent months developing trusted relationships with people who weren't necessarily to be trusted. Perhaps Sheik Aws was the key.

The stout man returned promptly, contemplating what to do as he paced back and forth across the room, my press card in one hand, his cane in the other. I had no time to explain to Amir who James was and why Khafaji was important. I didn't know Khafaji or anything about him, but he was our only hope.

"Amir, tell him I am a friend of James, that James knows Khafaji."

No response from Amir.

"Amir, tell him."

Amir tried, but the man ignored his words.

"He does not want to hear anything," Amir said, resigned, still holding his jaw.

The stout man ordered a young man nearby to tear a cloth banner lying on the floor into strips. The young man paused for a moment to read the message praising Sayed Muqtada al-Sadr scrawled across it in blue paint, then ripped it in half. He removed my watch, tied my hands behind my back with the cloth, and used wire to bind Amir's hands. Then he blindfolded us.

"Ana sadiqi James, James araf Khafaji, ana sahafi . . ." I am a friend of James, James knows Khafaji, I am a journalist. I repeated it again as the cloth went around my eyes, trapping my words midsentence in darkness. There was no response.

A man pulled me up by the arm, and I was led out the door. Disoriented by the sudden darkness of the blindfold, I struggled to maintain my composure as I lost my footing. Outside, patches of light flickered under my blindfold. I could hear voices and an engine running. I felt my way with my bare feet as I was pushed into what must have been a van.

"Amir?" I called out, afraid we were being separated.

"I am here," Amir said, trying to reassure me from behind his blindfold.

We were pushed down side by side onto the floor of the van, with our backs against a seat and our legs stretched out in front.

"Amir," I repeated, needing to hear his voice, needing to do something, to know what was happening, what was going to happen. Amir had no answers, but my fear compelled me to ask, to keep prodding with words through the darkness.

"Amir," I pressed, as if my words could somehow soothe our condition.

"Yes."

"What's going on?" I attempted to sound calm and purposeful.

"I don't know."

"Where are they taking us?"

"I don't know. Be quiet."

After a moment I tried again. "Amir . . ."

No response.

I stopped, worried that my constant questioning might make things worse.

As the van lurched out onto the street, someone pushed my head down. *Remain calm,* I thought. *Focus.* Which direction are we headed? How long are we driving? Like a trail of clues, those details might be the only way back.

In the distance I thought I heard the deep, muffled sound of explosions, like rocket-propelled grenades hitting a building. I wondered if it was another Mahdi Army attack on Nasiriyah or, perhaps less likely, the Iraqi police responding to our kidnapping.

A few days before the kidnapping, Amir and I had driven though a Mahdi Army attack at eight A.M. in the city of Kut, two hours north of Nasiriyah. A guard from the Nasiriyah Museum drove the small red Directorate of Archaeology pickup truck; Mr. Hamdani sat in the passenger seat, and Amir and I in the back seat. Traffic was at a standstill, which usually meant a roadside bomb or a passing Coalition convoy. We inched forward for an hour, until we came to the bridge leading into Kut. A

Mahdi militant dressed in black with a keffiyeh, the checked headscarf worn throughout the Middle East, and a Kalashnikov stood in the middle of the road directing traffic. The Mahdi Army was attacking the governor's office, and had set up a checkpoint along the main road so that civilian traffic could be directed away from the attack. The Ukrainian Coalition forces assigned to protect the city had retreated to their base and the fledgling Iraqi police were trying unsuccessfully to defend the government buildings now under siege.

The small red pickup truck turned left and followed a group of cars racing through the center of town, accompanied by the thunderous roar of rocket-propelled grenades hitting buildings and the steady pounding of machine-gun fire echoing through the city. Fighters dressed all in black—pants, T-shirts, and keffiyehs—crouched on either side of the road, some bent backward from the weight of heavy machine guns held in both hands, others with rocket-propelled grenade launchers propped on their shoulders. I wanted to film, but we were in a government vehicle, and I was worried that someone would see the camera. Mr. Hamdani stared straight ahead, unflinching, pointing out the museum in Kut as we sped by, while Amir looked out the window, nervously stroking his goatee. We made it out of the city and pulled over at a rest stop for tea about fifteen minutes north, congratulating one another for still being alive. American forces bombed the city later in the evening. Sixty-one people were killed that day and another 150 injured. I got out and looked at the side of the truck. Mr. Hamdani had had the foresight to remove the sign for the Directorate of Archaeology, Dhi Qar province.

A hand kept my blindfolded head pressed down to my knees as the sounds of fighting disappeared. Soon the van went over a series of bumps that signaled a dirt road. My wrists bound behind me, with my fingers I could feel a small hole in the bottom of the van through which a mixture of hot exhaust and dust was coming up. The fumes were beginning to make me sick. Maybe it wasn't the exhaust but the situation. I caught myself. *I can control this*, I told myself. *I have to find a way to break free.*

Information. I needed information—anything that could give some sense of their plans, intentions, weaknesses. Pretending my shoulder was cramping, I leaned forward and twisted my neck to signal I was in pain. A man sitting directly behind me began to massage my shoulder. It was an odd gesture, and I was not sure if his sympathetic act meant everything would be fine, or if he was being compassionate because he knew what lay in store for me. My hope for control vanished in the gap between those two divergent possibilities. I stopped twisting and he stopped massaging.

"*Shokran,*" I said, tilting my head slightly in his direction. Thank you. He patted my shoulder but said nothing.

The van stopped, the door slid open, and I could hear several people get out. There were voices outside. Then others got in, the door slid shut, and we drove off. A few minutes later we stopped again. The man sitting behind me got up, patting my shoulder one more time as he left. I had hoped he wouldn't leave, not wanting to lose any sympathy. The seat remained empty as the van drove off.

With no one behind me, I began working on the knots that bound my hands. Soon, with little difficulty, a knot on my right wrist was undone. As each knot came loose, my confidence grew and my resolve deepened. In another minute my hands were free. Keeping my hands behind my back, I brought my knees up to my eyes and carefully nudged the blind-fold down by pretending to scratch my forehead against my legs, until I could just see over the top. The inside of the van came into view as a haze of shadows and colors. I nudged the blindfold a little farther and details emerged: a man to the left and in front of me in a sort of jump seat with an AK resting on his lap; two in the front, a driver and a man on the passenger's side.

I cautiously felt around under the seat behind me for a weapon and found four long, thin metal tubes with sharp ends. Must be the barrels of AKs that had been taken apart. I felt around more. No guns, just the barrels. As the van came to a stop, I grabbed one and held it tightly behind my back. The door slid open.

"Amir." No response.

"Amir."

"Yes."

I spoke carefully and deliberately, so Amir would understand exactly what I meant with no need to repeat myself. The kidnappers might understand English, but it didn't matter; I had to take the chance.

"My hands are free. I have a gun barrel in my hand. What should I do?"

There was a long pause.

"Do nothing."

.   .   .

Part of me wanted him to say that, but I thought this might be my last opportunity to escape; otherwise I feared I would end up chained to a wall in a dark room somewhere. I had not made a run for the window in the Sadr office. Now we were in a van heading toward an unknown fate. We had to take control.

My plan was simple. I would take the sharp gun barrel and plunge it into the side of the head of the man sitting in front of me, then grab his AK and kill the two men in the front seat, dump the bodies out the door, and untie Amir. He would drive and I would look out for others as we returned to Nasiriyah. Or should I drive and give him the gun? No, Amir probably wouldn't fire it.

There was little chance of this actually working. I was plagued with questions: What was it like to plunge a metal bar into someone's head? How much force was needed? What if I just hit him and made him angry? How do you even fire an AK? Can you just pull the trigger, or do you have to load the thing? I was a documentary filmmaker and journalist. I knew how to interview the man, not kill him. Besides, I hadn't fought anyone since the fourth grade, and that was a wrestling match in the snow. And for all my plotting, I'd forgotten one simple fact: my glasses had been stolen in the market. I could not see beyond ten feet without my glasses. Amir would have to drive.

The door slid shut and we were off again. A moment of decision had passed, but the opportunity still existed. My hands were still free.

"Amir." Silence. "Amir."

"Everything will be okay. Be quiet."

Quiet? Quiet meant acceptance, and I was not willing to give up control of my life to someone else, even Amir, whom I trusted.

I thought about which direction we were headed. South toward Basra, east into the marshes, or north through the desert? Since we seemed to be driving roughly thirty miles per hour over dirt roads, I feared we were headed north. Any direction but north. North of Nasiriyah there were looters and militants. An hour north, Rafa'i, two hours, Fajr, twin sin cities of looters and militants. To the northwest was Diwaniya, where back in March I had narrowly escaped a group of fundamentalists looking to "kill the journalist." West of Diwaniya were Najaf and Kufa, where the Coalition forces had launched an assault on Sadr's militia. North of Najaf and west of Baghdad were Fallujah and Ramadi, western cities in the Sunni Triangle. Worst of all, between Hillah and Baghdad was the road through Mahmudiyah and Latifiyah, the Triangle of Death, where extremists killed any foreigner, journalists in particular. Since the beginning of the year the mounting death toll had been conclusive evidence: two CNN employees in an ambush, two American aid workers, two Japanese journalists, and a newly arrived veteran Polish journalist who had mistakenly put a PRESS sign in his car window. Any direction but north. To the north was Zarqawi, a shadowy al-Qaeda operative responsible for the kidnapping and videotaped beheading of foreigners.

I kept a tight hold on the gun barrel, gathering strength from the cold steel and trying to work up my courage. If they were going to kill me, I would fight back. If they weren't set on killing me, I would wait. But there was no way to know their intention.

Soon the van stopped again. The door slid open. Several people got in and sat behind us. My moment had passed.

By then, my blindfold had slipped down so far that it no longer covered my eyes. Trying to nudge it up with my knees, I succeeded only in making it slip farther. Closing my eyes, I lowered my head, hoping no one would notice. The man directly in front of me with the AK on his lap said something to the man sitting behind me, and I opened my eyes just enough to see him gesturing in my direction. I had been found out. I closed my eyes. The man seated behind me leaned down, slipped his arm behind my back, and felt my hands. Discovering that I had untied them, he became angry, and I braced myself for a brutal beating, or worse. He struck my right shoulder with a surprisingly light blow, just enough force to warn me. Confused, I couldn't decipher their intentions from their actions.

He retied my hands so tightly they began to go numb.

With no options, I became desperate. Some animals, when confronted with a life-threatening situation and no means of escape, experience tonic immobility; they feign death. I didn't know what it would do, but it couldn't hurt. I dropped my head back, held my breath, and stopped moving.

I felt a splash of cold water, and someone removed my blindfold. I leaned forward, wiping my face on my knees. A young man with large rectangular plastic glasses and a round, intelligent face looked directly at me and spoke softly in English.

"Don't worry, we are not Zarqawi."

Not Zarqawi? I was stunned. Just the mention of the name meant that Zarqawi was on their minds as well. The man across from him stared at me, holding his AK with an earnest expression. Why were they letting me see their faces, I wondered. This might mean they were telling the truth. I was a journalist; they shouldn't harm me. Would they release me once they checked my credentials, or were they simply saying whatever they thought would keep me from untying myself again?

"If you are innocent, everything will be okay," the man with the glasses added.

They retied my blindfold. *Innocent.* What did that mean exactly? Did they think I was a spy? Would nationality determine my fate? Was it possible for an American journalist to be innocent in their minds, or was being an American an automatic confession of guilt?

In July, when I'd interviewed the director of Nasiriyah Television, he'd recounted how, in the midst of a Mahdi uprising, he had been dragged out of bed by fundamentalists and put on trial in a Sharia court, a court governed by Islamic law, hastily set up in the TV studio. The Sharia court found him guilty of broadcasting pornography and sentenced him to death. In fact, he was guilty only of exercising his neutrality as a journalist, having refused to broadcast a propaganda video left by the Mahdi Army at the TV station a day earlier. His death was narrowly averted when the Italian army bombed the building that evening in a counteroffensive.

Were these the same people? Was I about to be tried by local Islamists bent on finding an American guilty in a mock trial? There was nothing I could do at the moment. I held on to his sincere tone, a lifeboat to keep my spirits afloat.

The grinding of stones under the tires was the only sound as we drove deeper into wherever they were taking us.

The van stopped again, this time for good. The door slid open and we were led out. I was angry at myself for having lost track of time. Had it been an hour? Two hours? A car passed nearby and our captors forced us to the ground—another clue. Even out here, the kidnappers had to keep us hidden. When all was clear, we were led barefoot, hands bound, across a field and then on our knees through a low passageway. They instructed Amir and me to sit, retied our hands in front of us, and then allowed us to remove our blindfolds.

The fading afternoon light illuminated our prison: a small natural enclosure formed in the space between four six-foot-tall date palm trees—dark, dense, and spiked like the top of a pineapple—growing closely together. Newly cut date palm fronds were stuck vertically in the earth as walls and laid loosely on the ground as covering. The leaves of the date palm trees came together in a dome branching out at eye level, the sky visible through a small opening where the palm fronds didn't meet. The entrance, a six-foot-long tunnel also fashioned from date palm fronds, made the enclosure feel like a sort of marsh igloo. With just enough room for two men to lie down, and hardly enough height to allow us to stand, the space was suffocating.

The kidnappers checked the restraints around our wrists, then went back out.

"Are you all right, Amir?" I whispered.

"I don't know. My jaw hurts," he said, touching it lightly. "I think maybe it is broken. It is painful when I speak."

I felt guilty that the stout man had struck Amir instead of me, but I didn't know what to say that could comfort him. There was no time to reflect on what had happened; we might both be facing something much worse.

"Where do you think we are?"

"In the marshes, somewhere."

"How do you know?"

"That is where they would take us, certainly."

The cold damp earth, a wind moving through the palm branches, the disappearing sun, the sounds of birds, cows, a car, and children in the distance provided some comfort, a reminder that I was alive. A certain calmness set in, a sense of resignation.

Then I noticed a dirty red blindfold on the ground. Amir looked wearily at it, then back at me. I wondered who had been there before and what their fate had been. The enclosure, the blindfold—these were experienced kidnappers.

On the ground near the blindfold was the familiar blue cover of a packet of cigarettes. I picked it up. Roseman.

"Amir," I said, showing him the name.

He made a slight noise of acknowledgment and perhaps surprise, then lowered his head, the heaviness of the situation too much for him to process this new information.

Amir was naturally optimistic. He wanted to believe this would end well. I was somewhat pessimistic, but my outlook came from being pragmatic, not fatalistic. My only hope was to somehow regain control, and the only way to do that would be to face the awful reality: captive several hours into the marshes, a used blindfold, and an empty pack of Rosemans.

Marie-Hélène had been fascinated with the colorful names of the different cigarette brands in Iraq, photographing them everywhere we traveled: Ishtar, Pleasure Lights, Miami, Souvenir, Gilgamesh, and Roseman. Roseman had a special meaning. At each looted archaeological site we visited, Mr. Hamdani would inevitably find packets of empty cigarettes left behind by the looters; they were a sort of calling card, clues to a group that routinely evaded capture. The brand of cigarette favored by looters was Roseman. In Mr. Hamdani's mind, smoking Rosemans was proof that you were a looter.

Four days earlier, I had gone on my last archaeological-protection patrol with members of the Carabinieri, the Italian paramilitary group tasked with protecting cultural history. The site, Dahala, just twenty minutes from the Italian base in Nasiriyah, had been heavily looted eight months earlier, and now there was evidence of fresh looting at a third-millennium B.C. burial ground. Mr. Hamdani looked grimly at each new hole. But he was happy just to have gotten the Italian Carabinieri to go on patrol, their first in more than three months. There were no looters to arrest that day, just recent remains left as evidence of how frustratingly close they were: shovels, teapots, plastic bags with stale bread, and an empty pack of Rosemans.

Had we been kidnapped by looters? Or was this just an ordinary pack of cigarettes, the last pack smoked by the man who'd worn the red blindfold? I found a small stick from a palm frond and tore off the front cover of the packet, about the size of a cuneiform tablet. The back was white. Digging into the soft, damp ground, I carefully used my primitive stick-and-earth pen to scratch a message in capital letters:

MH
ZEUG
LOVE

I put the packet cover in my left shirt pocket. *This will be with me for the rest of my time,* I thought. With Marie-Hélène and my dog, Zeugma, close to my heart, everything will be fine. And if these men kill me, I want to have some way to communicate, to say what I feel. To say good-bye.

Zeugma was our adopted dog. Marie-Hélène and I had found her on our first project together, a documentary film at the archaeological site of Zeugma in southeastern Turkey, in the summer of 2000. Marie-Hélène, Zeugma, and I were a little family unit. Crammed into a studio apartment in Manhattan's West Village, we formed a small nucleus of love and support, and faced everything together. I had fallen in love with Marie-Hélène for many reasons—her intellect, her beauty, her sense of humor, and most of all her kindness. People were always drawn to her magnetic energy and honesty, and her presence in Iraq had made our journey much easier, unlocking doors with simplicity and sincerity. Amir admired her for that, nicknaming her Dignity Candle. I wanted Marie-Hélène to know that whatever happened to me, I was thinking about her until the end.

Amir looked defeated. Was this his fault? We depended so much on the judgment of translators and fixers, people with local knowledge and connections who could unlock doors that we could never open on our own. They helped gauge risk, but at the same time were eager to please. Amir had said it was okay to go to the market and film. I knew it was dangerous, he knew it was dangerous. Why did he say it was okay? "Why not?" were his words. Why not? Because someone could kidnap us, that's why not. Why didn't I just stick with the footage of the market I had shot before? It was not Amir's fault. Ultimately it was my decision. But then was it my fault?

I knew that thought would be fatal. This was no one's fault. It was a risk we faced, part of the work we were doing. I knew the risks and had prepared myself mentally. We would have plenty of time to kick ourselves later, and the way things were going, we would likely have help doing that.

"Amir, why did you tell them I am an American?" This question had weighed heavily on me since we had been brought to Sadr's office.

Many journalists in Iraq from Coalition countries took refuge behind other nationalities, typically Canadian but sometimes French. It was surprising just how many Canadians there were in Iraq. Iraqi translators and fixers encouraged it, along with Iraqi clothing, haircuts, and mustaches, fearful that they would be targeted as well. Proud, mustached Munawar, who had taught me the phrase *ana bisharbic,* complimented me on my mustache as it grew bushier, a facial hedgerow thick enough to hide behind. "From Iranian TV," Amir would say as Marie-Hélène and I mutely nodded, not a word of Persian between us. In the first few months after the war, saying "American" typically elicited smiles and the comment "Good," with a thumbs-up. But now all we got were cold stares or worse.

"It is better to tell the truth. They will find out anyway," Amir responded.

"How would they find out? My press card is from the *International Herald Tribune* with a French address. I told them in the market I was French. Marie-Hélène is half French. Why did you say American? We talked about telling people I was French, right?"

"I don't know. I thought it is better to be honest."

I was deeply frustrated that he had said American. Everything might have been solved in the Sadr office. We had worked so hard to maintain the illusion of not being American that to just go and tell them seemed foolish. Marie-Hélène had dual citizenship, French and American passports. Moving around Iraq, we carried only her French passport and told everyone we were husband and wife.

"Please tell them I am French. If they ask, just say French, okay? Don't say anything more about my being American."

Amir reluctantly agreed.

It was too late anyway, but I thought it would be better for us if they thought of me as French-American.

I surveyed my surroundings again, trying to remember details from a two-page U.S. Embassy handout on what to do if you are kidnapped. I had read it while registering as a U.S. citizen in Baghdad at the Green Zone in June, hoping I would never actually need it.

Befriend your kidnappers
Be prepared for a long stay
Don't show weakness, they don't respect weakness
Look for opportunities to escape and take them if you can

Since America's policy was not to negotiate with kidnappers, I took that last one to heart. I interpreted it to mean that if you are kidnapped, chances are no one is coming for you. It was up to me to find my own way out.

The rustling of the palm branches was more than just the wind. Two men holding AKs, their faces wrapped in keffiyehs, emerged through the entrance, and ordered Amir and me to face the back. We shifted our positions as they sat down behind us.

Befriend your kidnappers. I needed to be friendly. No, more than friendly: ingratiating. They should feel we were their guests, not hostages. You don't kill your guests. We were honest, we were innocent, this was just a misunderstanding.

"*Salaam alaikum,*" one of them greeted us. Peace be upon you.

"*Wa alaikum salaam,*" And peace be upon you, Amir replied.

"How are you?" the kidnapper continued in Arabic.

"Fine, but I think my jaw is broken," Amir answered.

"Ahhhh." Not the American "ahhhh," pronounced clearly with a strong *a,* but a deep exhalation, more of an "oooooooohhhh." A response that meant many things: they were sorry for our situation, they were not going to let Amir see a doctor, there was nothing to be done but live with the pain, they were not too sorry.

"What did he say, Amir?"

"He asks if we are fine."

"Tell him we are fine and thank him for allowing us to remove our blindfolds."

Amir reluctantly translated my words.

"*Afwan,*" one replied. You are welcome.

I was searching for words, a dialogue, as I stared at the back of the enclosure.

"Where did they pick you up?" one asked, his tone quick and monotonous, displaying more curiosity than emotion. It seemed strange that they did not know about us.

"In the market," Amir replied.

"What were you doing?"

"Filming. We work for the Directorate of Archaeology," Amir said curtly. There was a great deal more he understood about them than I did. This was his country, his language, and these were his neighbors. But I knew that we needed to be polite, that we needed, against our will, to befriend them.

"Amir?"

"Yes, Micah?"

"What do they want?"

"I don't know."

"Can you ask them?"

Amir asked and I listened to their long response in Arabic, but couldn't understand anything. I had studied Arabic for close to two years, but in Iraq, dependent on translators and fixers to keep us safe, I had little opportunity to practice my Arabic.

"They want money."

"What?"

"They say this is only about money."

"I thought they will let us go when they confirm that we are journalists, that we are innocent."

"No, they say they are just thieves and this is about money. They say they are not the ones who kidnapped us."

Had we already been sold off? What about Sadr's office? What about the man with the glasses in the van who assured me they were not Zarqawi, that everything would be fine?

The tension that had been building suddenly released, like a dam collapsing, and a torrent of pent-up emotion swept away the foundations I had been constructing in my mind, leaving me both angry and relieved. Our captors were not religiously or politically motivated, just common criminals. I remembered Munawar's words: "Everything in Iraq has a price, *habibi.*" Forget ideology, forget being friendly, forget being innocent, and forget being a journalist. None of that mattered in this enclosure, only money. At least I could try to bargain with criminals.

"Do their words make sense to you, Amir?"

"I don't know. That is just what they say. They say they are not the ones who kidnapped us, they just want money."

"How much do they want?"

"Seventy thousand dollars," they replied.

"I'm a journalist. I don't have that kind of money."

"What about the company you work for?" they asked.

I knew my only hope for a quick resolution was for them to understand that I didn't have money and was of no value to anyone except my family, who loved me.

"I'm independent. The newspaper I work with doesn't care about me. My country does not care about me," I said glumly, continuing to negotiate, letting my words sink in.

After considering it for a moment, they gave their answer to Amir.

"They say they need money," Amir repeated.

"I have some money in Nasiriyah. If you take us there now I will give it to you. It's all I have."

"How much?" they asked.

"Three thousand dollars." I had three thousand dollars in a small envelope in my video bag in Amir's office. Three thousand dollars was about six times what most Iraqis earned in a year.

"Not enough. We need seventy thousand dollars," they replied.

How had they arrived at that number? Why not one hundred thousand? It must have been based on experience. My family didn't have that kind of money. And even if I agreed to seventy thousand dollars, they would certainly ask for one hundred thousand, or one million, maybe ten million. The sky was the limit once they thought I was a potential source of money.

In the distance I recognized a faint, familiar sound; a steady, resonant beating of air. No one spoke as the sound grew louder. Suddenly a green helicopter appeared directly overhead at about one hundred feet. An Italian helicopter—I could tell from the color, and that it was flying alone. We must still be in the Italian sector.

The Italian air force in Nasiriyah flew helicopters, the key to protecting the archaeological sites. Originally situated along the banks of the Euphrates, the sites now lay in remote desert, the river having migrated west over the past several thousand years. Overland, it took eight hours round-trip by four-wheel drive. A helicopter could make it out in less than thirty minutes and scare away looters for days.

Marie-Hélène and I had struck up friendships with several members of the Italian air force in Nasiriyah. The air force general often invited us to dinner, where we talked about everything from archaeology to our shared love of flying.

Had the Italian air force heard about our kidnapping? It seemed unlikely that they would know so quickly. I thought about how to signal to the helicopter, but the presence of two guards with AKs convinced me not to try. Oblivious to our troubles, the pilot was probably looking out over the beautiful marsh landscape, a deep red in the fading light, waving to the women and children standing in the fields, who would wave back when no men were around to notice.

The helicopter passed. I listened as it faded into the distance and silence enveloped us again. I made a mental note of the day, time, and direction of flight: Friday, early evening, left to right of my enclosure facing the back. This could be important information when I got out, if I got out. But it was of little use now. I had to find my own way out. As any hope of immediate rescue faded with the last sound of the helicopter, I tried again to negotiate.

"I may be able to get a little more, maybe five thousand dollars. My family does not have much money, but I can get them to send that because they love me. If you let us go now, we can give you three thousand, but only if you let us go now. Then I will go to Baghdad and get the rest."

"Not enough," they replied.

I paused for a while, thinking carefully before making another bid. "Okay. I may be able to get ten thousand, maybe, but I will need to go to Baghdad and contact my family. It will take three days for the money to arrive. Then we will come back."

"How do we know you will return?"

"I am a man of my word." I knew that wasn't good enough. Even I didn't believe it. Of course they would need something as collateral. They pointed to Amir.

"He can go."

I think Amir could read the terror that flashed through my eyes. Without Amir, no way to communicate and no options to negotiate, I would probably not survive.

It was a chance at freedom that I was certain Amir longed to accept, but he had not left me in the market, and I did not think he would leave me now.

Amir considered the man's words, trying to weigh what was best for both of us.

"Micah, I could go, but what will happen to you?"

"Amir," I said, "if you leave, I don't think I will get out alive. When they realize what it means to have an American, things will get much worse." I feared that the longer I remained captive, the worse it would be for both of us. Amir nodded; he was thinking the same thing. We were in this together.

Kidnapping of Iraqis following the war was rampant, mostly for ransom but also for political reasons, revenge or who knows what. It went largely undocumented, and ransom in the south was often less than five thousand dollars. Amir had told us about a man from Nasiriyah who had been kidnapped three times in the past year. Each time his family would pay a ransom, and they would kidnap him again.

An American was different. If these kidnappers were not associated with Zarqawi, how long before Zarqawi heard the news and drove down to buy an American hostage? If we were both going to survive, I reasoned, it would mean my getting out before the end of the evening. I would then bring money to get Amir out.

"Amir, if I don't get out tonight, I don't think I will ever get out."

"What do you think I should tell them?" Amir asked.

"Tell them my family won't send money unless they hear from me directly. I can go to Baghdad and get more money. It will probably take three days. Can you wait three days?"

"Yes, I can wait."

"You know I will come back, don't you?" I said, my hand on my heart.

"Yes, I know."

I tried imagining three more days in captivity. It seemed an eternity. Amir's courage was remarkable. He was calm, hardly a note of concern in his voice. Almost resigned, but not quite that; he showed patience and fortitude. What did it take to endure such a situation? Twenty-three years under Saddam. Stretched across the often inhospitable geography was a human landscape of unimaginable suffering, countless stories of tragedy hidden in the heat and dust. A man I'd met in Nasiriyah in June 2003 had just returned after thirteen years of exile and imprisonment in Iran. He was searching for his family, whom he had not heard from since fleeing Saddam in 1991. He had changed his name to Lucky because he had made it back to Iraq alive. Mr. Hamdani's brother-in-law had been a political prisoner for seven years. Even Mr. Hamdani had been imprisoned for six months. I didn't think I had the strength to survive three days in captivity.

"No," they said, pointing to Amir. "He can go, you stay."

"Amir, tell them that my family won't send any money if they don't hear from me directly."

"How do we know you will return?" they asked again. I sensed progress, and a possible opening. We just needed to convince them that I would return.

"Amir, tell them I am honest, I am a man of my word." I put my hand on my heart, an Iraqi sign of sincerity. "And besides, Amir is like a brother to me, I would never abandon him." I didn't think they believed me. An American come back for an Iraqi? Not plausible.

"No. He can go." They pointed to Amir again. "You must stay."

Frustrated with their responses, I decided to test the limits of the negotiation.

"Tell them to forget it then."

Amir repeated my words. They were not happy with my tone of voice. I had overstepped the line.

"Be careful what you say or a wolf will come in the night and steal your balls," the man said, and with that, negotiations ended. I had blown it, and felt sick thinking that someone might actually come in the night and cut off my balls.

They left our enclosure, pausing briefly to speak in hushed voices just outside.

"Can you hear what they are saying?" I asked Amir in a whisper. Amir strained to listen.

"No."

The voices faded, but someone remained to keep watch.

My failed negotiation exacerbated the oppressiveness of our enclosure, but how much worse it would be if we were locked inside a room. My fear was mitigated by being outside. In nature I felt connected to life around me and there were places to run and hide.

Be prepared for a long stay. I tried to remain calm, breathing deeply.

In the darkness I thought more about bargaining my way out. The three thousand dollars in my video bag in Amir's office was a donation from the Carr Foundation, a human rights and arts organization based in Cambridge, Massachusetts. The Carr Foundation had funded our documentary film and had recently decided to support Mr. Hamdani's effort to protect the sites. The money was the second installment for salaries for new civil guards Mr. Hamdani had hired to protect Umma, one of the most important Sumerian sites, several hours north of Nasiriyah.

Because of its rich history, Umma was also the most heavily looted site, where several hundred looters dug every night, illuminated by electric generators, kerosene lamps, and truck lights. Umma had been transformed into a moonscape, with hundreds of craters dug by looters, some twenty feet deep, connected by underground tunnels.

Late in July, after yet another unsuccessful attempt to get the Italian Carabinieri to go on an archaeological patrol, Mr. Hamdani sat dejected at his desk in the Nasiriyah Museum. He looked up at Marie-Hélène and me and said, "Everyone wins except me, Mike. The looters get what they want, the Coalition gets what it wants, and even you get your film. What do I get? Who is going to help me? I ask you, Mike, who is going to help me protect the sites?" Our camera dutifully captured his plea. There was no one left for him to ask, and the looters were working at their leisure.

On our way back to the Italian base that night, Marie-Hélène and I decided to ask the Carr Foundation to help Mr. Hamdani pay the salaries of the civil guards to protect the sites.

"Sumerian history is not just Iraqi history, it's world history," Mr. Hamdani repeated often. No one could lay claim to it, since the Sumerians had disappeared in the early second millennium B.C. They had left behind remarkable works of art and literature, including Gilgamesh and the Atrahasis myth of human origin, with their dramatic narrative parallels in the Old Testament, written over one thousand years later. Through an accident of accounting or sublime ingenuity, the Sumerians had developed one of the most profound advances in history: the invention of writing, etched out in cuneiform script with simple reed pens on clay tablets. Though humankind has been around over one hundred thousand years, we started documenting our thoughts only five thousand years ago. Everything we know about ourselves—our stories, musings, histories, ideas—started at Uruk, just thirty miles north of Nasiriyah.

The 2003 war dealt a severe blow to many of the sites already under attack by looters working in the power vacuum that followed the 1991 Gulf War. The amount of looting in the first three months following the 2003 war, according to Mr. Hamdani, equaled the total in the previous ten years.

But from September 2003 to March 2004 the situation improved. Mr. Hamdani had received limited funding from the Coalition Provisional Authority (CPA), based in Nasiriyah, to hire fifty additional civil guards for the sites. The Italian Carabinieri, who had taken a particular interest in preserving Iraq's cultural heritage, were doing an excellent job of protecting the sites with regular patrols.

Then in April 2004, shortly after I arrived on my third trip to Iraq, things fell apart again. The Mahdi Army rose up to battle the Coalition, and in the ensuing chaos the looting worsened, reaching postwar levels. Viper 5, the Carabinieri unit assigned to protect culture, was under new leadership and guarding archaeological sites was no longer a priority. After the June 28, 2004, transition to Iraqi sovereignty, the CPA disappeared, along with the money to pay the additional civil guards, who were subsequently dismissed.

From April 2004 on, Mr. Hamdani tried everything to protect the sites in the Dhi Qar province. Despite the escalating conflict, he went out every day in his red pickup truck to beg for help. The local police told

him, "The looters' tribes will ask for blood money if we arrest them."
The customs police claimed, "It's not our jurisdiction." The Iraqi
National Guard said, "We don't have the weapons to battle the looters,"
the Italian Carabinieri insisted, "We are on a humanitarian mission."
The Iraqi government in Baghdad maintained, "It's the responsibility of
the Coalition"; but the U.S. forces answered, "It's the responsibility of the
Iraqis." There was always an excuse.

Mr. Hamdani had enough funding to employ only one hundred civil
guards, who were paid one hundred dollars a month to protect more
than eight hundred sites. By comparison, Amir's brother, who worked
for the oil-protection force in Nasiriyah, took us to see the slick, well-
funded operation. The Coalition had provided funding to hire more than
eight hundred guards for the Dhi Qar province and outfit them with
brand-new uniforms, guns, and trucks to guard the oil pipelines. The
British security firm Erinys had been awarded the $40 million contract,
and boasted how there had not been even one terrorist attack against the
pipelines in the Dhi Qar province.

The Carr Foundation agreed to a small donation to pay for civil
guards, so it made sense to concentrate the efforts on a single site. Stopping the looting at Umma might send a message. Mr. Hamdani came up
with a plan to hire twenty new civil guards at Umma. They would guard
the site for four months, until a new Iraqi archaeological-protection
force being established in Baghdad could take over. He enlisted the help
of a local tribal leader, Sheik Saleem, encouraging villagers to care for
their history. Within a week, Mr. Hamdani received approval from the
State Board of Antiquities and Heritage, and the Italian Carabinieri offered to train the guards. The Nasiriyah Museum buzzed with activity
and enthusiasm. "The bog that is Iraq is beginning to move," Amir said
with delight.

I had come down on my final trip to Nasiriyah to film the new civil
guards' first day at Umma. Five months of hard work on our documentary culminating in that one day, a note of hope and optimism in an otherwise dismal story of looting and destruction. Instead, I had been
kidnapped. This couldn't be happening.

Through the darkened entrance two guards emerged, commanding
Amir and me to face the back. One of the men began retying our blindfolds.

"Where are they taking us?"

"To eat," Amir translated his reply.

"Do you believe them?"

"I don't know."

I tried again: "What about the money? Tell them if they take us to Nasiriyah now, we can get the money."

"They say it is too late to go to Nasiriyah tonight. Perhaps tomorrow," Amir said.

We both knew it was just an excuse. With yet another opportunity lost, my heart started racing. I didn't want to be moved. As long as we were stationary, things were probably okay, I reasoned.

They led us, blindfolded, out through the narrow passageway. When we got to the opening, I could feel someone pushing broken plastic slippers in my direction. *"Shokran,"* I said, slipping my feet into them. Thank you. There was only one pair. Amir had to walk barefoot. I was told to hold Amir's arm while one of the kidnappers led him by the other slowly across rough ground. Counting the steps, I tried to determine which direction we were headed, but couldn't orient myself. After about thirty steps, we were told to sit down and face away from them; then they allowed us to remove our blindfolds. It hardly mattered; by now it was too dark to see their faces, which were wrapped in keffiyehs.

They had brought us to a small field surrounded by low trees, no more than six or seven feet tall, with larger palms in the distance. The night was luminous, the sky a deep blue muslin turning to black, with bright stars beginning to pierce the fabric, and a rustling wind. I supposed, now, that they were telling the truth: we were being brought out to eat. It was another opportunity to speak to them, and perhaps find a solution.

A man began to speak to Amir, and they talked animatedly for a while. I listened for words I could understand but was unable to pick up anything except a notable shift in Amir's mood. Amir, still looking away, exchanged good-byes when the man left.

"He said he recognized my voice, that he was a student of mine," Amir said with delight. Amir had taught English for many years. Most translators in Nasiriyah had been students of his, including nearly all the translators who worked for the Coalition. Working with the Coalition paid considerably more than Amir made at his small translation bureau, but he enjoyed his work, and his freedom.

"Did you recognize his voice?"

"No. He says he respects me and will do everything he can to help us."

What a break, I thought. We needed allies.

"Don't worry," Amir added. "Everything will be okay." For a moment, I shared his optimism, as we sat quietly, waiting for them to bring food.

"Do you know who the number one enemy of Islam is?" one of the guards asked, breaking the silence.

America? I thought. *Me?*

"Israel," he answered. I shuddered at the implication—that they might possibly think we were spies—and tried to redirect the conversation.

"It is very beautiful out here, very peaceful," I said.

They didn't respond at first.

"It's a difficult life," one said after a while.

"*Nam,*" I said, agreeing with them. Yes.

One of the men got up, handed the AK to the other man, walked about ten feet away, laid out a rug, and started to pray. I studied the outline of his body in the darkness. With his back to us, he stood at one end of the mat, raised his hands to the sky, and then knelt down, placing his forehead between his hands on the ground.

I asked Amir to ask the other guard if I could pray when he was finished.

"Are you Christian?" the guard asked.

"Yes," I replied, hoping to gain his trust.

I was brought up free of religion, as my father liked to say, raised in a secular family, my parents both scientists at Yale University. I am not religious and I have never prayed, but it didn't matter; I thought I might be able to gain their sympathy if they considered me as a man of faith. The guard continued praying for about ten minutes, then gathered his rug and sat down near us.

I got up, stood at the end of my mat, put my hands in front of my heart, and remained still. I could feel them watching me. My mind focused on many things: escape, Marie-Hélène, my family, but not God. After five minutes, I sat back down.

"How do you pray?" one of them asked.

"You stand still and meditate on God," I responded. They stared at me. I couldn't come up with anything better. I stared back at them, my false identity hidden in the darkness.

They asked Amir about Islam, quizzing him on the three prayers that a devout Shi'ite Muslim would say during the day and the five principles of Shi'a Islam. Amir couldn't answer them. They silently absorbed this, branding him a *kafr,* an unbeliever.

Born in Nasiriyah, Amir was raised in a traditional Muslim family, but had adopted the intellectual and cultural traditions of the West. Once, in his small translation office, he had proudly showed Marie-Hélène and me a faded picture of himself as a young man doing his best imitation of James Dean: slicked-back hair, dark jacket, rueful look. He could have been any kid growing up in America; it could easily have been a picture of me. Amir was a proud intellectual, a man of letters, a fan of Foucault, and not a practicing Muslim. He did not try to hide this, though he avoided the topic. I admired him for sticking to his convictions. Was I giving up on my convictions? I knew that if the kidnappers thought of me as a practicing Christian, it would improve our chances of survival. A bad Muslim, as Amir was in their eyes, was worse than a Christian. They could forgive me. After all, Jesus was a prophet in Islam. They could not forgive Amir.

A figure emerged from the dark, carrying a pail of water with soap to wash our hands. A while later two more figures appeared, bearing a round metal tray with food and a plastic pitcher with water. I drank as much as I could, splitting the jug with Amir. The food was difficult to make out in the dark but seemed to be a simple rice dish with sauce. I folded some rice in a piece of bread and tried to eat, but I didn't have the stomach for it. When I was done, I thanked them for the meal. Mosquitoes had come out in force with the setting sun, and I wrapped the mat I was sitting on around my bare ankles, buttoning my shirt at the neck. It was of little use. With ferocious appetites, the mosquitoes quickly found their way to any exposed skin.

"*Akou moushkilah?*" the guards asked as I slapped at my face. What's wrong?

"*Dood tayyar,*" I responded, remembering the words for flying insect in Arabic. They didn't understand, so Amir explained.

"Ahhhh," they responded with mild interest.

"In France the mosquitoes are not as aggressive as they are out here."

"Your skin is too soft," they said. "The mosquitoes don't bother us."

After several hours, we were blindfolded again and led across a field, over rough ground covered in plants with long thorns. Amir walked barefoot, every other step landing on a sharp spike. He cried out in pain, and I winced at each cry, asking the guards to give him slippers, but they ignored me. The one pair of plastic slippers was for me. Perhaps because

Amir was an Iraqi, perhaps because he didn't pray, they showed him no mercy. Defying the guards would not help. I had to gain their sympathy, convinced that whatever ultimately happened to me would also happen to Amir.

After about fifty steps we were instructed to sit and they removed our blindfolds. We were in a large, empty field and I could see lights from a house in the distance. Amir massaged his feet, trying to pull out thorns that had become embedded in his skin. Six men, some carrying AKs in one arm and rugs tucked under the other, approached from the house. They told us to lay our mats side by side and tossed two blankets in our direction. One was a thick wool blanket, the other a dirty gauze window curtain with tears in it. Leaving the thick one for Amir, I lay down, beside him, both of us staring at the sky. With my hands tied, I tried to carefully tuck the window curtain around my body so that nothing was exposed, but the mosquitoes found their way in through the many holes.

I wondered if Marie-Hélène knew anything about what had happened, still hopeful that this would all be settled before anyone found out. Exhausted, I managed to drift into a semiconscious sleep, only to be awakened by another bite and incessant itching on my feet.

"Oooohhhhh." A deep resonance sounded near my ear.

Returning to consciousness with a rapid beating of my heart, my muscles tightened as I lay motionless. The night was cool, and the miniature world around my head—small breathing hole through the curtain, the horizon a faint phosphorescent line in a black sea—resolved around that sound as adrenaline began coursing through me, a thousand pinpricks of panic waking my skin. A man was speaking to Amir in a deep, commanding voice that echoed with indignation, a voice of sinister authority. Amir answered each question with rapid, plaintive responses. I listened intently, unable to understand anything they said. After an hour the conversation stopped and I could hear Amir lying back down. Raising my bound hands to my forehead, I wiped the sweat away from my eyes, trying to imagine the nature of the conversation. Since six kidnappers were lying next to us, I decided to wait till morning to ask Amir.

I carefully untied my hands under the gauze blanket, thinking about the wolf that might come in the night.

Marie-Hélène, Friday, August 13

Paris

My mother, sister, and I flew from Milan to Paris, a one-night stopover on our return to America, celebrating my mother's birthday in a small restaurant near Notre-Dame cathedral. After my mother's birthday dinner, we went to Le Centre Internet to check our email for the first time in a few days. Micah's most recent message was dated August 11:

```
How is your vacation?
Drove from Nasiriyah to Baghdad this morning. The
Mahdi Army had taken over Kut and we had to drive
straight through the fighting with Mahdi Army on
both sides and lots of shooting. The Mahdi Army was
actually directing traffic while the fighting was
going on, how polite of them.
```

It was typical Micah humor, and I was glad to see he still had it after so long in Iraq. The chair behind me scraped the floor as my sister, Chantal, turned to ask, "Did you see this?"

I was still reading Micah's message.

"A British journalist was kidnapped in Basra," she said, reading from an Iraq news alert she had signed up for when I left in May. Every bomb registered on her mental map of the country as she'd compare the attack with where I might be working. She'd called me on my cell phone one morning minutes after we had arrived to photograph a car bombing in Baghdad. I'd assured her that I was okay as young police recruits collected body parts in large, clear, oblong plastic bags.

"What?" I asked. Basra was so far south. The kidnapping of foreigners in the south was rare. Most kidnappings happened in the Sunni Triangle, between Baghdad, Tikrit, and Ramadi, though more recently, foreigners had been abducted along the road south from Baghdad to Najaf.

I finished reading Micah's email.

```
I am in Baghdad with Amir for a couple of days,
then one last trip to Umma then back to NY on Tues-
day or Wednesday. Talk to you soon,
    xo
    m
```

"Oh, wait a minute. Here's an update." Chantal turned again and faced me. "It's good news—he's been released."

"That's great news, so quick." One day was an unusually fast resolution.

I sent Micah a quick message, then clicked "check mail" one last time before we left. No new messages.

At the hotel, we watched the end of the opening ceremonies for the Olympics. Iraq's team was welcomed with a standing ovation, and I felt proud for them but estranged, having difficulty separating emotionally from a place I had worked so intensely. I missed being there. I missed Micah.

I woke with the sensation of someone watching me. Cold damp cloth, mosquito bites, hard ground, still in my clothes—where am I? A man shook me. He had been kneeling near my head watching me as I slept. An AK dangled loosely around his stomach, slung across his white dish-dasha, a full-length robe often worn by men in rural areas of Iraq. His head was wrapped tightly in a keffiyeh. It was still dark, with only a faint illumination from the coming dawn. I rose and looked at his eyes through the narrow opening in the cloth. Catching my gaze, he adjusted the scarf tighter around his head and motioned for me to turn around. There had been at least six guards when I'd fallen asleep; now there were only two. One guard retied my blindfold, checked that our hands were still bound—I had retied mine during the night—then told Amir and me to get up and take our mats.

Again they pushed the only pair of plastic slippers toward me. Amir's feet were still sore from walking through the field the previous evening, and now he had to walk back. I felt guilty taking the shoes. Walking bare-foot through a field of thorns was their punishment for Amir, a bad Muslim who worked with the Americans. The guard took Amir by the arm. I was instructed to hold Amir's other arm and we were led back together, the faint glow of dawn creeping under my blindfold, across the field toward our enclosure. Amir moaned constantly as he stumbled over the thorns, sometimes letting out a deep gasp.

We crawled though the opening of the enclosure, set out our mats, me on the right and Amir on the left, and lay down. I removed my blind-fold and untied my loosely bound hands as I listened to the guard shifting position every now and then outside. He remained quiet and I wondered if he knew anything about us, or even cared.

Cars passed slowly every half hour or so along the road. They came from a long distance to the south and disappeared to the north. What would it be like to be on that road? How much hope and optimism in those cars, just to be in one driving somewhere, free and alive. I fell back asleep thinking about that road.

. . .

The sound of bleating woke me. The sun was up, and I could hear the voices of children. Just outside our enclosure, sheep being led to pasture made their way down the gentle slope near us toward the road. I strained to see them through the thick palm leaves, but could not make out any movement. Through the opening above us was a gentle blue with no clouds. It must have been beautiful outside. The temperature was mild, and there was even a slight breeze. Thinking about the previous night's conversation, I became optimistic about the day. If our kidnapping was about money, we could go to Nasiriyah and settle it quickly.

"Amir, what did the man say to you in the middle of the night?" I asked in a hushed tone.

"The same thing as the others," he whispered. "He talked about money, about how to get money. How much we had. I explained everything."

"What do you think?"

"The man said it was about money. I think today we will know more."

"How is your jaw?"

"It's painful, I have trouble talking. I think it's broken." He turned his cheek toward me, and I examined it closely. "Do you see anything?" His jaw was swollen, which could mean a bruise, a fracture, or a break, possibly a serious medical problem. I said little, not wanting to upset Amir, since there was nothing I could do.

"I don't know, it's a bit swollen. I am sorry about your jaw."

A young man crawled into our enclosure. On his command, we turned away from him. He set down a tray with two glasses of hot tea and some *khubz*, a flat bread usually served at every meal; a typical Iraqi breakfast. Still facing away, I asked Amir to thank him.

The man replied simply, "It is my duty."

Amir asked if he knew anything about our situation. He said that he knew nothing; he was just a guard.

"Does he think we will be released soon?"

"*Insha Allah,*" the guard responded, backing out. God willing.

"He knows nothing," Amir said.

Toying with a piece of dry *khubz*, I looked into Amir's eyes. "What do you think will happen, Amir?" I asked, trying to decipher his true feelings.

He considered my question carefully before replying.

"I don't know, but I think in the coming days you will discover your personality. We will learn who we are."

The tea and bread gave me confidence that my effort to be friendly had been rewarded, even in small ways. Amir tried to eat the *khubz*, gnawing tenderly at a piece, then putting it back on the metal tray.

"It hurts when I chew," he said.

My feet itched madly. I counted the mosquito bites—more than fifty on my right foot alone—then found a small stick and scraped until they started to bleed.

At noon they brought us a plastic container with water and some food, which was again rice in an aluminum pot with a watery sauce that tasted of beans. I could eat only a small amount, but it was comforting that they were feeding us. About an hour later, a guard came to remove the pot. I thanked him again.

"It is our duty," he said.

"*Akel moumtaz,*" I added, trying to befriend him. The food is excellent.

"It is the same food we eat," he replied, and backed out through the mouth of the enclosure, holding the half-full pot of rice.

In the afternoon a large man wearing a white dishdasha replaced the guard. The man sat inside the enclosure on a mat with his legs folded and an AK resting on his lap. He was the first guard to sit so close, and he didn't mind that I looked at him, although he made an effort to cover his face with his keffiyeh. He instructed Amir to look away. I wasn't sure how to interpret this. If they were going to let me go, they wouldn't want me to see their faces. But since I was a foreigner, perhaps they assumed I wouldn't recognize them. I thought about what it would take to over-power him and grab his gun. He must have weighed two hundred pounds and was at least six feet tall. It was not a good idea.

Amir mentioned the conversation about the money to the new guard. He responded in a soft voice, saying not to pay attention to the two men who spoke about the money the night before.

"He says it's bullshit, they have no authority," Amir told me, some-what bewildered. "He says the two who spoke last night are just guards, they don't know what they are talking about."

"But what about the man who woke you up late? You said he spoke about money."

"Yes. But this man says it's not about money and they have no authority. He says a group has gone into Nasiriyah this morning to discuss our situation and should be back in the evening with news."

"Do you believe him?" I asked quietly.

"I don't know," Amir replied, trying to make sense of this new information. Someone was lying, but we didn't know who. If this guard was telling the truth, his words were both disappointing and heartening. Our kidnapping couldn't be solved with money. But perhaps we would be released as soon as they confirmed that we were journalists.

"Amir, ask him if he thinks we will be released today."

"*Insha Allah,*" the guard responded, with a positive note in his voice.

"Can we speak to someone in authority?"

"Don't worry, they will come if they need to. They know about your situation."

I asked Amir to remind him that we were just journalists and to pass that message along to those who had authority.

Amir relayed his words: "Believe me, you would not be alive now if you were not innocent." Innocent. What did that word mean to them exactly? Neutral? That I understood their side of things?

Then a thought occurred to me.

"Tell him about the ambulance."

• • •

After the uprising in April, the Mahdi Army regularly swept down into Nasiriyah from the north, seizing the northern half of the city and stopping at the Euphrates River which bisects Nasiriyah. The local police would disappear. Italian forces would emerge from their base southwest of the city and occupy the city south of the river. For several days they would fight across the river, until a truce was brokered and the Mahdi Army withdrew.

On Thursday, August 5, a week before Amir and I were kidnapped, the Mahdi Army again took over the northern half of Nasiriyah in a surprise offensive. Iraq was officially sovereign, following the transition of power on June 28, and so the Italian army got involved only after a call for help from the governor of Nasiriyah. I watched as new Italian tanks rolled out late in the evening, traveling at fifty miles per hour along a road that had recently been cut across the desert for quicker access. By Friday morning, the fighting had stopped and the situation was under control, according to Captain Ettore Sarli, chief spokesman for the Italian forces in Iraq.

"There was a car-bomb attempt last night," Sarli told me when I inquired. "Not so safe in Nasiriyah, is it?"

A car bomb in Nasiriyah was unusual. I had not heard of a car bomb in that part of Iraq since the bombing of the Italian headquarters in Nasiriyah, known as "Animal House," in November 2003, eight months earlier. Nineteen Italian soldiers had been killed, and the Italians had moved their operations out of the city soon after.

I went with a group of Italian journalists to report the fighting. The press office escorted us only to the edge of the city, but there was nothing to document and we returned to the press compound at the base.

A retired Italian general who had decided that he wanted to become a journalist and see the world was staring at a map of Nasiriyah pinned to the wall. He was interested in archaeology and we had struck up a friendship, discussing it as best we could in a mix of broken English and Italian. Had I been to the bridge? he asked.

"Which bridge?"

"The bridge where the car bomb had been," he said. Something had sparked his interest. I found the official press report in Italian: there was a car-bomb attempt against the Italian soldiers, the soldiers shot at the vehicle, the car exploded, and four people were killed. Since when are car bombs stuffed with people? I wondered.

I emailed Amir and arranged to meet him the next morning at the main gate. We were headed to the Directorate of Water to learn about the Saddam Canal, a large saltwater canal started by the Belgians in the 1950s and finished by Saddam after the 1991 Gulf War. By some accounts, the construction, which ran near several important archaeological sites, had unearthed precious artifacts, prompting the subsequent looting.

I told Amir about the report of the car bomb, suggesting that we stop by the bridge to have a look. When we arrived, a group of Italian soldiers were stationed at the foot of the bridge, but the bridge was open and traffic was moving smoothly. I asked the Italian soldiers about the car bomb, but they said they were not allowed to speak to the press.

We circled around the square a few times, then stopped to talk to people on the street. No one knew about a car bomb. Pointing toward the bridge, they said an ambulance had been shot at by the Italians as it tried to pass, and a pregnant woman, her unborn baby, her sister, mother, and husband had all been killed. Everyone in Nasiriyah knew that story, they said.

"The bodies were left until noon the next day," one man told us. "Dogs came to sniff them." This was a common insult in Islam. "Go see for yourselves," he said. "The ambulance is still on the bridge." I remained skeptical. At every car bombing in Baghdad, there were plenty of witnesses who would point to the sky and swear that it was a missile from an American helicopter.

We drove halfway across and parked. The charred remains of a large vehicle lay opposite, the Arabic words for ambulance, SAYARAT IS'AF, written clearly on the side. I took out my video camera and filmed as curious onlookers slowed to watch. I asked Amir to stand in front of the ambulance and speak into the camera, describing the story we had heard and pointing out the words on the burned vehicle that translated to "ambulance."

We left and went to our interview with the manager at the Directorate of Water, which was informative but dull. When I finished the interview we headed to the Directorate of Health, where the ambulances were dispatched.

A dozen men were gathered in the small office building. They invited us in for tea and confirmed the story. The number twelve ambulance had been dispatched at three A.M. on Friday to transport a pregnant woman who was going through a difficult labor and her family from the general hospital in the north of the city to the maternity hospital on the south side, across the river. The Italian army, stationed on the southern end of the bridge, shot at the ambulance as it came across. The ambulance burst into flames and the four passengers inside were killed. The driver and two people with him in the front seat managed to escape. Six similar ambulances were parked outside, with the large numbers that the Italians had assigned for identification painted on their fronts. The number twelve ambulance was missing.

A man from the Directorate of Health took us to interview the driver, Sabah Khazal Kareem, at his house in Nasiriyah. He was surprised that a Western reporter would show interest in the story. Having survived with a minor leg wound, he was bitter about what had happened. His had been the first ambulance on the scene to help survivors of the attack on the Italian headquarters the previous November, making five trips to the hospital with wounded Italian soldiers. He considered himself a friend to the Italians.

In a startling coincidence, he was the same celebrated driver who had rescued Jessica Lynch, also in ambulance number twelve, transporting her from the Mukabarat, the Iraqi secret police, to the hospital in Nasiriyah. He showed us several thank-you letters from Pfc. Lynch that he had received for his good work.

When I returned to the base I sent an email offering details to *The New York Times*. It was an important story, and since two Italian television journalists from RAI 2, one of four state-owned Italian stations, were unable to travel into Nasiriyah to cover it, I offered them the videotaped interviews. They were interested, but had to clear it with their editors in Rome. When I returned from dinner, the RAI 2 journalists were in a rush to get the material. The editors had approved it, and they wanted to air it on the seven o'clock news in Italy. They ran to General Corrado Dalzini's office with one of my tapes to get a comment. The general doubted the story but said he would look into it.

The scene became frenetic as the Italian journalists scrambled to broadcast the material: a clip of Amir in front of the ambulance and a clip of the interview with the ambulance driver. Adding to their desperation, my camera format was incompatible with their equipment. Airtime was just ten minutes away.

At the last minute, a Turkish technician working for the Italians somehow found a solution, and my footage made the final seconds of RAI 2's evening news. General Dalzini had come by and was standing silently, watching it all in the glowing light of the satellite truck.

Most soldiers were at dinner in the giant mess hall, where televisions tuned to RAI 2 broadcast the evening news. When the story aired, it was as if a different kind of bomb had been dropped squarely on the general's quarters. General Dalzini disappeared for a while, then reappeared standing outside the press area, doing an improvised interview for RAI 2. He denied that the Italian forces had shot an ambulance. I got my video camera and came back out to film his interview. Captain Sarli stopped me, claiming that I was not authorized to film.

"I didn't know your translator was an ambulance driver," he added.

"What do you mean?" I responded, baffled. "He is *not* an ambulance driver."

But Sarli had already turned and was headed back to where General

Dalzini was standing, silhouetted in the bright light of a camera spot against the thick black night.

I turned back to my tent, my walk interrupted by a loud voice directly behind me. General Dalzini was yelling at me in Italian; Captain Sarli, at his side, translated: "If we find out that your translator is not an ambulance driver, you will have to leave the base in the morning."

I still had no idea what he was talking about. "My translator is *not* an ambulance driver—" I began. They both turned around and left before I could finish. I walked slowly back to the tent, trying to piece together what had happened. The two journalists from RAI 2 came in, looking pale.

"The story created a scandal," one said. "It's a very big deal in Italy. They are not taking it well. The general denied they shot an ambulance."

I knew the story was important, but I didn't think that the Italian army would react this way.

"Eighty percent of the Italian population does not support the war," the RAI 2 journalist continued. "We are supposed to be here on a humanitarian mission. This is the first time such a report of our troops killing innocent civilians has come out."

"Why are they asking about my translator being an ambulance driver?"

"When we broadcast the story, the station back in Rome put the wrong caption on the video feed. It said 'ambulance driver' under the part where your translator was standing in front of the ambulance."

In their rush to air the story a mistake had been made, and I was paying the price. I went out looking for Captain Sarli, but he was gone. I went back to the video truck to talk with the Turkish technician. While I was standing there, a soldier from the press office came out.

"You must leave the base first thing in the morning," he said bluntly and walked away.

"Well, I guess I'll be going," I joked to the Turkish technician, hiding my shock. He shook his head in disbelief.

"They can't kick you out."

"They just did," I replied.

"Where will you go?" he asked.

"I don't know. I will stay in Nasiriyah, or maybe go back to Baghdad."

As I packed my things, I told the journalists from RAI 2 what had happened. Shocked themselves, they said they would try to talk to General

Dalzini and left, offering me their computer and satellite phone to file my story with *The New York Times*. I tried reaching John Burns back in Baghdad, but he was away covering the fighting in Najaf. I called New York and got an editor on the line. He commiserated but acknowledged that if they kick you out, they kick you out. "You can file with me—just send it to my email," he suggested. I sent a quick email to Marie-Hélène, wanting her to know what had happened.

I finished the story at around eleven-thirty P.M. and filed it by email just as one of the RAI 2 journalists returned, this time escorted by the Italian Military Police. They had spoken to General Dalzini and explained to him that it would look bad if they kicked an American journalist off the base for reporting a story. Americans value freedom of speech above everything, they said. The general agreed that I would not have to leave in the morning, but the Italian army had opened an inquiry into the incident and I would have to answer some questions. The Italian MP stood in the door of the tent, waiting to escort me to the police headquarters.

The MP brought me to a small mobile interrogation office in the general's compound. The RAI 2 cameraman sat inside, smoking nervously. At their insistence, he was trying to make a copy of my tapes for the Military Police.

I was told to wait until another MP showed up. The second MP questioned me for several hours. He typed carefully: first name, passport number, address, then everything I knew about the ambulance in detail. He said they were opening an inquiry into the alleged shooting of an ambulance. I gave him the names of everyone we had interviewed and suggested that they go to Nasiriyah and interview them personally, though I didn't think they would.

Because of the format problem, the cameraman was unable to copy the tapes and the MPs said they would just keep them. I protested, since these were my original tapes, and offered to make a DVD copy of the material. They reluctantly agreed. I stayed until four A.M. copying the tapes, and then was escorted back to my tent. The journalist from RAI 2 was still awake, lying on his cot. We exchanged stories, both shaken by what had happened. He knew he was no longer welcome at the base and he didn't think he would last his full month-long assignment.

With only an hour of sleep, I met Amir at the main checkpoint at nine A.M. I told him what had happened, but he didn't seem concerned. "So what are you going to do?" he asked. Because of my relationship with

Amir, I was the only Western journalist who could travel to Nasiriyah safely and I felt a responsibility to document the story, both for the public and for the Iraqi family who had been killed. "I want to keep following the story," I said.

Amir and I drove to Nasiriyah to interview the hospital director, but he wasn't in. Instead, the head of the hospital guards took us to film the bodies of the family that had been killed. They were being kept in a freezer behind the hospital. In Islam it is customary to bury the dead within twenty-four hours, but since the entire family had been killed, the hospital was having difficulty finding a relative to claim the bodies. I covered my mouth with a cloth and tried several times to film inside the freezer. The smell was so strong I could manage only a few seconds at a time. The bodies had been severely burned, a dark mass of charred and mangled flesh wrapped in clothing. I could see a man's steel gray face perfectly preserved, his eyes closed.

"Baby," the guard said in English, pointing to what might have been a stomach ripped open. I couldn't see a baby. About to throw up, I quickly left.

The hospital director caught up with us as we walked across the courtyard. He pulled Amir aside and spoke to him sternly in Arabic. Amir managed to placate him, and he walked with us back to his office.

"Everything is fine," Amir assured me. In a quiet voice he continued: "He says we should have come to him first before filming the bodies. He doesn't want any trouble. He does not want to upset his relationship with the Italians." I knew how he felt.

On our way out, the hospital director introduced us to two men who were just being released from the hospital. They had also been in the front seat of the ambulance with the driver, and their story was consistent with everything I had heard. When we were done with the interviews, we were invited for tea with Colonel Suleiman, the head of the hospital's Facility Protection Service, the organization responsible for guarding essential infrastructure in Iraq. Colonel Suleiman showed us a large file of documents and photographs about the ambulance incident. During previous clashing between the Italian forces and the Mahdi Army, he had tried to transport wounded civilians across the bridge. In order to allow the ambulance to pass safely, he had stripped down to his underwear, walking slowly up to the Italian army so that they would not take him for a suicide bomber.

Two FPS guards had also been killed in the fighting, and Colonel

Suleiman was upset about the unusual heavy-handedness of the Italian forces. But it was the outright denial of responsibility by the Italian army that angered him.

There is a concept in Iraqi tribal society known as *diyya,* or "blood money." If you accidentally injure or kill someone, you work out a fair price with the family—often cash, but sometimes a daughter—and all is forgiven. I'd been introduced to this concept by Sheik Abu Fetah, a local tribal leader in Nasiriyah and a close friend of Mr. Hamdani. His tribe had guarded Ur, one of Iraq's most important archaeological sites, for more than eighty years. Sheik Abu Fetah's grandfather had worked with Sir Leonard Woolley, the famous British archaeologist who had excavated at Ur in the 1920s and '30s, uncovering the fabulous burial treasure of Queen Pu'Abi and the purported house of Abraham. Abu Fetah was a large man with a magnetic presence, an infectious laugh, and nine and a half fingers—half a finger left on a battlefield during the Iran-Iraq War. He would show up on occasion at the museum in an old black GMC, wearing his trademark white dishdasha, with one or two tribal members in tow. One day Sheik Abu Fetah appeared in the courtyard of the Nasiriyah Museum with a member of his tribe who had shot a gun in the air in celebration during a wedding. Sheik Abu Fetah waved his pistol as he explained how the bullet had come down and landed in a woman's foot. He had settled the matter for less than one hundred dollars. Blood money worked in Iraqi society, but the precarious politics of the Italian presence in Iraq meant the issue could not be settled so simply, at least not in Italy.

From the hospital, we went to the museum to meet Mr. Hamdani. He was proud that I, a Westerner, had shown such concern for the Iraqi family killed in the ambulance, but he was worried about what this meant for the archaeology. He had carefully cultivated a good relationship with the Italian Carabinieri, since he needed their help to protect the sites. It was a tenuous political balancing act, and he didn't want to be associated with the volatile story we had just uncovered.

He had a meeting scheduled with the Carabinieri that evening to convince them to send a patrol to the sites, their first in many months. Mr. Hamdani, Amir, and I returned together to the Italian base. I worried about going back, knowing I was no longer welcome. "You worry about nothing," Amir assured me. "Nothing will happen."

As we drove back to the base, I asked Amir if he thought we had done the right thing reporting the ambulance story. "Yes," he said firmly. After

the way I had been treated, I wasn't so sure. "It's the truth," he continued. "Your job is to report the truth."

We arrived at the gate, and the Carabinieri escorted us to a meeting
with Major Antonio Frascinetto, the new Carabinieri commander in
charge of the Italian effort to protect archaeological sites. I had known
him for several weeks, a kind, courteous, professional man with a sincere
interest in stopping the looting. As we waited in the courtyard, two MPs
entered and said they wanted to talk to Amir for ten minutes. They left
together, one of the MPs walking stiffly as Amir held his hand. Holding
hands between men is a custom in Iraq. Most Westerners fortunate
enough to experience this level of hospitality, myself included, stand uncomfortably, waiting for the moment when they can reclaim their hand.

Forty-five minutes later I was still sitting in the courtyard when the
MPs returned and asked me to come with them. They led me back to the
same room I'd been in the previous night. Through a closed door, I could
hear Amir speaking excitedly in the adjoining trailer but could not make
out the words.

"How can I help?" I asked. No one responded.

One MP held up a set of handcuffs, swinging them slowly, watching
my reaction. I stared at him and then laughed, turning to the other MP.

"So, seriously, what do you want?" I repeated. The MP put the handcuffs down.

"We just have some questions," he said. "The tapes from yesterday,
well, we need the original tapes."

"I stayed up all night making you a DVD copy. Besides, there is nothing that you can't get yourself. Go talk to the ambulance driver. I told you
everyone we interviewed. Just go out and interview them yourselves."

"Yes, but you see, it's not possible for us to go to Nasiriyah now." I
doubted this was true since Italian troops were stationed by the bridge.

"That may be, but it has nothing to do with me," I said.

"Si, si. Okay, just wait a minute."

They considered what to do as I waited. After a half hour an MP came
out from where Amir was being questioned.

"It appears we have a problem," he said, looking at the ground and
shaking his head.

"What?" I asked.

"Did you go to Nasiriyah today and interview people about the ambulance?"

"Yes. I'm a journalist. I go and interview people."

"And you filmed the"—he tried to remember the word in English—"corpse?"

"Dead bodies," another man added.

"Yes, they're in storage at the hospital."

"Well," he said, looking around. "That is a problem. We will need those tapes as well."

"Listen," I said, growing impatient. "You cannot just ask me for my tapes. These are my tapes. You don't have any right to ask me for this material."

Another man came over and tried to explain. "*Sì, sì.* But you see, sometimes the job of a police officer and the job of a journalist"—he searched for the right words—"get confused. Sometimes a journalist becomes like a police officer investigating. Sometimes. You understand?"

"No, I don't understand," I protested. "I have my job, and you have yours. They are different. I told you everyone we have interviewed to be helpful, and I even gave you a copy of the interviews yesterday. I was filming in Nasiriyah, in sovereign Iraq. I did not film the shooting of the ambulance, I only interviewed people about what had happened after the fact." The Italian army was a member of the Coalition, so I assumed it respected basic laws protecting freedom of the press. But this was Iraq, and I was at the Italian base. No longer knowing what to expect, I told them I was headed back to Baghdad for a few days and would make another copy. They reluctantly agreed.

When they were done speaking with Amir, we walked back across the base together to meet Mr. Hamdani. I felt terrible that Amir had suddenly been dragged into this.

"What did they ask you?"

"They insulted me," Amir said. "One of them said, 'Tell the truth.' It is an insult to suggest I am not a man of my word. 'Am I a criminal?' I asked. 'Have I done anything wrong?' He said, 'No.' So why treat me like a criminal? I said to him, 'I will tell you everything, I have nothing to hide, I will tell you the story of the ambulance,' and he said, '*You* say it is an ambulance.' They don't believe it. It is shameful."

We couldn't find Mr. Hamdani at the Carabinieri headquarters, so Amir and I went to the mess hall and sat alone at a table. There were several hundred soldiers in the tent, and it felt like all eyes were upon us. We were no longer welcome. Two months of camaraderie and shared dinners ended abruptly. Overnight I had gone from being the reporter who covered the archaeology to the reporter who reported false stories to destroy the good reputation of the Italian army. Amir and I ate in silence. I was so sickened I could hardly touch the food.

We found Mr. Hamdani back in the courtyard behind the Carabinieri office. Oblivious to our troubles, he had had a good meeting—they had promised a patrol the next day—and was ready to head back to Nasiriyah. I asked Amir if I could come with them. "Why not? You are welcome." I left the base that evening with most of my belongings.

"Where will I sleep?" I asked Amir as we drove away from the base, toward a darkened Nasiriyah.

He thought for a moment. "At the museum, of course." Sleeping at the museum involved locking myself in with a chain around the front door while two guards slept outside. "Don't unlock the door for anyone, even the guards," Amir said as he disappeared into the night. The Nasiriyah Museum had been burned a few months earlier during a Madhi uprising by militants who had come to kill Mr. Hamdani because of his work to stop the looting. Several of the rooms had been destroyed, and the building still smelled of smoke.

In the morning, I made the mistake of unlocking the door and going out to wash my face with a hose. When I returned, my small camera was missing. One of the guards shrugged his shoulders and pointed to a plaster statue of Gudea, ruler of the ancient Sumerian city Lagash, suggesting the statue had gotten up in the night and snatched it. He helped me look for it, but it was nowhere to be found. The other guard sat on the steel bed frame outside the front door, showing no interest in my lost camera. When Amir appeared an hour later he chided, "I told you not to unlock the door." After several months working at the museum, I had trusted the guards, and was angry at their betrayal. Mr. Hamdani, also angry, assured me that he would find the camera.

I returned to the base for the rest of my things. Before leaving I ran into my friend the retired Italian general, who asked if it really was an ambulance. Knowing my reputation had taken a beating, I showed him the digital photographs. He shook his head in sorrow, wishing me luck as I left.

In the late afternoon Mr. Hamdani, Amir, and I met the Carabinieri for a patrol to the nearby site of Dahala, their first archaeological patrol in more than three months. One of the Carabinieri saw my camera and asked me not to film him, saying in broken English, "I didn't know your translator was ambulance driver."

I handed my Italian press ID to a Carabinieri soldier as they dropped us off by the American gate, requesting that he return it to Captain Sarli. As we drove back to Nasiriyah that evening, I turned to Amir and again asked him where I was going to sleep, since the museum was no longer an option.

He thought a moment. "At my house."

Amir was taking a risk. The neighbors couldn't know that a Westerner was staying there. We pulled over on the dusty street in front of his house. Amir went out to make sure no one was looking while I sat in the car, then told me to come quickly, locking the gate behind us. We rolled out mats in the garden courtyard of his home and slept next to each other that night. Saddened about what had transpired at the Italian base, I was comforted by Amir's generous hospitality and concern for my safety.

The next day, Amir, Mr. Hamdani, and I headed back to Baghdad, driving through the Mahdi Army attack in Kut. When we arrived, Amir and I went directly to APTN to see if they were interested in the ambulance story. Busy covering the fighting in Najaf, the director told me to come back the next week; the story would still be relevant.

On Thursday at the Dulaimi Hotel, my base in Baghdad, I noticed a small sticker on the door across the hall that read CPJ—COMMITTEE TO PROTECT JOURNALISTS. I wasn't familiar with the group, but a committee to protect journalists is exactly what I need, I thought. The room used to belong to our friend, photographer-writer Mitch Prothero, but I hadn't seen him in a long time. I looked up CPJ on the Web and emailed them a quick report of what had happened at the Italian base. To my surprise, a few hours later I got an email back from Mitch.

"Hey, Micah! It's Mitch and I now work for CPJ. Stop by my room at the Dulaimi on this incident you reported." Up all night preparing to film the first day of the civil guards at Umma, I didn't have time to stop by, and left at six A.M. the next morning for my final trip to Nasiriyah.

• • •

Amir told the story of the ambulance to the kidnapper. He listened intently, surprised that a Westerner would report such a story. Amir encouraged him to check the story and check my credentials.

"He says we did a good thing," Amir said. For a moment I felt a bridge had been built across a chasm of distrust, although my kidnappers' acknowledgment made me uneasy.

"*Shokran.*" Thank you, I said, ambivalent. I had reported the story because it was news, and because the family that had been killed deserved as much, not for any other reason.

"When will our dilemma be resolved?" Amir asked the large guard.

"Yours will be a short story," he assured us.

"What does short story mean?" I asked Amir.

"A week," the large guard responded.

"And a long story?"

"A month, or more. You will be released today, or tomorrow for certain. A British journalist was released today."

"When was he taken captive?" I asked.

"The day before you were taken captive."

"Where?"

"South, Basra."

"Why did they release him?"

"I don't know."

He assured us again not to worry. We thanked him and he left. Hearing about that British journalist made me feel better. I was not alone, and our story might end well.

"Do you believe him, Amir?"

"Somehow. We are journalists. We are innocent. They have to let us go. Believe me. Everybody knows about our story. They cannot harm us. Our driver Hatem must have told Mr. Hamdani, who, without a doubt, contacted the governor and the deputy governor, Adnan al-Sharifi. They will help us." Amir was laying out the argument carefully, hopeful that our problem would be solved quickly.

"I don't know, Amir," I said, studying the ground.

"What do you think?" he asked me, for the first time.

"I think it's fifty-fifty. I don't think they will let an American go."

He thought about this for a minute, then rejected it, saying I was being pessimistic. But I was pragmatically weighing the options, not letting myself be swayed by the words we wanted to hear. Though encouraged by this guard's words, the others had left a different impression, and I still didn't know whom to believe.

"You know what the man said yesterday when we were led out of Sadr's office?" Amir continued. "One man asked the mule who hit me if he should get the pistol. Do you know what that means?"

I shook my head no.

"It means 'Should we execute them?' The man said to him, 'No, they may be telling the truth.'" He paused for emphasis. "Believe me, it will end well." It surprised me that Amir had kept that detail quiet. What else was he protecting me from?

"But what if these men are looters and know we are following the story of the looting—then we are in trouble."

"Tch, tch." Amir shook his head. "Don't think about that." He leaned forward. "That mule, in the Sadr office, the one who struck me, when I said you were here for the archaeology, he said, 'He has come to steal our heritage.' That means they are against the looting."

"But the guard last night told us they are not the ones who kidnapped us."

"I don't know," Amir said, stroking his jaw. He had faith, but he did not have answers. Neither did I.

We had plenty of time to think that afternoon. I tried to keep my emotions from clouding my reason, but the positive words from the large man with the soft voice, the one Amir had told the ambulance story to, had lifted my spirits. The day grew heavy with the still heat and I lay on my back, trying not to move. A wasp flew in just above my head, silently circled the enclosure, and then disappeared through the palm leaves.

"What is the first thing you are going to do if we get out?" I asked Amir.

"I am going to see my family, then go back to work in my translation bureau. I am happy with my life; I would not change anything. But I would like to study abroad and finish my thesis." Amir dreamed of writing at length about politics and language, drawing heavily from Foucault. Linguistics and philosophy were his first loves. By studying language, he believed, one could understand human nature.

I sat up. "If we are released, the first thing I am going to do is take a shower. The second thing is to ask Marie-Hélène to marry me," I said, smiling for the first time since our kidnapping.

Amir smiled back.

Before Marie-Hélène had left Iraq, she had told me that our four years together had been a very happy time. What did I think about taking things to the next level? I was washing our dinner plates at the Dulaimi, and nervously began scrubbing the clean ones again. She suggested we think about it. "It," of course, was left open to discussion and interpretation.

The last four years had been a very happy time. Marie-Hélène and I were already partners in life. I knew I could spend my life with her, have children, and grow old—and not get married. I valued my freedom above all else. Formal commitment felt like a constraint. My hope had been to keep so busy I could avoid the conversation for as long as possible. Years, perhaps a decade. Alone in captivity, however, I had time to think about what I really wanted. The daily concerns of the outside world were gone. Layers of mundane worry had been peeled away. Stripped of everything, my life lay bare before me as a simple set of desires. What did I want? I wanted to live. I wanted to be happy. I wanted to live happily with Marie-Hélène and Zeugma.

Commitment no longer seemed confining; it would be liberating. The thought of marriage was a comfort. I tried to imagine her surprise when I proposed. "Do the right thing, *habibi*," Munawar, our large, jovial friend and driver in Baghdad, would say. "Don't take care about stones, take care about Marie-Hélène."

"No project is worth losing your life over," Munawar told me repeatedly in March as we drove back and forth from Baghdad to Nasiriyah to Hillah, each trip getting more dangerous. Insurgents had bombed three bridges that month, closing the main highway south, and all traffic had been redirected through the small towns of Mahmudiyah and Latifiyah. The line of cars moved slowly, often coming to a complete standstill for hours as American forces defused the daily roadside bombs. At times traffic moved off the main road, into the fields and through winding dirt paths. I wanted to document it, but you could feel the danger all around. "Can I film?" I would ask Munawar. "Why not, *habibi*?" was his typical response. Once, while we were navigating a dirt path somewhere between Hillah and Baghdad, an Iraqi man leaned out the window of a passing car and took a picture of me as I held the video camera focused through the windshield. "Why did he just take a picture of me?" I asked Munawar, knowing the answer: insurgents were tracking the movement of foreigners. "Who knows, *habibi*?" Munawar replied with a nervous laugh. A few weeks before that, I was with Munawar at an electronics shop in Baghdad, trying to buy a hard drive. Two men with long beards and white dishdashas put down a thousand dollars in cash for two brand-new small video cameras. "We are mujahideen," they announced proudly. The man behind the counter happily threw in two free packs of MiniDV tapes. "We should go, *habibi*," Munawar told me under his breath.

Eventually I had to lie down in the back of the car in order to travel at all along that road. Even Munawar Schumaker, as he liked to call himself, traveling at eighty miles an hour in his black Volkswagen Jetta, couldn't outrun the gangs waiting at checkpoints. Munawar lost a good friend in Mahmudiyah. He was an engineer traveling in a car with another friend and two children. The four were shot dead and left by the side of the road. The killers hadn't even bothered to steal the car. "Why?" "Who knows, *habibi*?" It was just more of what Munawar called the relentless pressure. I felt it. Five months of daily bombing, random killings, failing infrastructure, and no jobs.

Munawar had agreed to drive Marie-Hélène to Nasiriyah when she arrived in May, but that was the last trip out of Baghdad for him. He hated driving to Nasiriyah. Iraq is a very tribal place, and he had no relatives there, so he was out of his element. Amir saw it differently. "Spoiled Baghdadis," he would say, referring to their big-city attitude and the exorbitant prices they charged for a four-hour ride south, no less than one hundred dollars each way. Munawar was willing to forgo his relatively large salary for the relative safety of Baghdad. It had become too dangerous, and his wife wouldn't stand for it.

Amir had been married as well, but had gotten divorced ten years ago.

"Why did you get divorced, Amir?" I ventured during our hours in the date palm enclosure. In Iraqi tradition it is rude to ask a man about his family, but Amir and I were close friends by then, and given our immediate circumstances, why not. Once, in his office, he had shown Marie-Hélène and me a picture of his wife, a beautiful woman with long dark hair, wearing a modern dress.

"My wife's father would not let us be. He was constantly interfering in our lives."

The father of Amir's wife was a tall, imposing man, and the head of the Communist Party in Nasiriyah. Amir referred to him ruefully as "the stallion."

"It was so bad you had to get a divorce?"

"Yes, it was impossible to be together with him around."

"What does she do now?"

"She lives at home." It saddened me to think about her being alone.

"Would you like to be married again?" I asked.

"Somehow, I hope."

Sensing a shift in Amir's mood, I changed the subject. "Do you think Mr. Hamdani went to Umma today?"

"No, certainly not. I am sure Mr. Hamdani is focused on solving our problem."

I was distressed at the thought that our kidnapping had affected the important work of protecting the archaeological sites. Without Mr. Hamdani, the new civil guards would not start working at Umma, and the looters would be at it again—two hundred or more that night for certain. Maybe if they released us tonight, we could go to Umma tomorrow.

"I believe our situation will be solved tonight, perhaps. If not tonight then definitely by tomorrow," Amir assured me.

"You know, Amir, there is one thing I wish."

"What is that?"

"I wish I knew karate."

He laughed. I thought there had been, and still would be, many opportunities to free ourselves, if only I knew some form of martial arts. I wanted to solve our kidnapping myself, and not burden anyone.

"Remind me, when we get out, to take karate lessons," I told him.

"You must promise to send me two books when you go back to America," he said. *"The Encyclopedia of Linguistics* and *Karate for Dummies."*

The evening came and went. There was no news, and no more talk of money. We asked about the group that had gone to Nasiriyah, but were told they had not yet returned. As the last light of day faded, two guards led us, hands tied and blindfolded, with mats tucked under our arms, back to the field where we had eaten the night before. They brought a pail of water and soap to wash our hands, then food. After a few hours they led us out to the field to sleep. Amir again stumbled blindly through the thorns, alternately gasping and moaning at each step. Then, as before, they allowed us to remove our blindfolds.

About an hour after we lay down, the man with the deep, sinister voice returned.

"Micah," Amir said nervously, "wake up, he wants to speak to you."

I pulled myself up, frightened, folded my legs, and kept my eyes on the ground in front of me, not wanting to provoke him.

"He wants to know why you are here in Iraq."

"I am here to help. I am concerned about the destruction of culture. I am a journalist." Amir relayed my words in Arabic.

"Tell him about the ambulance," I continued. Amir told him the ambulance story, explaining how we had risked our work and reputations to report the truth. The man listened, but since his face was wrapped in a keffiyeh, I couldn't tell what he was thinking.

"He says you did a good thing to report the story of the ambulance," Amir said, relaying his words. The man continued, his tone more severe.

"He wants to know if you are a contractor or have ever worked for the military."

"Tell him that I swear I have never worked for the military," I said, putting my hand on my heart. "I am a civilian, a journalist, and am here only out of concern for culture and the Iraqi people." In the darkness I tried to look into the man's eyes as I said the words. Amir conveyed my message.

"He says to go to sleep."

"When does he think we will be released?"

"*Insha Allah.*"

I lay down, thinking about how they would verify that I was a journalist. Perhaps they would go to the Internet and search my name. They would easily find the website for the small media company Marie-Hélène and I ran, Four Corners Media. Among the many archaeology stories and images, I had just updated the website with a large picture of a marine holding a brick stamped with cuneiform writing, and a short documentary about a New York soldier training new Iraqi police recruits that had aired on PBS. How would my kidnappers view that reporting? Through the fractious and highly partisan lens of Iraq, nothing was neutral.

Eventually I drifted to sleep. *Tomorrow,* I thought.

Marie-Hélène, Saturday, August 14

I woke early to catch a seven A.M. flight from Paris to New York and boarded the bus alone to the terminal. My bags were still covered with Iraqi dust, full of my journals, *abaya, hijabs,* and several cameras.

Arriving at Charles de Gaulle airport, in a moment of panic I searched frantically for my handwritten list of Baghdad contacts. Without them, there was no way to reach anyone I knew in Iraq. Micah and I were hoping to return to Iraq soon for a month of filming, and the contacts were essential. I turned my bag upside down in front of the security counter as the security personnel shifted impatiently; the small notebook was the last thing to fall to the ground.

Bumped up to business class, amid plush space, looping films, and the eerie drone of jet engines, I began to think about what my life would be like after returning home. So much had happened, so much I had yet to process. The trip had been a transformative journey for me: making a difficult decision to go, despite deep concern, accomplishing what I had set out to do in a dangerous place, and returning safely.

Two paws pressed against my stomach, as Zeugma, our dog, met me at the door of my apartment. She seemed smaller than I remembered, and I was amazed at how memory reshapes things. I went in, Zeugma standing a few extra seconds at the door, waiting for Micah.

After throwing my bags down, exhausted, I slept until four A.M. Sunday morning. I woke before the sun and checked my email: nothing new from Micah. Uneasy, I pulled Zeugma up on the bed. Her warmth filled the empty space next to me, and I went back to sleep.

The day started the same way as the previous day. We were awakened before dawn and led across the field back to the enclosure. A pattern. Again, the guard pushed the only pair of plastic slippers in front of me, and we moved slowly as Amir stumbled barefoot and blindfolded through the thorny fields. But this time the guard had not retied my blindfold. He plodded along half asleep, holding Amir by the arm while I trailed a few steps behind, carrying my mat.

Having undone the knot on my left hand before getting up, I now held the cloth tightly between my hands, studying the sleepy guard's neck. His head was wrapped in a keffiyeh that draped over his shoulders, making it impossible for me to see my target. He was about my height and weight. He held the AK in his left hand and Amir's left arm with his right hand. I could jump him, I thought. I tried imagining how that scene would unfold.

Holding the cloth taut with two fists in front of my chest, I would reach over his head in a swift motion and bring the cloth tightly around his neck. Leaning back with all my weight, I would pull as hard as I could. He would kick and struggle as we fell to the ground. The gun would fall as well, his hands clawing at his neck, desperately trying to loosen my grip cutting off his air supply. "Now," I'd say to Amir in a loud whisper. Amir would pull off his blindfold and grab the gun as the man stopped struggling and lost consciousness. We would drag him into the enclosure, still alive, lay him in the corner, bind his hands and feet, and tie a piece of cloth around his mouth, then head back into the field and toward the road.

I replayed that scenario in my mind. There were other endings as well:

Unable to get the cloth fully around his neck, the guard would fire a shot from the AK, exploding into the morning stillness. Within moments, half a dozen men with AKs would come and disentangle us, beating us with their gun barrels, and drag us back to the enclosure.

Or worse still:

I wouldn't get the cloth tight around his neck. He would turn quickly and the gun would go off. Amir would fall to the ground holding his stomach as I lost my grip, tumbling back on my hands. The guard would pivot, pointing the gun at me.

Ours would be a short story.

The guard stopped, turned around, pointed the gun toward the ground in our direction, and held out his right hand. We had reached the mouth of the enclosure, and he motioned us on, standing to the side holding the AK as we crawled through the entrance.

"*Shokran,*" I said. Thank you.

He nodded. I rolled out my mat, lay down on my side, and went through the scenarios again in my head. It could work; it all depended on him not firing the gun. In any case, today was Sunday, the day we were sure to be set free.

A familiar rhythmic sound came from outside the enclosure, soft, like gurgling water. The guard was snoring.

The sun came and went that day in a long arc over our heads. I had never sat in the same place for twelve hours and watched the sun move across the sky, like the second hand on a clock. Within that arc, many small things happened.

"Amir, we need to have a plan in case things do not go well," I said as we drank the warm tea and gnawed the dry *khubz.*

"What is your idea?"

"In the morning, the guard who leads us here doesn't blindfold me, and my hands are untied. I can put the cloth around his neck and strangle him. You grab his gun."

"Do you think you can overpower him?" Amir asked, clearing his throat with a long drink from the small plastic jug of water. I watched him carefully, rationing the water, about a pint each. That water would have to last until the afternoon.

"Yes. He is smaller than the others. I think so. We need a code word in case we have to act." I thought for a moment. "How about *bingo*? If I say *bingo*, that means we act."

"Okay, *bingo*. But I think today we will be released. Let's see," Amir added.

"I hope you are right." I stared at the half-empty water jug.

"Do you know what *bingo* means?" I asked Amir.

"No."

"It's a game older people play, and what they say when they win. Bingo." He didn't understand, but it didn't matter; it was just a word.

"Bingo," Amir said, thinking about it.

"We also need to have a way to refer to the guards so we can understand each other when we talk about their conversations. The one who comes to speak with us late at night, let's call him the Grim Reaper. Who else?"

"There is the fat one," Amir said, referring to the large, friendly one with the gentle voice. I preferred to call him the large one with the soft voice.

"And the one with the long face," I added. They never allowed Amir to see their faces, so that was not helpful. "What about the two who were here the first night?" It was difficult to identify them, and I had trouble distinguishing their voices. That was it, the Grim Reaper and the large one with the soft voice.

I studied our enclosure. The palm trees were thick. An occasional gust filtered through, stirring the hot, stagnant air. Amir and I tried not to move too much or knock against each other in the oppressive environment. Just beyond, tantalizingly close, was an open field leading to the road. Without my glasses, I didn't know if the road was visible from where we were, but I could hear the infrequent sound of passing cars. Turning onto my stomach, I tried to look out between the palm leaves at the back, telling Amir to keep watch over the entrance.

In the morning the guard would sit outside the enclosure until the sun became too intense; then he would move into the shade just inside the entrance. Even outside he could easily hear everything we did: a slight movement on our mats, or the unusual rustling of the palm leaves. Carefully, I worked at one of the date palm fronds that made up our walls, looking for a way out. It took several minutes to remove the frond, digging in the dirt, then lifting it centimeter by centimeter, each motion creating a sound that we were sure would alert the suspicious guard. When I had managed to extract the large palm frond, I set it carefully on the ground and peered out. The palm branches were just high enough to fit under if I lay on my stomach.

I turned to Amir with a smile and gave him a thumbs-up. He looked back for a moment, and then kept his eyes on the entrance. I needed to clear the lower branches and ground cover so our exit would be as quiet as possible. Lying on my stomach, I put my arm through the opening and began to twist off small branches one by one. After a painfully slow half hour, having cleared most of the lower twigs and ground cover, I sat back up and carefully put the date palm frond back in place.

"I think we can fit through there," I said to Amir. "The field is just beyond. Let's call it Freedom's Gate." Amir smiled.

Freedom's Gate was the name of a frequent motif found in the paintings of Amir's friend Kamal, the best-known Iraqi artist living in Nasiriyah. It was represented by a bright red door, often the centerpiece of a complex tapestry of abstract houses and images, and signified the freedom he longed for.

Nasiriyah had been a modern city in the 1960s, with a thriving cultural center. During Saddam's reign, the Ministry of Information absorbed the Ministry of Culture, and most artists fled Iraq. Those who remained were closely watched, and were often told what to paint. Following the 1991 Gulf War, as Saddam exacted his revenge on the Shi'ite population, the city came heavily under the influence of Iranian-style fundamentalism. Women disappeared behind veils, and the cultural center all but vanished. For twenty years, Kamal had painted dark, tortured works that, when asked by the secret police what their meaning was, he had ironically interpreted as glorious visions of life in the south. Following Saddam's fall in 2003, Kamal's palette had changed dramatically to bright colors and lively scenes. Freedom's Gate began to appear in all his paintings. At first, it was an ideal well within reach. Then, as the Mahdi Army and fundamentalists exerted their influence in Nasiriyah, a distant myth.

Kamal would wave his thick fingers in disgust when Marie-Hélène and I told him about yet another public statue of his that had been destroyed by fundamentalists. Then, laughing like a child, he would recover himself, pointing to his latest work: a love story in the marshes.

Freedom's Gate was also the name Amir gave to the opening in Marie-Hélène's long black *abaya*, which parted occasionally, displaying a glimpse of skin, a view of the West, catching the eye of any Iraqi man close enough to see it. "You must close Freedom's Gate," Amir would say, pointing to her dress with a laugh.

. . .

Our plan would be to slip quietly though Freedom's Gate and be reborn into freedom, or simply run like hell. It made more sense than trying to overpower a guard with a gun.

"What do we do when we reach the road? Which direction should we go?" I asked Amir.

"We head toward the nearest town, then head west to Nasiriyah," Amir answered.

"Which way do you think the town is?"

"That way." Amir pointed parallel to the direction of the road toward the field where we were brought to sleep.

"How do you know?"

"It is the direction the cars travel in the morning. They must be going to town."

"And that is east," I said, pointing toward the entrance of the enclosure.

"How do you know?" he asked.

"The sun rises in the east and sets in the west."

"And that is south," Amir continued, pointing behind me.

"How do you know?" I asked.

"The man who prays at dinner, he prays toward Mecca, which is to the south."

I had not thought of that, and it confirmed that our directions were right.

"Do you think we can find a ride to Nasiriyah, or should we make our way through the fields?" I tried to imagine what it would be like without shoes.

"Somehow, I think we can make our way by car." Amir thought about it more. "But you know, we don't have money. It is not likely that we will find a ride without money."

"How about we promise someone one hundred dollars if they take us to Nasiriyah?" I suggested.

"Somehow," Amir said without conviction.

We were both doubtful that a car would pick up two dirty shoeless men without money and drive them an hour or more to Nasiriyah.

It occurred to me that Amir had lost his glasses as well.

"How will we know that the cars coming are not the kidnappers searching for us? We don't have our glasses. Are you farsighted, Amir?"

"Yes."

"That's good. Then at least you can be our eyes."

We should probably have a weapon, but there was nothing around except for date palm leaves. The new fronds as they appear low on the date palm tree are sharp and pointed. I slowly twisted one until it broke off. Then another, and a third. By slowly twisting the mature date palm leaves I could pull off a kind of natural string. I carefully wound the natural string around the three thin, six-inch spikes, tying them together to form one sharp spike. I had managed to fabricate a decent shiv, which also worked as an excellent mosquito-bite scratcher. I held it out to Amir. He didn't look convinced or intimidated.

Bingo, the Grim Reaper, Freedom's Gate, a shiv. The hours were passing slowly, with no sign of our release, but at least we were doing something.

"Can you teach me more Arabic, Amir?" I wanted more words in case we were separated.

"What do you want to know?"

"How about something useful. *Ana sahafi* means 'I am a journalist,' right?"

"That is right. *Ana sahafi. Ana ashtaghoul al athar. Ingil al haqiq.* I am a journalist. I work on archaeology. I carry the truth."

"*Ana français.*" I added with a smile.

"Of course, you are French." He laughed.

I repeated the words. He corrected my pronunciation and I repeated them again. After a few more tries, I lost interest. Improving my Arabic felt like a false exercise. My mind kept wandering back to Freedom's Gate and thoughts of escape.

As the morning dragged on, I tried again to engage Amir in conversation. An odd mix of anxiety and tedium, fermenting in the rising heat, began to dull my thinking. I wanted to keep my mind active with something other than the constant worry about captivity and what would happen next.

"Who was the philosopher you spoke of, Amir, the father of phenomenology?" Amir's conversations always seemed to lead back to either Foucault, a French postmodernist philosopher, or phenomenology. If it mattered so much to Amir, I wanted to know why.

"Hegel?" Amir replied.

"No, the other one."

"Husserl. Edmund Husserl," Amir said, sitting up straight.

"Can you explain it?"

Amir launched into a discussion about "subjective reality" and how it shapes our understanding of "objective truth."

Husserl meant nothing to me there, and I didn't understand a word he said. Talking philosophy was a way to pass the time, but in captivity I couldn't feign an interest in phenomenology, at least not as Amir explained it. We sat in silence for a while, as I applied the shiv to the mosquito bites on both feet, more than a hundred now, raw and bleeding.

"You said you wrote a thesis in college," Amir tried after a while. "What was it about?" I looked up, surprised that he remembered.

"It was based on the work of Henri Frankfort. You remember, the book you gave Marie-Hélène?" Amir had presented Marie-Hélène with a newly minted xeroxed copy of *Before Philosophy: The Intellectual Adventure of Ancient Man*, one of my favorite books, which I had read and reread while studying the ancient Near East. Amir photocopied everything, his simple publishing system born of necessity.

"It was about the impact of environment on religion," I started slowly, "and how religion is shaped by our experience with our environment. In ancient Egypt, the natural environment was stable and predictable. The sun came up and went down every day. The Nile flooded regularly, bringing fertile soil to the fields. Since the environment was constant, the Egyptians imagined a stable, hierarchical pantheon of gods with the sun at the top, reflecting the natural world around them. In ancient Mesopotamia the environment was unpredictable and unstable, with frequent storms, flooding, and other natural disasters. The gods the Mesopotamians imagined reflected this natural world of theirs, and were highly temperamental."

Scratching my bleeding feet and thinking about ancient religions influenced by their environment, I began to understand Amir's description of phenomenology. In the strangest of all possible worlds, our two ideas came together.

"The Egyptians' and Mesopotamians' ideas about religion were shaped by their natural world," I said, and then borrowing Amir's term: "the phenomenology of their environment." My mind started moving more quickly, a sensation that was liberating. "What religion would we invent if we were stuck here?" I put my hand on the date palm wall, our environment. "There would be demons based on the guards, malevolent gods and . . ." It was hard to imagine. We knew terror and captivity, but could there also be understanding and compassion?

Trapped and completely powerless in our enclosure, I thought hard about religious concepts shaped by the natural struggle between the weak and the strong.

"Think about Christianity," I continued. "Jesus, persecuted by the Romans, couldn't fight back, so instead of fighting, he embraced his weakness—turn the other cheek—finding an inner strength of will, mind, and spirit, and envisioned a God who gave strength to the weak. He discovered an understanding of God shaped by his captive environment."

In my mosquito-bitten delirium, I was borrowing liberally from thousands of years of history, philosophy, religion, and science, struggling to make sense of my fight for survival. From an evolutionary perspective, what would survival of the fittest mean in captivity; adaptation to my environment through cleverness, physically overpowering my captors, or something else? Should I strangle the guard as he walked us back to the enclosure in the morning? Should I try to run? Or should I accept captivity and try to overcome my kidnappers through patience, inner strength, and compassion?

Amir saw our world the way he wanted to see it: a short, difficult story that would have a happy ending. Be patient, wait, he counseled. I saw our world as I wanted to see it, a story whose ending depended on our actions. But the universe of our kidnappers remained a mystery, unknown to both of us. Our personal interpretations might have nothing to do with the reality of our situation.

Fighting back seemed like the worst option. That was sure to end badly, and that wasn't me. But I could still try to escape.

I lay on my back again and closed my eyes. I imagined Marie-Hélène and Zeugma, holding them, them holding me, feeling protected. Using the force of my thoughts I tried to send them a message: "I am okay."

Marie-Hélène started practicing Buddhism just before leaving for Iraq, after purchasing her bulletproof vest. Buddhists believe that the world is spiritually interconnected, entangled on a macro scale. I tend to approach life rationally: don't believe it unless you can see it, experience it, prove it is true. But I agreed with Marie-Hélène that there are many things about our universe that we don't understand. The classic scientific view is that objects exist and remain separate in space and time, influenced only by their immediate environment; a concept known as local realism—the moon is real even if no one sees it. A newer theory, however, speculates that the universe is governed by probabilities, not absolutes. Things can even be connected in strange ways, quantumly entangled, instantly sharing information even though they are physically separated. I thought about similar concepts of interconnectivity that appear in a number of religions, philosophies, and day-to-day observations, such as the butterfly effect: the idea that if a butterfly flaps its wings in the Iraqi marshes it can, through our interconnected world, create a storm in New York.

I turned on my side and watched as ants moved across the floor of the enclosure toward a few grains of rice spilled on the mat. Those ants would march away with the rice and be eaten by a chicken, who would be driven to Nasiriyah and sold to a buyer from Kellogg, Brown and Root, a Halliburton subsidiary. The chicken would end up on the plate of an American soldier, who would return to New York, where he would pass Marie-Hélène and Zeugma on the street. The soldier would bend down to pet Zeugma, who would sense something familiar in him.

Amir and I were experiencing a severe case of local realism. I preferred to imagine my quantum-Buddhist-butterfly-interconnected-entangled life with Marie-Hélène.

I lay on my back, rested my hands on my stomach, and pressed my eyelids tightly together. "I love you."

I woke again in the late afternoon, still jet-lagged, the apartment quiet. I checked my email, but still no word from Micah.

```
Micah
    I am really happy to be back. missing iraq. but
happy to be back alive and in one piece.
    when are you headed back?
    what is going on? did you get the camera back?
    travel safe sweet one
    xo
    mh
```

The small camera was important; it allowed us to film discreetly. I was disappointed to hear that it had been taken, and wasn't sure how Micah would get the final footage without it.

My sister, Chantal, had also flown back to the States and her home in Bloomington, Indiana, where she would begin another year of graduate school in music and comparative literature. She called Tante Olivia, our aunt who lives in Orlando near our mother, eagerly awaiting news.

"Fifty percent of the package is back," Chantal told her. "The wait is almost over. Two more days. Nothing can happen in two days."

After a visit to the gym, my first workout in three months that did not involve carrying body armor and media equipment, I had dinner at a new outdoor café around the corner, with Zeugma. Despite my enthusiasm at being back, I felt awkward, undone, uncomfortable, Micah's absence marked by the empty chair facing me.

Staying up late to readjust my internal clock, I checked my email one more time: still nothing. It was strange, and unlike Micah. "No news from you," I wrote. "Are you arriving tomorrow?"

Drifting into the fog of sleep, I thought vaguely about whom I'd try to reach in the morning if I still hadn't heard anything. Perhaps Micah wanted to surprise me and would arrive unannounced at the door. I fell asleep to that thought.

The morning passed, fading into a thick midday heat that sapped my energy and made it difficult to move or think. The small red plastic jug of water the guards left for us to share had been empty for hours, and I was beginning to feel weak and dizzy from thirst.

"*Maya barda, shokran?*" I asked the guard sitting outside. Cold water, thank you?

"Someone will come," he responded, uninterested.

After another hour, no one had appeared. Amir asked again. The man pointed the AK out the front of the enclosure at a forty-five-degree angle and fired a shot. The sound reverberated across the quiet afternoon. A single shot, apparently, was the signal to the others to come. He hadn't loaded the weapon. They must keep a bullet in the chamber, I thought. I waited to see how long the others took to respond. It was at least five minutes, perhaps ten, before someone arrived; just one person without a gun, somewhat surprised to hear the shot. The guard handed him the gun and went to fetch water.

"Any word about our situation?" we asked the new guard.

"None."

I hadn't expected an answer.

By the afternoon, the confines of the small enclosure were more punishing than my thirst. We were allowed to leave the enclosure briefly to urinate and defecate, using our left hand and the water to clean up. The guards would hand us a different red plastic jug with water and we would squat about twenty feet from the entrance; they would stand at the mouth of the enclosure, watching from a distance. Wrapping my arms around my knees for balance, staring at the dark yellow, urine-stained patches of parched earth, I basked for a moment in the strong sunlight. For the past two days I had urinated standing up, but Amir advised me to squat. Iraqi men always squat when urinating. The guards had told Amir that they thought my actions oddly foreign and indecent.

The few minutes outside the enclosure allowed me to stretch my legs and get my blood circulating. I was becoming desperate for those moments, but I rationed my requests, saving them for times of necessity, afraid the guards would say no.

The few minutes it took to relieve myself weren't enough. I had to exercise to keep up my strength. I asked Amir to ask the guard, who had moved into the mouth of the enclosure to avoid the strong sun, if I could stand up and stretch.

"Why?" the guard asked.

"To exercise," Amir explained.

He nodded and went back to reading to himself out loud from a small xeroxed religious pamphlet, sometimes singing the words softly.

With hardly enough room to move, I stood up in the center of the enclosure and began to stretch, going through some basic yoga poses slowly, not wanting to startle the guard. I closed my eyes and focused on breathing deeply for several minutes, then opened my eyes and stretched my arms up above my head, my hands reaching out through the small opening in the palm leaves. The guard must have thought it strange, and after a few minutes he told me that was enough.

"*Shokran,*" I thanked him, sitting back on my mat. He nodded, wrapping his keffiyeh tighter around his head, and kept reading.

"What kind of stretching is that?" Amir asked.

"Yoga. You should try it,"

"What does it do for you?"

"It builds strength and compassion. It helps you to focus, relax, and to stay calm. It's also good exercise."

"Can you teach me yoga?"

Amir sat up as I instructed him to breathe deeply and close his eyes. Not noticing any immediate impact, he relaxed after a minute, his frame slumping over.

"Muslims don't practice yoga?" I asked.

"No. The Hindus practice yoga; Muslims considered it paganism. It is not Islamic."

A few months earlier I had photographed the Iraqi wrestling team for *U.S. News & World Report,* lying on the old mat with my camera as wrestlers tossed each other around in preparation for the summer Olympics. The surroundings were a sad testament to thirty years of neglect: torn mats, shattered windows, and a single broken-down weight machine listing in the corner. The hope for the Olympic team was a determined young man who had been tortured by Saddam's son Uday for losing a competition.

"People don't exercise much in Iraq, do they?"

"No. People don't exercise the way they do in the West."

"What are you discussing?" the guard asked Amir.

"We are talking about Islam," Amir replied.

"Ahhhhh," he said.

"Thank him for allowing me to stretch," I said. Amir passed along my message.

"*Afwan*," he replied, not lifting his eyes from the book. You're welcome.

"What is he reading?" I asked Amir.

"A holy book from an Imam," Amir replied.

How ironic, I thought as Amir and I shared a look.

"Are we the first hostages he has had to guard?" I asked. Amir relayed my question.

"No," he said, looking over, "there was a man here before."

"The red blindfold," I said to Amir. "A foreigner?"

"No, an Iraqi."

"What happened to him?"

"He was released after a month." A week, a month, a year; what seemed the same to them was an inordinate amount of time to me. "We take people for a reason," he continued. "Sometimes former Baath Party members. After careful research we pick them up, usually at their home. Your story is unusual."

Although Amir did not say anything, he thought he knew who had been kidnapped before us, remembering a man from Nasiriyah who had told him of twenty-seven days in captivity in an enclosure in the marshes; his had been a long story.

"*Inta mitzawig?*" Are you married? the guard asked me, looking over.

"*Nam.*" Yes. I could never explain to them my close relationship with Marie-Hélène without saying I was married. And since Iraqis respected marriage, I felt it was better to be married, in their eyes.

"*Fee taleb?*" Children?

"*Nam, wahid.*" Yes, one.

"*Zane,*" he said. Good. "*Walid?*" Boy?

"*Bint,*" I replied, referring to Zeugma. Girl.

He nodded, smiling politely. A girl wasn't as good as a boy, but better than nothing. I loved Zeugma like a child, but since dogs are considered unclean in Islam, I didn't elaborate.

As it became dark, two guards blindfolded us and led us out to the field again to eat.

"What happened with the delegation from yesterday?" Amir asked after we had laid out our mats and sat down. They said they didn't know.

I turned to Amir. "What about the man you spoke to Friday night, your former student?"

"He has not returned. Maybe he is ashamed since I was his teacher." I was afraid his absence meant there was nothing he could do for us.

The mosquitoes had returned. I untied the cloth that bound my hands and wrapped it around my ankles to protect them. The guards watched me, but said nothing.

"The guard asks if you can teach him some English words," Amir said, as I sat with my mat folded around me, trying to fend off the mosquitoes.

"What does he want to know?" I offered, hoping to continue building our connection.

The guard spoke the words slowly in English. He already knew them; he just wanted to make sure he was saying them properly.

"Where are you from? What is your name? Sit down. Be quiet." A kidnapper's vocabulary. I stopped responding.

After we ate they blindfolded us again and led us back into the field to sleep. It was our third night in captivity. Marie-Hélène must have returned to New York by now, and Mr. Hamdani would certainly have contacted her. I lay awake trying to imagine how she would react to news of my kidnapping, and what was happening in New York. After two days, no word back from the group that had gone to Nasiriyah was a bad sign. It meant our situation was complicated. I feared that the longer we remained in captivity, the worse things would get.

Late in the night, the Grim Reaper returned.

I woke at five A.M. gripped with worry, feeling disconnected. My eyes focused on the shadowy outlines of our small apartment until I fell back to sleep. The phone woke me a little while later. The answering machine picked up. I recognized the voice. It was Micah's mom.

"Marie-Hélène, this is Suzanne." The words entered uninvited into the dark room. The Iraq trip and my vacation lay around me in half-emptied bags and piles of souvenirs, *hijabs*, journals, books, photographs—a still-undeveloped picture in my camera of my sister and me in Florence in front of the old bronze pig statue that brings good luck.

I turned over. Suzanne's voice was tired and drained. "Please call me back as soon as you can." I righted myself, leaning forward to see the time: 5:41 A.M. Something was wrong.

I called her back. "Suzanne, this is Marie-Hélène."

"Alan just called me." She stopped, unable to go on, and I wondered why Alan, Micah's dad, would be calling her so early. Her voice trembling slightly, she continued, "He got a call from the Associated Press." She paused again. "A journalist is missing in Iraq." She was being careful with her words. I took a deep breath. "They think it might be Micah."

I exhaled, sharp and loud. "What?"

"Micah is missing," she repeated. "I called the Associated Press and they told me, too. They picked it up from Al Jazeera."

I felt nauseated, the dizziness that comes from realizing the ground has disappeared beneath you. A story about Micah, not by Micah. On Al Jazeera, the Arab world's largest satellite TV station. The network had become the first stop for information about kidnapped foreigners and hostages. Al Jazeera was often the first to broadcast this kind of information, and it was usually correct. I was convinced that Al Jazeera knew what had really happened.

No matter how softly she spoke, she couldn't blunt the reality of her words. They created a canyon in my mind into which all my thoughts fell. I had to instruct my body: breathe in, breathe out.

Everything around me confused and dark, only one thing was clear: Micah needed us and we had to act. I had just returned from Iraq; I knew the country, I knew people there, I could help him. Words formed inside of me, and by speaking them, I could make them true.

"Suzanne, he is okay. He will be okay. I promise you. He will come home, I promise you we will bring him home."

Speaking deliberately and slowly, the words thick in my mouth, I asked Suzanne whom she had talked to at the AP.

I heard her shuffling papers, and I searched for a pen and something to write on, finding an old envelope from *Archaeology Magazine* in the trash. I wrote down the name and number: Nick Wadhams at the AP.

"What else did he say?" I asked.

"Not much, that's all he knew. He was nice. Then he asked if it was okay to ask me a couple of questions."

I froze. "What kind of questions?"

My gut told me that we shouldn't talk about Micah to the media until we knew more. I told this to Suzanne.

"I understand. I didn't tell him anything, really."

"What did he ask you?"

"He asked if Micah was French."

"Why?"

"I don't know. I think he said the Al Jazeera report said that the missing person was a French-American journalist."

"And?"

"I said I didn't know. I tried to explain that you had a French passport, you had talked about Micah getting one."

"That's good. We've got to keep it out there that he is French."

"He asked me if Micah was married. I said I didn't know. Maybe you'd gotten married in Iraq. I didn't know. He stopped asking me questions, because I kept saying 'I don't know.' I really didn't know, I couldn't think, and I didn't know what I should say. But I asked him *not* to say that Micah is not French, and to leave my comments out of it for the moment."

"Is he writing a story?"

"I think so—I don't know. He suggested I call senators and representatives for help, and the State Department, that they would probably be the ones tracking information. He also said I could go to Google and type in Micah's name to find the latest news."

"All right. Let's just coordinate what we are going to say. Let's all check in and agree on what we are doing before saying anything to the press. I'll call you back in a few minutes. Don't worry."

"Okay," Suzanne said quietly. "I'll make some calls, too."

I hung up. Missing. If he was detained or dead, Al Jazeera would have said that. To me, in Iraq, in a story on Al Jazeera, missing meant one thing: kidnapped. I thought, *Micah*, then *kidnapped*, unable to put those words together. They were live wires that would short-circuit my thoughts.

5:51 A.M.

Before calling me, Suzanne had called Micah's younger sister, Eva, and when Eva didn't pick up, had left a message telling her to go to her dad's house. Eva, who was finishing her Ph.D. at Yale University, lived just two blocks from Alan, a professor in molecular biology. Eva had already gotten a call from Sally, Alan's partner, at 5:30 A.M.

"They took him," Sally said.

"What, who . . . what are you talking about?" Eva asked, waking from sleep.

"They took him . . . they got him . . . they took Micah."

Eva began to scream, "No no no no no no no no . . . who has him . . . who?"

"The kidnappers."

By the time Suzanne called, Eva was already running down the street to Alan's house.

Eva wanted to be strong for her parents—she had to protect them, keep them from the pain of the news, afraid they might not be able to stand it. She fought hard to control her own fear.

She rushed into Alan's house and found her dad upstairs, Sally desperately trying to console him.

5:53 A.M.

"Let's do this, let's do this," I said aloud, willing myself to move. "You can do this." The only response came from Zeugma, who raised her eyes at me from her corner. She stayed tightly curled around herself. I looked for the phone. It was on the floor. I realized I had dropped it. My paralyzed fingers kept punching the wrong numbers. Waiting for the ring, I closed my eyes for a few seconds and held them shut, squeezing tightly. I wanted to pull my eyelids down like draperies, to shelter myself from what was happening, to hold on to a last moment of peace. When they opened, I would have to face the awful truth.

5:54 A.M.

"AP news desk," someone said hurriedly after the second ring.

I looked down at the envelope, already full of notes from my conversation with Suzanne, searching for the name of the reporter who had called her.

"I'm looking for Nick Wadhams."

"Nick here." There was newsroom clatter in the background.

"Micah Garen, my partner, is missing in Iraq," I said, forgetting to introduce myself.

"I'm very sorry," he responded. His voice was gentle.

"What have you heard? What's going on?" I asked.

"All we know is what we picked up on Al Jazeera early this morning, that a reporter is missing in southern Iraq."

"Why do they think it's Micah?"

"The deputy governor of Dhi Qar has identified the missing journalist as Micah, saying that his translator's family, the family of"—papers rustled as he searched—"Amir Doshi, had said they hadn't seen Amir in three days, which was when they reported it to Al Jazeera." He spoke slowly, not wanting to overwhelm me. We both paused, Nick waiting for my reaction, me waiting for his. Silence echoed between us.

"Are you still there?" I asked Nick.

"Yes, I'm here."

"Is there anything else?" I asked, afraid.

"That's all we know right now. When did you last hear from Micah?"

"Are you writing a story?"

"Yes, we are. If it's okay with you, I have a few questions," Nick continued.

I hesitated. It wasn't even six A.M. I was in shock, unable to handle questions. But I realized a story would go out with or without my input. This was possibly an opportunity to help Micah, since people would see the media coverage. It was important to get the right information about him out in Iraq, because it would clarify who he is: a documentary filmmaker and journalist. A civilian should not be harmed. More importantly, if it had been reported that he was French, I hoped that it would continue to be reported that he was French. My hope clung desperately to that fact.

I wanted to tell Nick to protect Micah; I didn't want to answer questions. "If Al Jazeera is reporting that he is French, that helps him. If the people who have him know he is French, it will protect him. People in Iraq feel better about the French than the Americans. They would always say, 'French, good' and give the thumbs-up when they heard I was French. If they think he is an American, it will make things much more dangerous for him."

In a conversation with a reporter you normally answer questions, not give instructions.

"Is he French?" Nick asked.

I explained to Nick that I was half French—I had dual citizenship, both French and American—and had worked and traveled in Iraq with Micah, and just gotten back home. Micah and I always traveled with my French passport, leaving our American passports hidden in our room at the Dulaimi Hotel in Baghdad.

"So Micah is not French?" he pressed, trying to clarify.

I did not want to lie. But if for some reason people thought Micah was French, it had to stay that way. I wasn't sure why it had been reported he was French. Had Micah told someone? Had someone who knew us said he was French?

"Well, I have a French passport," I continued, "but Micah is American, he has an American passport."

Anticipating Nick's response, I continued, speaking louder, cutting him off.

"But the question of nationality could mean the difference between life and death for Micah. Do you understand? If they think he is an American, he could be killed."

As a journalist, Nick would understand, I prayed. Journalists in Iraq were becoming targets. An American journalist was a prime target.

"I understand," Nick replied. "But we can't lie."

"I know, I know, I don't want you to lie. Please don't say he is an American. At least not until we know more. It's already out there about his being French," I pleaded.

"I'll tell you what. I'll talk to my editor and call you right back."

"Please call me right back. Please call me right away."

Micah and Amir had been missing for three days. Three days was a long time. I didn't feel that Micah might already be dead, and so it didn't cross my mind. I believed I would know, deep within, if he was dead.

5:58 A.M.

Suzanne called Jonathan, Micah's older brother who lived in New Jersey with his wife, Nieves, and their newborn baby, Tomas.

"This can't be happening," Jonathan responded when Suzanne told him Micah was missing. "This can't be happening. I can't handle this. I have a new baby. No, no, no, no, this can't be happening," he repeated over and over, part cry, part wail, that grew louder, something she had never heard from her son.

With that terrible sound, Suzanne too began to come undone. She tried to comfort Jonathan, but his anguish was so deep she couldn't console him.

6:10 A.M.

Nick didn't call back fast enough, so I called him.

"I talked to my editor about the French thing," he answered. "We can't say something that is false, but we don't have to focus on it either. We will just leave the initial information out there."

It was a small but important victory that anchored me. If I thought of Micah's disappearance as a series of small, solvable problems, I believed I could handle it, and contain my fear.

"Micah is a reporter, he's only a reporter," I began. "He has nothing to do with the military or the government. He was in Iraq covering a story about culture, a story Iraqis would care about. It's important that no one associates him with the government."

"Yes," he assured me.

"Have you heard anything else?" I asked anxiously.

"No, nothing new." If it's okay, he continued, "I have a few more questions. "When did you last hear from Micah?"

"I haven't gotten an email from him in a few days." I checked my email. August 11, Micah's last email to me: more than three days.

"What is your relationship to Micah?"

It was complicated, less definable than nationality. I didn't really want to answer, because I didn't want to be drawn into the story. Micah was missing, and all I wanted was to get more information to try and help him. Now the story spotlight was widening, and I wasn't sure what role to play.

"We are partners," I began, "in life and work. Micah and I work together as documentary filmmakers, photographers, and journalists. We have a small media company, Four Corners Media, and we were in Iraq together working on a documentary film about the looting of archaeological sites. We've also been together for a long time. You could say we are life partners."

The explanation was too long and hard to digest. We were partners in life, in love, in business, and as parents to Zeugma. We were committed to each other, and *girlfriend* did not convey the depth of our love and fidelity. There was no title for someone between girlfriend and wife other than *partner*, and that sounded like a business relationship.

If I was going to be quoted, and speaking for Micah, I had to be taken seriously. Though this was an AP story, my audience was Iraq. Any comment to the media would circulate around the world. *Girlfriend* held no meaning, and little respect, in Iraq. *Wife* did.

"Fiancée," I told Nick.

"Okay."

"Please, call me right away if you hear anything new."

"I will," Nick promised. "I'm heading off my shift soon, but the guy who comes in will know everything. Call us anytime. Good luck."

How would "the guy who comes in" know everything I had just explained to Nick?

I was beginning to realize that there would be many people involved in this, with different ideas and efforts, and not all of them as patient and understanding as Nick. Someone needed to coordinate the information to make sure the people who cared about Micah were speaking with one voice, so the media would get the right message. We all needed to be focused on the same thing: bringing Micah home alive.

6:24 A.M.

I called my sister, Chantal. *Please pick up, please pick up.* The phone rang and rang. I was desperate to hear her voice. "Please leave a message," an electronic voice instructed.

"Chantie, call me back. Call me back right now."

I tried again, hoping the ringing of the phone would wake her.

"You have to call me back right away."

She picked up after the third call.

"Babycat, hi, what's going on?" she asked in a sleepy voice. I couldn't find the words.

"What's going on, tell me," she prompted.

"Micah is missing. We just got a call from the AP. It's on Al Jazeera."

She was quiet. I could hear her straightening up in bed, pulling herself together.

"I'm on my way to the airport. I'll be right there."

6:32 A.M.

"I just heard, what can I do to help?" Scott Heidler, a friend and reporter who had been in Iraq for eight months, called from Kabul.

"Anything I can do?" Bob Sullivan, a journalist friend of ours who had also worked in Iraq, asked by email. The emails and phone calls from our friends and colleagues began pouring in from Iraq, Afghanistan, France, Egypt, Japan.

Bob, Scott, and I began an email dialogue about what to do next. Getting more information about Micah and putting out the right message was our biggest concern.

Bob suggested contacting Al Jazeera to have the journalism community vouch for Micah's credentials, and to drive home the message that he was a dedicated archaeological journalist. He said that Al Jazeera would probably know how to contact someone who knew how to contact someone, though they wouldn't admit it. We all agreed that behind-the-scenes contacts were more important right now than making a public statement.

"You tell me if you want me to contact Al Jazeera for help," he said.

"Go for it."

6:40 A.M.

As Scott, Bob, and I continued to talk over email, I was interrupted by ringing phones, my home phone and my cell phone: first one call, then two, then call-waiting, then someone on hold as the media picked up the story. Soon the rings were like rain, filling the apartment. I phoned close friends, wanting to keep them informed and hoping they could help. I called Aparna Mohan, a friend from graduate school at SAIS, the Johns Hopkins School of Advanced International Studies, who now worked in public relations.

She burst into a welcome song. "Oh my goodness! Welcome back! How was Iraq? How was Italy?"

"Aparna, I just got a call. Micah is missing." I tried to be calm for both of us.

Though she was composed, worry hung on the edge of her words. "Okay, we'll figure this out. What can I do?"

"Please monitor the news; I can hardly handle the phones."

After we hung up, she called another friend from SAIS living in Toronto, who immediately emailed a friend of hers, Dan Senor, who had been the spokesperson for the CPA in Iraq until the transfer of sovereignty in June 2004. "A friend and journalist Micah Garen is missing in Iraq," she wrote.

He responded right away. "I'm working on it."

7:31 A.M.

After leaving three messages on his cell phone, I woke Noble Smith of the Carr Foundation, who offered to come down to New York to help me, even though his wife was due to have their first baby in a few days.

Greg Carr told me he would talk to media friends for advice on making a statement, and get names in the Arab media who might know something.

"We'll get through this," Greg assured me. Both Greg and Noble felt an enormous sense of responsibility. "Come back," Noble had written Micah recently, concerned about what he called the *"Year of Living Dangerously* syndrome," where a reporter keeps digging deeper and deeper, taking increasing risks on a never-ending quest to break the big story.

7:28 A.M.

There was no refuge from the calls, even for a minute, but I had to act, not just react to the ringing phone. Who would know the most about Micah's recent movements, I thought. Where he was and who had last seen him. Perhaps he had spent the night at Umma to film the first night of the new civil guards, and been ambushed. Perhaps his recent coverage of the ambulance story had put him in danger.

I remembered Micah's email about an Iraqi ambulance that the Italians had shot during fighting with the Mahdi Army, killing the family inside. After the story came out in Italy, Micah wrote that he felt unwelcome, and had decided to leave the Italian base. The Italians had been our friends, and had been very hospitable while I was there. Had the ambulance story changed their view of Micah? Had they detained him? If Micah had left the base and stayed in Nasiriyah, had he been followed?

I emailed Captain Sarli, the Italian press officer in Nasiriyah, hoping for clues and their help: "We really need your and the Italian military's help to save Micah."

8:14 A.M.

My SAIS network, friends and colleagues from graduate school, was fully engaged. Soon, like a strong wind, the memos, emails, and phone calls saying that Micah had disappeared in Iraq filled offices in Congress, government agencies, development and humanitarian organizations, media organizations. Several SAIS friends at the Operations Center at the State Department in Washington, D.C., assured me that the State

Department was doing everything it could. "My contacts are your contacts. What can I do?"

Quickly, a U.S. embassy contact in Baghdad whom Dan Senor had been in touch with wrote back, saying that the only thing they knew about Micah was from the news wires. Because Micah was not embedded with any of the multinational units at the time of his abduction, they did not have a record of his movements. It would be hard to create a time line of Micah's last several days.

Aparna was scouring the news, sending me every news article. Most of them were the same, except for one report from AFX News, a subsidiary of Agence France-Presse, about the ambulance story.

"The head of archaeological services in Nasiriyah, Abdul Amir al-Hamdani, said Garen has been living for the past few days in a hotel in the city . . . he had fallen foul of Italian troops in the area after accusing them of killing civilians. . . . As a result, the Italians banned him from their base and he moved into the city, Hamdani said."

In Baghdad, the U.S. embassy contact sent another email saying that they were piecing the story together on their end. They had spoken with the Italians and learned that Micah had been staying with them, and that he had gone with his translator on Friday to the Nasiriyah market, where he was supposedly abducted. The Italians said they were following the story closely, and that the Carabinieri were investigating and searching for him. "I guess he was very well liked by the Carabinieri, so they've taken a personal interest in the matter," he wrote.

Why weren't the Italians saying he had left the base? "Supposedly abducted" concerned me as well. It expressed doubt. If either the United States embassy or the Italian forces were not certain he had been kidnapped, they might not be pursuing it with all their resources. It also lacked urgency, and there was no time to waste.

Sheryl Mendez, a photo-editor friend at *U.S. News & World Report* in New York, was on the line. "I am talking to Rita in Baghdad," she said.

Call-waiting broke in. "Hang on," I said, picking up the other line. I heard, "Hi, this is *Good Morning America.*"

"Hold on."

I switched back to the other line. "Sheryl?" The line had been disconnected.

My landline rang. "This is Suzanne."

"Hi, Suzanne, hold on." I clicked back.

"Scott, I'm talking to Sheryl, who is talking to Rita in Baghdad. I'll get right back to you."

Another ring. "Hi, this is the *ABC Evening News.*"

8:49 A.M.

An official from the U.S. embassy wrote: "So you know, both the Italians and our embassy are very committed, from the ambassador's office all the way down to the Navy Seals out searching for him with the Carabinieri."

Happy that the U.S. embassy seemed to be taking a strong interest, I was still concerned that they would not be able to do much.

My first instinct had been to reach out to friends and colleagues—journalists and my SAIS network—not the U.S. government, because I knew firsthand how difficult it was to get things done in Iraq. Helping Micah meant having the right contacts, and being able to act on that knowledge. Insurgent attacks, daily and deadly, made it dangerous for soldiers and government officials to move around Iraq, and even more difficult for them to build ties to the community.

In Iraq, the Coalition and local Iraqis coexisted like oil and water, rarely mingling. The Coalition lived on military bases or in the Green Zone, the large, fortified, and heavily guarded compound in the center of Baghdad surrounded by fifteen-foot blast walls. Once Saddam's palace and the seat of government, the Green Zone now housed the U.S. embassy, other U.S. government offices, and contractors. The rest of Iraq, including foreign journalists and relief workers, lived in what the Coalition called the Red Zone. How could the military or government agencies, operating from the Green Zone and military bases, gather information about Micah, learn who was holding him and where?

I began calling and emailing people I knew who had connections with Iraqis, mostly journalists, who had friends and sources, who could make contact immediately and, ultimately, negotiate.

. . .

News that Micah was missing quickly spread in Baghdad. The community of freelance journalists, who always look out for one another, sprang into action. Rita Leistner, a Canadian photojournalist friend who was also staying at the Dulaimi Hotel, heard the news from a *Rolling Stone* correspondent. The humble Dulaimi, rumored to have doubled as a brothel before the arrival of foreign correspondents, had become the hotel of choice for freelancers and journalists on a budget. Dulaimi family members and friends who worked in the hotel would drink tea and watch television in the red-carpeted lobby and greet us warmly when we returned from a long day of filming. "Hello, Mr. Mike, hello, Mrs. Helen, *Salaam alaikum, alaikum, salaam, sheku maku, maku shi, sholnik,* good. Tea?" Peace be upon you, and peace to you, what's going on, nothing, how are you, good. Tea?

The Internet was down at the Dulaimi, as it often was, so Rita ran to the *USA Today* office in the neighboring al-Hamra, the tall white hotel where larger U.S. and foreign media companies stayed. The upscale al-Hamra had a pool and satellite dishes.

Because the wires reported that Micah was French, Rita contacted the U.S. embassy in Baghdad to let them know he was also an American citizen. The embassy asked for a picture, so she convinced Hamza Dulaimi, the hotel manager, to let her into Micah's room. Moving gingerly among Micah's scattered belongings, she found his driver's license, photographed it, and emailed the image to the embassy.

She ran upstairs to tell Andy Berends, an American documentary filmmaker and friend, about Micah's disappearance. Together they wrote a profile of Micah for the consulate that included a detailed physical description: "He has green eyes and is 5 ft 9 inches tall. Approximately 150 to 160 pounds. His hair is more gray than in these photos. In fact, mostly gray salt and pepper. He kind of looks Iraqi, wearing a mustache when I last saw him Wednesday or Thursday night. Dresses casually in dark trousers and plaid shirts." Andy reread the description and said, "He sounds like every Iraqi man." Rita wondered how she could make him stand out. She added "trim and attractive."

Andy sent an email to James Longley, another friend and American documentary filmmaker who had spent a lot of time in Nasiriyah working on a film about the Mahdi Army. From Erbil in northern Iraq, James emailed back quickly that he had already heard the news, and agreed to try to contact Sheik Aws al-Khafaji, a young, ambitious Shi'ite cleric and the top Sadr cleric in Nasiriyah who had studied at the Hawza, a Shi'ite religious school in Najaf. James knew him well.

8:55 A.M.

My cell phone rang and I leapt to the wall where I'd plugged it in. "I'm at the airport catching a flight to New York," my sister said. "Thanks, Chantal, hang on." I jumped to pick up the ringing landline; it was the U.S. embassy in Baghdad, asking for Micah's fiancée. Bob Callahan, who worked in media relations, was soothing and tried to put a positive face on the situation.

"Sometimes people show up again. We've had several cases where people show up after a couple days—their cars broke down or they didn't have access to communication and they were out of touch for a while, then they turned up," he said.

I didn't believe for a moment that Micah was simply missing and would reappear. That wasn't Micah, and that wasn't Iraq. If someone was missing, there was more behind it.

"He's not missing, he's kidnapped—it's on Al Jazeera," I told Bob. "There is no time to waste."

He asked me about Micah's nationality. I told Bob the same thing I'd told Nick. "He's American, but he traveled under my French passport, and—"

"Stop right there," Bob interrupted. "The fact that he is an American citizen is a good thing. It is good for us to know that. We can put one hundred percent of our assets into helping him."

If Micah had dual nationality, he explained, it would make it harder, because two governments would have to cooperate and that could slow things down.

"Yes, that's great," I told him. "But you have to know how important it is that it continues to be out there that he is French. It could save his life."

"I understand," he said. Internally, they would operate with the knowledge that Micah was American, and would not interfere with any media reports about his nationality.

"By coincidence, there's a team of hostage negotiators traveling through Baghdad," he continued.

"Are they working on Micah's case?"

"They are now. You're very lucky," he told me. "They're among the best we have."

I didn't know what the hostage team could do, or where they had flown in from. If they were new to Iraq, how would they be able to operate quickly and effectively on the ground? Still, I was thankful that many people were working from different angles. But I wasn't going to take chances with Micah's life.

Mitch Prothero, the Committee to Protect Journalists' "new man in Baghdad," got in touch with Joel Campagna, CPJ's Middle East Program coordinator in New York, the minute he saw the news. Eva contacted Joel early Monday morning, after being given his name by a friend, and they spoke every few hours. Joel told her they were trying to find out who was holding Micah.

The network of our friends, families, and colleagues continued to grow and overlap: Erbil, Baghdad, Kabul, Tokyo, Boston, New Haven, Washington.

The morning was complete chaos. My cell phone and landline never stopped ringing.

9:02 A.M.

A Pentagon official in Baghdad called. I told him what I knew, everything about our film project, my concern about the strange Italian situation, and my fears that the U.S. government would not help Micah. What's one hostage in the middle of a war?

"The government takes it seriously," he told me, "and I take it seriously. It's like it happened to someone I know. We will be working for your fiancé as if he were one of ours. I'm going to say a prayer for him," he added.

Prayer? Pentagon! Prayer was powerful, but it was not the answer I was looking for.

"Thank you, I am sure that will help," I told him.

"It can," he said. "I believe in it. I'm Catholic."

"I'm Catholic, too," I said.

"I'd work for him and pray for him no matter what—Catholic, Muslim, whatever. No one deserves this."

His personal interest, frequent phone calls, and position at the Pentagon encouraged me.

He sent over a form to be filled out right away. I was to list everything we knew, every detail, including Micah's personal information: The Hostage Report Checklist.

In New Haven, Alan had received a forwarded email in which Micah had expressed concern about how he'd been treated after reporting the ambulance story. When Alan read that email, he was certain that Micah had been made to disappear because of his reporting. "We'll never know what happened to Micah." He covered his face with his hands. "We'll never know."

The news continued to come out online in the press, but it still wasn't clear what had happened to Micah. "A French-American journalist has disappeared in the southern Iraqi city of Nasiriyah," wrote the AP. Dow Jones referred to "the journalist reported missing in southern Iraq."

Most wires still carried the news that Micah was missing or had disappeared and that's how I talked about it with friends, not wanting to create panic, but in my heart, I thought, *Kidnapped.*

9:54 A.M.
CNN emailed me to confirm the earlier Al Jazeera report, which I had not yet read, including it in their email.

```
Micah Garen, a French journalist who also carries
the U.S. citizenship has been kidnapped along with
his translator in the Iraqi Southern city of
Nasiriyah.
```

Kidnapped. Seeing the word made it real. If I didn't force myself to act, I would slip into darkness. Being kidnapped in Iraq had been our worst fear, something Micah and I had talked about but, because we'd worked mostly in the south, never thought would actually happen. With great effort, I clenched my fists, I breathed, I blinked, I stood up, willing myself back to action.

Micah had been kidnapped. Now I needed details. The details might hold clues to help me find him.

Something wasn't right. It was the fourth day; the kidnappers would certainly have called the *International Herald Tribune* to check my credentials. They would know that I am a journalist. Mr. Hamdani would have made contact long ago. The question of innocence would have been settled. Unless . . . *Unless* led down an endless road of possibilities. Unless they had connections to the looters in Fajr. Unless they were waiting for someone to buy us. Unless, being an American, I was shit out of luck.

In the morning, a new guard, a boy who could not have been more than sixteen, came to watch us. I sat on my mat with my legs crossed and my shirt off, facing forward. He perched at the entrance looking at me, keffiyeh covering his face, then raised the AK to his eyes and sighted it at my chest.

I knew what an AK could do; an AK fires a high-velocity round that can penetrate several layers of steel. On Christmas evening in Baghdad, I had left a holiday dinner at the Sheraton Hotel to find my driver terrified. He had been caught in a hail of AK gunfire from two drunken men in a passing car, a bullet cleanly piercing the steel hood of the car and lodging somewhere in the engine. An AK round could easily penetrate the Level III Kevlar vests that we often wore hidden under our clothes. The only protection was an inch-thick steel or ceramic plate on top of the vest, not practical if you want to look like an Iraqi.

Here in the enclosure, from a distance of five feet, a single shot to the chest from an AK would certainly be fatal. The boy kept the gun pointed squarely at my chest, staring down the barrel. This was the first time since I had been brought to the enclosure that a guard had pointed a gun directly at me. The risk of the gun going off and accidentally killing your captive was too high. I knew now there was a bullet in the chamber, which meant one wrong move and my story would be over. Was he keen to kill me because I was an American? Was he just playing around? Was he afraid? I maintained eye contact, trying to appear friendly. I thought it would be harder to kill me if he had to look me in the eye. After a minute he lowered the gun, then turned and went out.

The boy was nervous, perhaps because he was young. He never spoke, ignoring our questions. He would sit outside the enclosure, then run in, pointing the gun at us, perhaps expecting to find that we had escaped. Eventually, he would go back out, wrapping his keffiyeh tightly as he went.

After a few hours, another guard came to relieve the boy, relieving me as well. The new guard was probably in his late teens or early twenties, with a long face and soft eyes, and wore a white dishdasha. He sat in the entrance of our enclosure with a small xeroxed book, instructing Amir to face the back of the enclosure, but didn't mind if I looked at him. I recognized his voice from the day before. He smiled as he readjusted a red-and-white-checked keffiyeh over his head, looping it loosely across his face and settling it on his shoulder.

"Any news about our situation?" Amir asked, turning his head slightly in the guard's direction.

"No, but another group is headed to Nasiriyah to discuss it. Your story is not so important. There are other things more important."

"Such as?" Amir asked.

"They are preoccupied with the fighting in Najaf. It will be settled, it takes time."

Starved for information, I could understand from his words only that the fighting in Najaf had not improved, but that was all. Any connection to Najaf, a conflict whose outcome was neither quick nor certain, frightened me.

His keffiyeh slipped down, revealing his oblong ocher face, brown eyes, and shy expression. He readjusted it to cover his face, then asked why I had come to Iraq. Amir told him about my interest in archaeology. My first trip to Iraq, in June 2003, was a strange confluence of events springing from a newspaper article.

• • •

Headline: IRAQI LOOTERS TEARING UP ARCHAEOLOGICAL SITES, May 23, 2003. The front page of The New York Times displayed a picture of a looter at the archaeological site Isin, carrying away a pot on his head as other looters stood by, guns in hand. I had read about the looting of the Iraq National Museum a month earlier, and Donald Rumsfeld's casual dismissal of the tragedy: "It's the same picture of some person walking out of some building with a vase . . . 'My goodness, were there that many vases?' " The looting of the museum took place over a period of three chaotic days in April during the fall of Baghdad. But the archaeological sites were being destroyed en masse almost a full month after the declared end of major combat operations.

I had spent the war deep in the bowels of corporate America consulting at a bank in New Jersey. It was the cost of being an independent journalist. To fund our work, Marie-Hélène and I spent half the year on various consulting projects. Independent generally meant independent of money, but it also meant we could focus on the stories that we really cared about. Since 2000 we had filmed and photographed the destruction of the Roman archaeological site Zeugma in southeastern Turkey, recorded an oral history of American's thoughts following the September 11 attacks, and, working with Sheryl Mendez at *U.S. News & World Report*, our entrée into freelance photojournalism, photographed the plight of Afghan refugees in Pakistan in 2001.

The article in *The New York Times* motivated me. With the money I had saved up I decided that day I was headed to Baghdad to cover the story of the looting. My father was worried and did his best to talk me out of it. "The story of the looting has already been covered," he insisted. "What more can you add?" I understood why he was saying this— anything to keep me from going to Iraq. "One story is not enough. You have to keep the interest alive in the media," I told him. We were very good at picking opposing sides of an argument and playing them out in two-hour volleys over the phone. No one ever won, and I was headed to Baghdad.

The State Department couldn't advise me about visas to Iraq. A frustrated consular officer told me that the Pentagon controlled everything, and wasn't telling them anything.

Before I hung up, she added, "When you get to the border, can you email me and tell me what is going on?"

I flew to Amman, Jordan, on June 1, 2003, and picked up a journalist visa at the Intercontinental Hotel, where I met up with a seasoned Hungarian journalist, Jozef Maki, and a young man from England, Mark Gordon-James, fresh out of college. Mark was in his early twenties and had come to Iraq to spend the summer starting an English-language newspaper, the *Baghdad Bulletin*. The three of us hired a GMC and hooked up with an NBC convoy to make the twelve-hour overnight trip from Amman to Baghdad. The Australian NBC security team supplied a walkie-talkie so that we could keep in radio contact as we raced across the desert at eighty miles an hour to avoid a possible ambush.

Approaching Ramadi for the final two-hour leg into Baghdad, a voice crackled across the radio in a strong Australian accent: "Put en yer Kevlar." Jozef and I were already wearing our vests. He had a wife and child, I had a girlfriend and a dog; we both had families to return to. Mark was in possession of only a well-pressed pink oxford shirt.

In the months following the fall of Baghdad, thousands of veteran journalists, freelance journalists, humanitarians, missionaries, soldiers, returning exiles, contractors, criminals, terrorists, and everything in between poured into the country, waved on by a few U.S. soldiers who stood at the Iraqi side of the Jordanian border directing traffic.

For a brief moment it was an atmosphere of celebration and opportunity. Iraq was free and open for business. Amid the euphoria, there was a chronic sense of doubt. Many Iraqis had electricity for only two hours a day, hospitals had little equipment or medicine, 60 percent of the country didn't have jobs, the Iraqi army had been dismissed with no way to feed their families, and there were not enough Coalition troops to secure the country. And, of course, my issue: world history was rapidly disappearing. As the stories began to emerge, the atmosphere darkened, and by late summer, the climate had changed considerably.

The *Baghdad Bulletin* was short-lived. It had to survive by paid ad sales, but the left-leaning editorial perspective didn't resonate with its advertising base: corporations looking to take advantage of the new lucrative contracts coming out of the country. The advertisers disappeared and, before Saddam emerged from his hidey-hole in December, so did the fledgling newspaper.

Arriving in Baghdad, I took a room with Jozef in the Flowerland, which we shared for eighty dollars a night, switching to the cheerless al-Musaffir two days later for forty dollars a night. It was across from the cheapest option, the Dulaimi Hotel, for twenty a night.

Jozef spent his days poking around, trying to find out who this Sadr was. At that time, Muqtada al-Sadr was a little-known Shi'ite cleric, rumored to be in his late twenties and rapidly gaining popularity in the Shi'ite slums of Baghdad. Once named Saddam City, the Shi'ite neigh-

borhood had been renamed Sadr City in honor of Muqtada al-Sadr's father, Grand Ayatollah Mohammed Sadeq al-Sadr, who'd been killed,
along with two of Sadr's brothers, by Saddam in 1999 in Najaf. Muqtada
al-Sadr's uncle Grand Ayatollah Mohammed Baqir al-Sadr had been a
widely respected intellectual and the head of the populist Islamic Dawa
Party in Iraq. After leading demonstrations against Saddam and the
Baath Party, he'd been executed by Saddam in 1980. Following the deaths
of his uncle, father, and brothers, Muqtada al-Sadr had gone into hiding,
under the tutelage of Iranian Ayatollah Kadhem al-Ha'iri.

Jozef had heard that Muqtada al-Sadr had recently organized his own
militia in Sadr City. Jozef knew this was an important story, and I accompanied him to a Sadr-linked mosque in Taji, north of Baghdad, where a
young cleric acknowledged that they had organized civil patrols for their
own protection in their neighborhood but denied that anyone carried
weapons.

"How do you protect yourselves if you don't have weapons?" Jozef
persisted. It wasn't a militia, the young cleric insisted. After the interview,
we headed to the roof of the mosque to take pictures of the neighborhood, stumbling on shell casings and military uniforms scattered everywhere.

During my first two weeks in Iraq, I was cautious about traveling to archaeological sites located in remote areas of the desert. Instead, I went to
Babylon to get my footing. The site of Babylon just outside of Hillah was
encircled by a marine base, Camp Babil. During the advance on Baghdad, the marines had swept north through the desert, turning east at
Najaf and moving up through Hillah, then on to Baghdad. The marines
often set up camp in Saddam's former palaces. Babylon was the site of
one of Saddam's more elaborate palaces, situated on top of a man-made
hill just beyond the archaeological site.

Three days after the marines pitched camp, several Iraqis asked the
marines to stop the looting that was beginning at the historic ruins.
The marines obliged, extending the barbed-wire perimeter to encom-
pass the ruins.

The marines appeared to have things under control. A public affairs
officer gave frequent tours to soliders, reading the history of Babylon
from a two-page xeroxed pamphlet.

"I didn't find any looting," I told Jozef on my return to Baghdad. He was having trouble turning up any reliable information about Sadr. We were both rapidly running out of money, and frustrated with our dead-end stories.

My story was at the remote archaeological sites. I had to find a way to Isin, the site described in the *New York Times* article, located in the desert two hours south of Baghdad. Since the article had detailed the looting from the perspective of local Iraqis and the looters, I focused on the Coalition's efforts to protect the sites.

Hiring a translator, car, and driver, I made the trip three times that week to the marine base in Diwaniya, the town closest to Isin, to find out if the marines were patrolling the sites, and if I could ride along.

Twice, I was turned away at the base. On my third trip, I arrived at eight-thirty A.M. in a small yellow taxi. It was already well over a hundred degrees. By the front gate a small sign painted in English read STOP LETHAL FORCE WILL BE USED. Iraqis walked cautiously up to the gate with pieces of paper, trying to ask questions. There was no interpreter, so they were told to wait. A few had gathered near a single tree across the road.

After another half hour, a marine came out to meet me and accompanied me across the base, stopping by a set of stairs that led to the command center. Through an open door across a courtyard I could see a man in a white dishdasha sitting on the concrete floor in a small room, blindfolded, with his hands tied behind his back.

"What did he do?" I asked.

"He's some local leader. He used to work with us, but we found out he was plotting attacks against us."

There seemed to be little infrastructure, legal or otherwise, to deal with that situation.

Upstairs, in the command center, I was greeted by a tall, obliging soldier standing in front of a wall-sized map of the surrounding area. Their small battalion was charged with securing Qadissiya province, about the size of Rhode Island.

"You came at the right time—we're just about to send out a patrol," he said, introducing me to the patrol leader. I described the looting at the archaeological sites, and requested to go to Isin. "Great," the patrol leader said. "Can you point it out on the map?" No archaeological sites were marked on the map.

Though the sites hadn't been bombed during the war, nothing had been done to protect them from postwar looting. A leading archaeologist from the University of Chicago had provided the Pentagon with the site coordinates, warning them about the likelihood of looting, but the information had not made it to troops in the field.

I had only a map of Iraq purchased at Barnes & Noble and a simple site map in Arabic that Donny George, head of the Baghdad Museum, had given me, wishing me luck. Using my Barnes & Noble map, which marked a few ancient archaeological sites with black dots, and my Baghdad Museum map, which used only the modern Arabic names, the patrol leader and I struggled to establish coordinates for Isin.

"As long as we have the coordinates, we'll find it; we have GPS," he assured me.

"You get the seat of honor," the patrol leader joked, directing me to the passenger seat in the lead Humvee, otherwise known as the death seat, where bullets usually hit first. We set off down the road, my translator and driver following behind in the yellow taxi.

About thirty minutes south on the highway we came to the spot where we would have to turn left into the desert. The marines pulled over and radioed the base, standard procedure. There was no response. They kept trying for fifteen minutes, then decided that without a working radio we had to head back. "We'll get it working and come back," they assured me. The other Humvee had to be jump-started, while a few of the marines stood guard on the empty road. A long line of camels made their way past us, traveling north along the highway. By the time they had disappeared, the Humvee started, and we headed north.

It was another hour at the base before we headed out again. By now it was the middle of the afternoon.

"Some idiot was tuned to the wrong frequency," the patrol leader said, explaining what had happened. Thirty minutes south at the turnoff, the patrol pulled over again and tried to radio in. Again, no response.

"Shit," the patrol leader said, staring out the window. He thought about it for a minute. "Fuck it, let's just go." Without radio contact we were on our own. If anything went wrong, the patrol wouldn't be able to phone in for support. He tested the GPS, but it wasn't working either. He tried getting coordinates from a satellite phone, but that also didn't work.

"They give us all the shitty equipment. The army gets all the good stuff, we get the crap. Not even armored Humvees. It's all ten years old, from the first Gulf War. I'm not kidding."

Since the GPS wasn't working, our plan would be to follow my trans-lator and driver in their yellow taxi. The small convoy of two Humvees trailing an Iraqi cab set out across the desert in search of Isin.

"You know, there could be several hundred heavily armed looters there," I warned as we headed out.

"Ten marines against a few hundred armed looters? That's not a fair fight," one of the guys in the back shouted, laughing.

The driver, no older than twenty, with a boyish face, wore dark glasses and a serious expression. He just wanted to complete the mission, what-ever it was, and get back safely to base.

We made our way slowly through the desert, stopping to ask direc-tions from Bedouin who looked with curiosity at this strange caravan. The machine gunner on top, called Squirrel because all you could see were his legs as he pivoted quickly around the turret, trained the .50 cal-iber machine gun on the Bedouin as my translator got directions.

I pulled the folded May 23 *New York Times* article from my left shirt pocket and gave it to the marine sitting behind me.

"This is where we're headed," I told him, pointing to the worn newsprint. He read the entire article on the bumpy ride across the desert, occasionally asking details about the history. I explained to him how the sites had not been protected after the war, and how important it was to protect them now.

"You know, we're marines," he said. "We're not trained for this kind of thing. We're trained to kick in doors and kill people."

When we finally made it out to the site, the sun was beginning to set-tle low on the horizon. As the patrol pulled up, we could see about fifteen looters on top of the mound disappear, some running off into the sur-rounding desert, others down into holes.

At least it wasn't the several hundred looters I was expecting. I set out across the mound to photograph as much as I could in the short time we had.

There were hundreds of holes, some as deep as twenty feet, covering the large mound. Piles of fresh dirt were evidence of the assault on his-tory, now only negative spaces in the human record that had previously lain largely undisturbed for thousands of years. Sadly, I had my story, and confirmation that the looting was still taking place.

The marines had fanned out in all directions, walking slowly, with their guns raised. At the base of the mound on the opposite side was a carefully laid cloth with a teapot and a few shovels. Two marines had rounded up three looters who had run off into the surrounding scrub, and I ran down to catch up with them. The three looters stood there with their hands in the air, smiling and joking with one another, which made the marine who had read the *New York Times* article furious.

"You think it's funny?" the marine shouted at one of the looters, who stopped smiling. Spotting a silver ring on his finger, the marine grabbed his hand. "You think it would be funny if I stole your ring?" Holding his rifle in the other hand, he put the gun barrel up against the man's finger. "You think it would be funny if I blew your fucking finger off?" For a moment no one moved. The looter looked grim. I was hoping the marine wouldn't blow his fucking finger off. He let go of the looter's hand.

"I hate fucking looters," he said walking off.

The marines searched them and confiscated their shovels. Worried that they would alert others and there would be an ambush, the marines instructed the looters to sit down and not move for half an hour after the patrol left.

"Can't you arrest them?" I asked.

"There is no room in the Humvees," the patrol leader said.

As we drove off I looked back to where we had left the looters. They were patiently sitting in the sand at the base of the mound, watching us. They would be back at work in a few hours.

The marine who had threatened to shoot the finger off the looter leaned forward and looked at me. "What a fucking mess," he said, shaking his head.

I arrived back in my room in Baghdad at around seven P.M. Jozef was lying on his bed smoking, and I showed him pictures of the marines detaining looters at Isin.

"You got your story," Jozef said, congratulating me. He left Iraq later that week, having run out of money and unable to complete his story about Sadr.

I took my Isin pictures to the Associated Press. Through the AP, they could potentially reach thousands of newspapers around the world. The AP bought four images for two hundred dollars. The three trips down had cost five hundred, but I was just happy that my pictures were out, my first published pictures from Iraq.

The *Baghdad Bulletin* eagerly published my first article on the looting, as did the Hungarian newspaper *Magyar Hirlap*. It didn't stop the looting, or do much to further my career as a journalist, but it was encouraging.

When pressed about the looting at the sites, the Coalition's response was always a variation of the same: it was a question of priorities. With only 150,000 troops on the ground, not everything could be protected. Although eighty-eight countries had ratified the 1954 United Nations Hague Convention mandating the protection of cultural property during times of armed conflict and occupation, the United States was not one of them.

However, I learned over the next week just how effective the Coalition could be when protecting culture was a priority.

I was almost out of money but wanted to go farther south to Nasiriyah, in the Dhi Qar province, which had some of the oldest and richest Sumerian sites. I convinced one of my translators to go with me to Nasiriyah and for five dollars we boarded a public van packed with Iraqis.

Arriving in the late morning, we found the marines camped out at the Nasiriyah Museum. They directed me to Major Visconti in the town of Shatra, an hour north. Major Visconti, an affable, thirty-three-year-old reservist from Long Island, was a successful pharmaceutical salesman in his civilian life. Like the marines I had met in Diwaniya the previous week, Major Visconti's men were also busy fixing schools, acting as local police, and settling disputes. Unlike the marines in Diwaniya, they were also protecting the archaeological sites.

"Eighty percent of my men have college degrees," he said, explaining their concern for culture. "And besides, we're from New York. When I get back I'm gonna take my wife to the Sumerian exhibit at the Met so she can understand some of what I'm doing out here."

Major Visconti was sending an archaeological patrol out that day and invited me to join them. It was on that patrol that I first met Abdul Amir Hamdani, the newly appointed inspector of antiquities for the Dhi Qar province, and Amir Doshi, a childhood friend of his, who'd come along as his translator. Mr. Hamdani had approached the marines right after the war and pleaded for their help to protect the sites. Major Visconti had immediately organized a patrol to Umma, where they'd broken up a virtual looters' city and arrested sixty looters. Since that day Major Visconti had arranged regular patrols to the sites, often three times a week.

"You from *National Geographic?*" the patrol leader asked me, spitting tobacco juice in the bright sand.

"No, I'm from Four Corners Media. We're a small media company based in New York. We work with different magazines."

"Uh-huh," he said. "What's your blood type?"

"O, I think."

"Don't worry, we'll pump you full of something. Those guys are from New York," he said, motioning to a few men sitting in a Humvee with a small picture of the World Trade Center painted on the side.

"You press?" a young marine in the Humvee leaned out to ask.

"Yeah, he's from *National Geographic,*" the patrol leader answered.

"Four Corners Media," I corrected him.

"Uh-huh."

If you cared about culture, you must be from *National Geographic,* he figured.

Mr. Hamdani carried a small notebook and camera, meticulously documenting the looting at each site we visited. Amir wouldn't stop talking, his arms conducted a never-ending symphony of stories, regaling me with countless historical details, an outstretched hand somehow ending up in almost every photograph. His endless stream of ideas was maddening, but as I came to know Amir I found his intensity to be one of his more endearing qualities, indicative of an active mind and a profound interest in the world around him.

"Come back in two days—we're sending out another patrol," Major Visconti told me. "You should have been there when we caught sixty of 'em."

Although busy with many other responsibilities, his unit was working to protect the sites, and it was clear to me that with a reasonable amount of effort on the part of the Coalition, the looting could be stopped.

Returning to Shatra two days later for another patrol, I found Major Visconti busy packing up and transferring control to the Italians. He had just learned that the marines were shipping out soon, real soon. The new Iraqi police, whom his men had been training for the past month, were going to do the patrol instead. Major Visconti apologized and suggested I go with them.

"They need to start to learn to do this on their own," he said.

A dozen Iraqi police recruits in ill-fitting uniforms piled into a single small white pickup truck, a few of them holding old AKs. As I prepared to follow them, a young marine from Pennsylvania, Troy Merrell, walked by carrying an ancient brick stamped with cuneiform writing. He had made a quick trip out to see the archaeological sites and brought back the cuneiform brick, left behind by looters, to give to the museum. After taking the requisite photograph of the Iraqi police commander, who awkwardly draped an arm around the young marine, I got the portrait I wanted of Troy, alone, holding the brick: a striking contrast between the soldier's youthful optimism and the irreplaceable ancient history.

Instead of heading to the sites, the Iraqi police headed south and pulled over in Nasiriyah, arguing that they could not go to the sites because their vehicle would get stuck in the sand.

"But it's a four-wheel drive," I protested. They shrugged their shoulders. "Why didn't you say something when we were at the marine base?" I asked. They shrugged again. Since powerful tribes near the sites controlled the looting, they feared retribution if they arrested anyone. They didn't have the equipment, training, or motivation to do the job and could not be convinced.

The day was a bust, so I decided to head to Ur, located in the heart of Tallil Air Base, twenty minutes from Nasiriyah.

The checkpoint to enter the base was about a mile from the ziggurat at Ur, a fifty-foot-high stepped pyramid made from mud brick, built in 2300 B.C. to honor the moon god Nanna, clearly visible straight down the road. Arguably the most famous archaeological site in the world, Ur is known to most soldiers as the birthplace of Abraham.

I told a soldier at the gate that I wanted to see someone in public affairs, saying, "It's about archaeology." He radioed back my request and stared at the ground.

"What's archaeology?" he asked.

I thought about how to put it simply. "It's the study of old things," I said.

"Is it like that movie *Broken Arrow* when they step on some old dirt?" he asked. I had sat through *Broken Arrow* on a recent plane flight, a film about a stolen nuclear weapon, a situation the military calls a broken arrow. I didn't remember a scene where they stepped on some old dirt. Perhaps he thought I had come to the ziggurat in search of weapons of mass destruction.

"No," I said. "It's more like that movie *Raiders of the Lost Ark*."

"Oh," he said. It didn't seem to ring a bell. He looked to be about nine-teen, which would mean that Harrison Ford was from his father's gener-ation.

"I hate this fucking country," he continued as we stood there in the blistering midday sun. "There ain't shit out here and it's a thousand de-grees." It felt and looked like hell that day. The air was choked with fine white dust, earth and sky indistinguishable, all one fiery continuum.

After we'd waited for an hour, his radio crackled, and he told me there was no one in public affairs. I headed back to Baghdad, stopping in Shatra to explain to Major Visconti what had happened with the Iraqi police. He shook his head in disappointment, saying he would fire them that day, and invited me back later in the week to go on a raid of the antiquities black market in Fajr, something he was determined to do before shipping out. "You can camp out with us before the raid," he offered. "Come by anytime." I said I would try to make it but was running out of money.

Major Visconti never made it to Fajr, turning over control to the Ital-ians in mid-July. I never made it either. Having run out of money, I re-turned home two days later.

When I got back from that first three-week trip in late June 2003, Marie-Hélène and Zeugma met me in New York. I emerged from another yel-low taxi, caked in dust and ten pounds lighter, to hugs, kisses, and licks. August was my month of redemption—the week my photograph of Troy Merrell with the recovered Sumerian brick ran in *The New York Times Magazine.*

I met my father for lunch in New York. He had come to see the Su-merian exhibit at the Met, and brought me a present, a copy of *Science* magazine, *his* magazine, in which there was an article about the archae-ological looting in Iraq. "That's my photograph," I said. "Really?" he ex-claimed, looking down at the small picture of three looters with their hands high in the air. "You're kidding?" he said, thrilled. For him, being published in *Science* was validation of my efforts. I was happy to see that my pictures were being used and that the story of the Iraqi looting was finally getting out.

In December 2003 I cashed in my remaining savings and headed back to Iraq for another three weeks, hoping to lay the groundwork for a documentary film on the looting that Marie-Hélène and I could work on together.

In the six months since my first trip, the Coalition had made an effort to address the looting by hiring two cultural advisers in the fall of 2003, Italian Ambassador Bandiolo-Osio, the senior adviser for culture, and John Russell, an American archaeologist from the Massachusetts College of Art, the deputy adviser for culture. John was hard at work rebuilding the Baghdad Museum and, together with Ambassador Bandiolo-Osio, fighting the labyrinthine bureaucracy to implement a plan to protect the sites that no one could agree on.

With billions of dollars pouring into Iraq, there was only $2 million available to protect both the museum and the thousands of archaeological sites throughout the country: $1 million from the Packard Foundation and $1 million from the U.S. State Department. On this modest budget, John Russell and Ambassador Bandiolo-Osio purchased twenty trucks and radio equipment, and began trying to organize and train an archaeological protection force.

In his small office in the Green Zone, John, delighted to have someone to talk to, spoke at length about the archaeology and the difficulties he faced, until his appointed Coalition press minder cut him off with a shake of her head.

In a rare coup, at the request of a VIP guest of Paul Bremer, administrator of the Coalition Provisional Authority, John Russell and Ambassador Bandiolo-Osio flew down to Nasiriyah by helicopter to survey the sites in the south.

John invited me along, but although there was space on the two helicopters, I never made it onto the flight. The Coalition press officer coordinating the trip wanted to give the story as an exclusive to FOX News.

The only way down to Nasiriyah was a four-hour journey by car. I left the day before the flight with one of my Baghdad drivers, Amer, and a friend he had brought along for security, too friendly to be menacing, who carried a knife with a curved blade and colorful handle, like those found in tourist shops.

We checked into two drab rooms at the Al-Janoub Hotel, and Amer and our friendly bodyguard went across the street to an open-air café. I knew the helicopter would be arriving in the morning, but the press officer had not given me any details. Communications from Nasiriyah were nearly impossible; my satellite phone and satellite modem were not working. I slipped out to find an Internet café, certain that Amer and our friendly bodyguard wouldn't allow me to go into Nasiriyah at night.

As I walked down the main street completely discouraged, I heard a familiar voice call, "Ahhh, Mike!" With outstretched arms, Amir ran up to me. "Mike, how are you? Are you going to the archaeological site tomorrow? Mr. Hamdani is going with the Italian Carabinieri to meet Ambassador Bandiolo-Osio and the helicopter, and you must come with us."

Over many teas at a nearby café, Amir and I talked about the trip to the sites, and my difficulty getting there. "Never mind," Amir said, "you are our guest now."

Overjoyed at this chance encounter with Amir, I had also found a way to meet the helicopter and, even more important, a way to work in the south.

Amir walked me back to the hotel through the dark, empty streets of Nasiriyah. I had been gone for almost two hours, and Amer and his bodyguard were searching for me in a panic, thinking I had been kidnapped.

"What do you think will happen to me if you disappear?" Amer said, furious. "What do you think your family will do to an Iraqi?"

"Don't worry, Amer, I won't be kidnapped," I assured him.

Mr. Hamdani, Amir, the Italians, and I met the helicopter early next morning. John Russell was delighted to see me, not surprised that I'd made my way out there. John had seen over a dozen sites for the first time and photographed looters running from the helicopter as they flew over Isin. Bob Sullivan, a producer friend of mine at Fox News who had come to do the story, offered me his video footage of the looters if I needed it for my documentary. The week before, I had given him footage from outside Abu Ghraib. Fox wasn't interested in the archaeology story, but at Bob's insistence they'd grudgingly allowed him to go, not sparing a cameraman. The press minder gave me a frosty hello.

The day was a success. John had seen the extent of the damage firsthand. My meeting Mr. Hamdani and Amir again added another angle to the documentary film. In addition to the Coalition perspective, I began focusing on Mr. Hamdani's efforts to safeguard his heritage.

On my return to New York a week later, Marie-Hélène and I, in an intense morning meeting with Greg Carr and Noble Smith, pitched our documentary film idea, showing them photographs and video clips from our previous projects. Greg told us that he had cried when he'd seen the footage of the looting of the Baghdad Museum, and he agreed right away to fund our project. I picked up everything I needed and had not had on the previous two trips—new video camera, health insurance, equipment insurance, Level III flak jacket with a picture of Marie-Hélène and Zeugma tucked beside the breast plate, helmet—and headed back to Baghdad on March 13. Finishing a consulting project, Marie-Hélène planned to join me in a month.

For the first couple of weeks, the film moved quickly. I was also at work on an article about the looting for *Archaeology Magazine*, and an article I cowrote for *The New York Times* was slated for publication in early April.

In late March, however, after months of tension, the Coalition closed down *al-Hawza*, the Sadr newspaper in Baghdad, provoking mass demonstrations. Then, on April 3, the Coalition arrested the cleric Mustafa Yaqubi, head of the Sadr office in Najaf, for the murder of Abdel Majid al-Khoei, a grand ayatollah recently returned from exile in London with moderate political views and ties to the United States. From Baghdad south, the country exploded in violence on April 4, as the Mahdi Army began battling the Coalition. On April 5, U.S. forces began a major offensive against the Sunni insurgency in Fallujah. Everything came to a standstill. The war had started again in earnest on two fronts.

Other than a few attempts to document the fighting in Fallujah, I was more or less confined to my hotel and the Coalition press office, where I videoconferenced with Marie-Hélène back in New York almost every day. I missed her terribly. We spoke at length about the dangers and whether or not she should come. Filming required a team and we worked best as a team, her personal touch and creativity always transforming our efforts into something deeply meaningful.

The offensive reached a stalemate by the end of April, and Marie-Hélène flew out on May 5, against much advice but eager to come to Iraq and work on the film. Munawar and I met her at Baghdad International Airport with outstretched arms and an *abaya*, which she quickly threw on as we headed to Baghdad down the dangerous airport road, leaving the next morning for Nasiriyah.

· · ·

Marie-Hélène and I spent May and June between Baghdad and Nasi-riyah. In Baghdad we filmed John Russell's battle to rebuild the museum, protect the sites, and stop the construction threatening Babylon. He had begun counting and recounting my nine lives every time we met: the time I was chased out of Diwaniya by militants looking to "kill the journalist," my trip to Fallujah at the height of the U.S. offensive down the same road the same morning Thomas Hamill was kidnapped, wait-ing for an Italian patrol at 3 A.M. in the darkened, emptied streets of Nasiriyah, and several other near misses I no longer remembered.

The trucks and radio equipment that had been ordered five months earlier were still stuck in Kuwait. John Russell postponed his departure from Iraq three times waiting for the trucks to be driven to Baghdad and trying to arrange a second helicopter survey of the archaeological sites. The trucks finally arrived in early June, and the site survey took place a week later, this time with Marie-Hélène and me on the helicopter. It was a gorgeous, sunny day, and we flew from the Green Zone to the Baghdad International Airport, refueled, and were on our way to survey the sites.

Half an hour into the trip, as we passed Babylon and entered the desert, Pazuzu, the Sumerian evil demon of the winds, appeared. A giant sandstorm reared up ahead of us, and the helicopter had to turn around. Landing at Babylon, dejected, we decided to tour the site while the heli-copter refueled.

Camp Babil had grown into a behemoth. In the fall of 2003, the Amer-icans had turned over control of the site to the Polish forces, who con-trolled Babil province. For eighteen months the Coalition had occupied Babylon, reshaping history with tires and backhoes. Pieces of the pre-cious lions of the Ishtar Gate went missing. Kellogg, Brown and Root re-moved barriers protecting the site, parked their vehicles right up on the ruins, and trucked in sand by the ton, contaminating the site. In May, new construction began, expanding a helicopter landing pad originally built by the marines on top of an ancient temple. That sparked a local outcry, and the work was halted.

John Russell and his replacement, Zaineb Bahrani, a professor of ar-chaeology from Columbia University, pointed out the extensive damage as we walked around Babylon, camera rolling. After lunch, we sat down at a meeting with an archaeologist from the Nebuchadnezzar Museum at Babylon, who began to detail the physical damage caused by the Coali-tion presence. Seeing the public relations catastrophe unfolding before her, the ever-present Coalition press minder told us to turn off our camera and leave the meeting. Two days later, perhaps anticipating an "Abu Ghraib of archaeology," the Coalition issued a press release saying that all new construction at Babylon had been halted and a team of archaeologists was being sent to investigate the damage. A month later, the Coalition announced that it would vacate Babylon entirely by the end of the year.

Over the next few months Marie-Hélène and I worked closely with Amir and Mr. Hamdani filming in Nasiriyah. With the Italian Camp Mittica as our base, we turned our attention to the continued looting in the Dhi Qar province, following the story from different angles: the Italian Carabinieri, the looters, but mostly Mr. Hamdani's desperate struggle to stop it. Amir provided a fascinating, insightful, and often humorous narrative, full of poetic and philosophical musings on the greater meaning of such horrific cultural destruction.

On July 30, after postponing her departure date several times, Marie-Hélène left Iraq, and I remained behind for the final two weeks of filming.

. . .

Amir explained to the guard that I had worked for the past eighteen months trying to document and protect Iraq's ancient history.

"Islamic history?" he asked, perking up.

"No, Sumerian and Akkadian," Amir corrected him.

"Ahh," he said, no longer interested, returning to his Quranic text.

Two guards came with food, the usual course of rice and sauce, which they set out on our mats. When they removed the aluminum pot, the large guard with the soft voice appeared, holding newly cut palm leaves in his arms. I sat back in a panic. He began sticking them into the dirt along the inside of the enclosure, carefully filling in the gaps to block any possible view, or escape. I didn't know how to stop him as he covered Freedom's Gate. Looking at Amir in desperation I pleaded, "Amir, tell him that's enough. Tell him I am claustrophobic. Ask him to stop."

Amir spoke, imploring him gently that it was not necessary to put in any more branches. His words made just enough of a difference. The guard stopped and spread the remaining fronds upon the ground. The new leaves blocked about half of the natural light that had filtered in, and the enclosure began to feel even more confining.

When he left, I spent a few hours carefully removing the new palm fronds in front of Freedom's Gate as Amir watched for movement outside. They might notice if too many of the new leaves were missing. After laying them on the ground, I cleared more of the ground cover inside Freedom's Gate, then quietly stuck a few of the palm fronds back in front.

The guards must have suspected something; perhaps they understood some of our conversation. Our opportunity for escape could vanish at any moment.

During the hot afternoon, the guard sang to himself outside our enclosure as I lay on my mat staring at the new thick walls. Generally these songs were passages from the Quran, or lamentations. After a while, he paused and called out to Amir, asking if I knew any songs. I thought of an Ian Tyson song sung by Nanci Griffith, "Summer Wages"; Marie-Hélène and I considered it our song, a ballad about gambling, separation, and romantic longing. Maybe "Plastic Jesus" was more appropriate; Paul Newman sang it in *Cool Hand Luke,* sitting alone in a prison cell with his guitar. It was, after all, a moment of cultural sharing. At least it had a nice melody. I decided to try it:

I don't care if it rains or freezes,
Long as I got my plastic Jesus
Sittin' on the dashboard of my car.

I went through four verses, pretty much humming it. There was a long silence when I finished. After a while the guard began singing to himself again.

In the evening, they led us, blindfolded and bound, out to the field. We rolled out our mats, sat down, and asked the guards for news, but the group that had gone to Nasiriyah had still not returned.

A guard brought a large metal pail with water and a bar of soap, and we were allowed to wash ourselves for the first time. I stripped to my underwear in the dark and splashed the cold water over my body, which was layered in sweat and dirt, taking time to wash my face. I dressed, sat back down, and Amir took his turn. The cold water cleansed my mind, and I tried again to build a personal connection with my captors.

"*Le pain, c'est bon*, the bread is good," I said, lifting a piece of *khubz* with a smile. I asked Amir to translate my words. Amir reluctantly translated as we ate the rice-and-sauce dinner from the aluminum pot. The guards remained silent. In Iraq, you "sit like a lion and eat like a wolf," which means you don't talk while eating and you eat quickly, fingers tearing at the meat.

Fishing around the pot in the dark, I noticed a single small piece of lamb in the sauce. If this was the same food they ate, then they had very little meat and probably even less money.

"What do you call this?" one of the guards asked, holding up the plastic jug of water.

"*Bouteille,*" I said, taking a guess. It would pass as long as I said it with a French accent. He seemed satisfied with my response.

"Have the guards ever been outside Iraq?" I asked Amir when we had finished eating.

"They say they have never been outside their village."

"When you go back to Paris, can you send us French perfume?" the guard continued.

"Is he serious?" I asked Amir.

"Yes, he is serious," Amir replied.

"Tell him that I will send him as much perfume as he wants, if he lets us go."

The guard replied with what had by then become their standard response: he had no authority.

"Ask him where I should send the perfume when I get back to France." Amir relayed my question.

He didn't reply. He had caught on.

"When I go back to France I will—"

The other guard cut me off. "Mike, no France," he said, shaking his finger. "No Paris."

His words were chilling. I became quiet. What else could I say?

10:42 A.M.

As the morning wore on, I received bits and pieces of information about Micah's whereabouts during the days prior to his kidnapping from calls, emails, and updated media reports. A record of his movements would give some clues about what he was doing, who he was talking to.

The calls and emails kept coming. Call-waiting on both my cell phone and my home phone meant I usually had four people on the line. The phone lines cut in and out; the battery on my home phone almost depleted, the cell phone refusing reception. CBS wanted to send a camera crew to our offices to interview a Four Corners representative. CNN wanted an on-camera interview, and wanted to talk to Micah's parents. *Good Morning America* wanted to talk to family and friends, Reuters wanted a high-resolution photograph, *The New York Times* wanted more background on Micah, and ABC News wrote, "HELP! We need to talk to coworkers about Micah Garen!" Media representatives were searching frantically for any information or reactions.

"Your boss has been taken hostage in Iraq," a CNN producer standing in Four Corners Communications' midtown Manhattan office announced to a startled woman at the front desk.

"That's impossible," the woman responded, confused and distraught. "My boss is in Scarsdale."

CNN, desperate for information, had confused Four Corners Communications with our small company, Four Corners Media.

Baskets of fruits and flowers with handwritten notes of concern and sympathy that ended in requests for interviews began to pile up at the apartment door.

Information from Nasiriyah was just coming out. An updated AP story reported that the deputy governor of Dhi Qar province, Adnan al-Sharifi, had said that a French-American journalist named Micah Garen had gone missing with his translator on Friday in Nasiriyah as they were walking through a busy market, and the translator's family had reported them missing a few days later.

The market—that was confirmation, and an important clue. The Italians probably had nothing to do with Micah's kidnapping; they wouldn't have seized Micah in a market. I wondered if Adnan al-Sharifi knew anything else or if he could be of help. Since he was part of the interim Iraqi government, and not popularly elected, I did not hold out much hope.

I realized I had to reach the right tribal leader or religious authority. The Shi'ite population in southern Iraq respected tribal and religious leaders more than political ones. Several journalist friends also wrote with that advice, one citing the successful ending to a recent hostage crisis when three Japanese civilians were kidnapped in Iraq in April 2004, one of whom was a journalist. The families had worked through Muslim clerics and tribal leaders to plead their case, and the hostages had been released.

Micah's and his brother Jonathan's childhood friend David Bloom, now a freelance journalist, suggested Imam al-Husainy, an Iraqi Imam who led the Karbala Islamic Education Center in Dearborn, Michigan, the U.S. city with the largest Iraqi population. The Imam had successfully negotiated other hostage releases. It was a long shot, but worth a try.

The Imam was warm and open when I called. He hadn't heard of Micah's kidnapping but did not sound surprised. He wanted details, which I took as a positive sign: where Micah had been taken, and the name and number of the local police chief. He wanted to find out more about Amir's family and talked about contacting Nasiriyah politicians, though, he cautioned, they would be hard to track down since they were attending a national conference in Baghdad that week.

"I will help you. If it is God's will, we will bring your fiancé home."

Many friends and family members turned to Washington, D.C., for help, contacting members of Congress. They hoped that their representatives, those in direct contact with power brokers and decision makers on foreign policy, could help Micah and speak on his behalf. I, too, wanted to hear from my representatives that they cared about Micah, to hear them voice concern and commitment to our family. Caring leads to action. Behind the scenes, they could encourage people at the highest levels to take Micah's kidnapping seriously.

Suzanne spent the morning calling family, the State Department, and one of her senators. A young woman answering the phone at the senator's office told Suzanne that she would have to send a fax. After expressing her disappointment with that response, Suzanne left her phone number, hoping to hear back, but never did.

Alan and Sally were in constant motion, juggling calls with the State Department as well as Senators Joseph Lieberman and Christopher Dodd, who immediately sent a letter to Secretary of State Colin Powell. Senator Lieberman promised to do whatever he could, calling the U.S. ambassador's office in Baghdad.

After hearing advice from Sally's daughter Alyssa, Alan and Sally decided that the best route would be to speak with relief agencies, which, like journalists, are well connected on the ground. They called many relief agencies, including the International Rescue Committee (IRC). A Canadian staff member of the IRC had been kidnapped and released several months earlier in Iraq by a group associated with the Mahdi Army, and now the IRC offered strong support, trying to reach other relief agencies operational in Nasiriyah.

10:59 A.M.

The pressure to talk to the media increased with each passing hour. Most people thought that it could help. Once information got out, I worried I wouldn't be able to control it, and the information could be used against Micah. We didn't know anything about the kidnappers, what they would respond to or what might anger them. If they were looters, we shouldn't say anything about the archaeology. If it was political, nationality was a question. I faced a terrible dilemma: should I make a statement or not? My gut told me to hold off. But I was torn, and worried that I would miss my only opportunity to help Micah.

Scott, Bob, and I continued our email correspondence, wrestling with this question. Publicity sometimes helps, Bob said. His nephew had been kidnapped by the PKK in eastern Turkey, and news coverage had helped get him out.

But we decided to stick with back-door channels for the moment, working through organizations set up to help journalists.

Bob was on the board of the Overseas Press Club (OPC), which had written a letter protesting the closing of the Al Jazeera offices in Baghdad, which the interim Iraqi government had accused of inciting opposition. Bob felt that a letter from OPC to Al Jazeera stating that Micah was just a journalist on the "smallest of budgets" could have a positive impact. We wanted them to know he was not a spy or a wealthy foreigner, a common accusation against foreign journalists in Iraq. Bob began drafting a letter, which OPC faxed later in the day.

Though I did not see it at the time, Al Jazeera had already updated their story from information they found on our Four Corners Media website. While our site featured many articles on the archaeology, Al Jazeera chose to focus on the video interviews with American soldiers posted at the bottom of the site, writing that our organization was "documenting the life and experiences of American soldiers on the front lines in Iraq"—an association with the American military that was dangerous for Micah, the very thing I was working to prevent.

11:02 A.M.

"What about Reporters without Borders [RSF]?" Bob had suggested earlier in the morning.

RSF had been one of the first to email me after news broke about Micah, but I had not yet responded.

Raphael Botiveau called from the RSF's Paris headquarters, wanting more details in order to release a statement on Micah's behalf.

"Is releasing a statement really the best thing to do right now?" I asked, the pressure on me building. RSF's position like CPJ's was that journalists are independent, journalists are civilians, and that as civilians, they must be protected. Publicity was good, he said. Anything—news coverage, a statement—that increases public pressure and awareness would help Micah.

"Is Micah French or American?" Raphael asked. I told him the same thing I had told Nick at the AP. "You should tell the truth," he replied, "it always comes out, and it's better that it comes out now, and from you." Talking to him, I felt I was already losing control of information. I went back and forth for two hours with RSF on the benefits of a statement, concerned most about the nationality question.

Though terrified of making the wrong decision, I relented, hoping that Micah's American citizenship would not be used against him.

"Publicity will help you," he repeated. "It helped with the British journalist that was kidnapped last week, and then set free."

I thought about James Brandon for the first time since Chantal had read me the news in Paris. A freelance journalist from the United Kingdom, a

Coalition partner, working on a story in Basra, Iraq's southernmost and second-largest town, Brandon had been kidnapped from his hotel by a group loosely affiliated with the Mahdi Army. They had demanded that Coalition forces withdraw from Najaf. He had been released twenty-four hours later, after Sadr made an appeal, saying that journalists should not be harmed. I knew then what we had to do: we had to contact Sadr himself. We had to get Sadr to issue an appeal on Micah's behalf.

Because Sadr had interceded on James Brandon's behalf, in part because he was a journalist, I hoped RSF's statement reiterating that Micah was a journalist might influence Sadr.

11:10 A.M.

"Mom, are you okay, is your heart okay?" Eva tried to comfort her mom, who was still in shock. Suzanne assured her she could make it by train to New Haven on her own. Though it was a beautiful late-summer day, Eva, working as hard as she was crying, felt as if the world was falling to pieces. With guilt and remorse, she remembered all of the childhood mishaps between her and Micah, and how they had drifted apart over the years, separated by their work in different parts of the world.

Together in New Haven, Eva, Alan, and Sally were on the Internet and phone constantly. Alan still feared that Micah could be the victim of a political cover-up. He remembered Micah saying he was working on a story about the looting for John Burns of *The New York Times*, and called the New York office. Alan was immediately patched through to John Burns in Iraq. The two men quickly developed a bond, and spoke often throughout the day. The conversations helped Alan talk through his fear of having lost Micah. Slowly, he began to feel more hopeful.

John was writing an article for *The New York Times* about Micah's disappearance, and he asked Alan to contribute something about Micah. Alan, composing himself as he went, sat for a long time facing his computer. Watching him as she made calls on her cell phone, Eva felt she was witnessing her father writing a letter of love for Micah:

Micah went to Iraq fully aware of the dangers, but determined to alert the world to the tragic loss of an irreplaceable archaeological heritage. His remarkable intelligence, charm and thirst for understanding led him to seek information from all available sources. He refused to turn aside in the face of injustice and inhumanity even from those with the power and responsibility to provide protection, and he is now in mortal danger.

John ran it in full the next day.

11:30 A.M.

A new AP story appeared, quoting the Nasiriyah police captain, Haidar Aboud, who said that witnesses had reported that the journalist and the translator were walking in the market when two men in civilian clothes armed with Kalashnikov assault rifles seized them.

The details, which I so desperately wanted, were horrifying. Micah had been kidnapped by men in civilian clothes armed with Kalashnikov assault rifles. Who were these shadowy men with Kalashnikovs?

The theories and suspicions about what had happened were proliferating. I received an urgent email from a professor at the University of Michigan and an expert in Sumerian translation. Micah had emailed him images of a library of looted tablets we had photographed. Worried they might have something to do with his kidnapping, he wanted to talk about the last few messages he had received from Micah.

Perhaps the shadowy men were looters, feeling threatened or exposed. Micah and I had wanted to know who the looters were, and to document their story. A week before I'd left, Micah and I had interviewed a man who'd claimed he had a library of cuneiform tablets that had recently been dug up from Umma. A local fixer spent a week setting up the meeting in Fajr, assuring the man it was safe for him and that nothing would happen. The man, afraid of arrest, warned our fixer, "Whatever happens to me, happens to you."

It was an important story since so little was known about who was doing the looting, or why. Micah was reluctant, feeling it was too dangerous, but with assurances from the fixer and Amir, and pressure from me, we decided to go.

At the edge of Fajr, a lawless city where more than 80 percent of the population is reportedly involved in the looting, we were stopped. The Iraqi police, in blue, questioned our driver, looking into the car. Micah, in his Iraqi shirt, and I, sweating in my *hijab*, lowered our eyes—I was just another Iraqi woman in a southern Iraqi town—only to see a bottle of water spilling onto the camera equipment we had stored out of sight under the seat. "The water, Amir," I whispered, but he cut me off through unmoving lips: "Do not speak." Mahdi Army militants, in black and clearly in charge, stood behind the Iraqi police. They looked over suspiciously, but waved us on to our first trip into the heart of Fajr, the city of looters.

On a remote farm surrounded only by a few sheep and the Bedouin women who tended them, the man unwrapped hundreds of cuneiform tablets, each one protected by brightly patterned cloth cut from an old dress, while we photographed. Reminded of a BBC special he had watched the previous week on the looting of Iraq's archaeological sites, he told us that he had studied political science at Baghdad University, and valued Iraqi history. Aware of the ugly contradiction, that he was destroying his own history, he explained that there were no jobs, and he had no choice; Saddam had destroyed the south. He looked lovingly at the tablets, which he said were as important to him as his children; he could never harm either. Upon leaving, he asked us if we could help him find a job in Baghdad, prompting Amir to dub him the postmodern looter—an antihero who only valued Iraq's history relative to his own needs.

Driving back to Camp Mittica, our fixer turned to ask us a question that had been bothering him. "What is the difference between a journalist and a police officer?" He, like many people in Iraq, was unfamiliar with the role of the media in society, the fourth pillar of a democratic state. To many Iraqis in rural areas, journalists were spies, and foreigners were there only to steal oil.

"A journalist seeks the truth," Micah told him. "A police officer enforces the law." Our fixer thought about it, unconvinced.

Perhaps the looters had been provoked by a recent Carabinieri raid in Fajr's antiquities smuggling market, where they had confiscated eighty pieces of antiquities, but had not made any arrests. Perhaps the looters knew we stayed at the Italian base, and associated the raid with us. Our questions, our filming, and the new Italian pressure might have pushed looters to act.

Before I left Iraq, I encouraged Micah to go back to the man with the tablets and take more pictures, but he was reluctant to go, not wanting to hazard the risk again. Had Micah gone back to photograph? Remembering my persuasions, heavy guilt, then a burning fear, settled in me. If Micah had been abducted by looters, it was probably my fault.

Looters, a criminal gang, the Mahdi Army? These men with Kalashnikovs could be anyone. The situation was a kaleidoscope of scarce information projecting a multitude of possibilities. The pieces came together in a swirling pattern of equally frightening scenarios, and Micah was at the center of all of them.

Juggling these theories—looters, Italian army, Mahdi Army—still in my pajamas six hours after learning of Micah's kidnapping, I sat at the edge of my couch in the center of my own chaotic kaleidoscope; images and information flooding my two phones and one computer. I couldn't shut any doors, not wanting to miss any clues.

Amid the horror, the small victories and the frantic pace of calls and emails helped me keep my emotions under control.

"Did you know about the Italian issue?" a family friend asked me on the phone.

"I saw a couple of emails from Micah," I told her, "but I really don't think the Italians are involved. Anything is possible, of course, but I don't think it's them."

"You knew and you should have said something," she told me. "Why didn't you say anything?"

Had I not been paying attention to the clues? Was this my fault? Her words hit hard and I began shaking, overcome by guilt and remorse for having left Iraq, and having left Micah, a decision almost as difficult as my decision to go there.

But staying in Iraq was Micah's desire and Micah's decision; I had wanted him to come back with me. "I just need to film the first night of the new civil guards at Umma," he'd told me. "Just two more weeks." And covering the ambulance story was Micah's choice; his conscience would not allow him to do otherwise.

Guilt, a paralyzing emotion, wasn't going to help bring Micah home, and getting upset would distract me from my goal. The only thing that mattered was action.

The phone call made me worried that with the family spread out in different locations, talking to different people, sending conflicting messages, and chasing different theories, we would all end up down the wrong road.

"Mom's on her way down from Boston to New Haven, and then we're heading down to New York tomorrow," Eva told me. "It makes sense to be in New York, and Jonathan's there, too. We can help each other. Dad and Sally are going to stay in New Haven, for now; they feel they can be most effective from there." Giovanni, Suzanne's husband, remained in Newton to manage the phone calls and media camped outside the house.

12:10 P.M.

By now, the story led every news report, but the information hadn't changed much. Reuters requested a picture of Micah. A picture could keep Micah's story alive in the media without giving away too much information.

I grabbed several photo albums and thumbed through pictures of Micah and me. There we were: walking in the West Village, at a friend's wedding in Sweden, family pictures with Zeugma, his send-off party in March—no mustache in any of them. It would be better if the photo had the mustache he wore now; he would look more familiar to an Iraqi audience. I wanted to use a picture of Micah with Zeugma, to bring him the comfort of home if by chance he saw it, but dogs are considered unclean in Islam. Grabbing three old photos of Micah, I threw on my clothes and sprinted to the photo store.

"I need some pictures scanned right away," I said.

"I'll be with you in a minute."

A thin man edged in front of me to claim his place in line.

Waiting was intolerable. "This is an emergency."

"Just a second," the man behind the counter said.

"I have no time, no time at all. You have to do this right now." I wanted to scream that Micah was a hostage, but Micah would be strong, and I had to be strong, too.

I pressed myself up against the counter.

"Right now!" I said.

Looking worried, the man behind the counter took the photos I pushed into his hands.

Scott sent the two scanned pictures of Micah to the news wires, and checked in with the Associated Press Television News in Baghdad. They had received the pictures and were feeding them. The pictures will soon be on air, APTN reassured Scott, "if subscribers can drag themselves away from Michael Jackson's latest court appearance." By 12:30 P.M., twenty minutes later, all the wire services had photos. Soon, Micah's gaze reached out to viewers around the world, and to me, from TV and computer screens.

A friend emailed me to say she had seen the picture. "It shows his kind eyes," she said, and I knew I had chosen the right one.

. . .

APTN also told Scott that Micah had been in the Baghdad office the previous Wednesday or Thursday with a video of a carload of Iraqi civilians
that he said had been shot in error by the Italians down in Nasiriyah. Interested, but too busy with Najaf, APTN had told Micah to come back
the following week.

1:11 P.M.

The RSF statement arrived in my email, waiting on my approval.

"I am appealing to Micah Garen's kidnappers to please release him—
he was just doing his job as a journalist by independently reporting on
the outcome of recent events in Iraq and by trying to help preserve Iraq's
archaeological heritage," my statement began. It said that Micah was an
American journalist working on a documentary film about the destruction of the archaeological sites in southern Iraq, and was now missing
along with his Iraqi translator, Amir Doshi. Reporters Without Borders
is very concerned, it said, and everything should be done to locate him
and release him, without harming him.

I told them to send it out.

1:15 P.M.

I dug through my luggage and found the small Iraq contact book I
thought I'd lost in Paris. "To Elowiya," Amir had written inside, an hon-
orary name for a female descendant of the prophet Mohammed, and his
cover for me while traveling. If stopped at a checkpoint, Amir's plan was
to say, "Elowiya is from the marshes in the south, and she has a sick kid-
ney from drinking bad water. We are on our way to the shrine in Najaf in
search of healing." I sifted through the names, looking for someone who
could help: reporters, soldiers, Iraqi clerics, museum personnel, fixers,
translators.

Of course! Amir's family. I should have contacted them first thing.
Since they had spoken with Al Jazeera, they would certainly have more
information. I immediately sent an email to Amir's account, which he
shared with his brother, hoping that someone would read it.

```
Hi,
    This is Marie-Hélène, Micah's colleague and fi-
ancée. We met several times—at the Iraqi Oil Pro-
tection Force, and then at your home.
```

I have heard the terrible news about Amir and
Micah's disappearance. The only information I have
so far is what has been reported from Al Jazeera,
which was then picked up by the global press. Can
you provide me with more details, such as when you
last spoke to Amir, where he was going, what exactly
you have heard.

I have spoken with people, and they are concerned
to help both Micah and Amir, so please know that
Amir is in our thoughts and actions as well.

1:23 P.M.

The phone rang. On the other end, someone with an Italian accent, speaking in a hushed voice asked, "Is this Marie-Hélène?"

I could hardly hear him. He wouldn't continue until he confirmed who I was.

"This is."

"I am an Italian journalist, and I worked with Micah at the Italian base in Nasiriyah."

The phone connection crackled.

"I can't hear you. Hi, hi, are you there?" I pleaded.

"Do you know about the ambulance story?" he asked me.

There was a loud snap.

"I know a little bit. Does this have anything to do with Micah's disappearance? What do you know?"

There was a shuffling noise.

"I cannot talk, I do not know if this line is secure. I will have to call you back."

"What is your number? Call me back! Send me an email if the line is not secure!"

The line went dead.

A few minutes later, the Italian journalist called again.

"Do the Italians have anything to do with this?" I asked immediately.

"I don't know," he answered, still whispering. "I cannot really talk to you, because the line is not secure. It is important you know about the ambulance."

"Why? How does this fit into his disappearance?"

"Do not tell anyone I am calling you."

"Okay."

"Micah was kicked off the base. He was upset and uncomfortable when they interrogated him."

"Yes, he emailed me."

"I have some information to forward you, some emails from Micah, and from the translator's family. They may help you."

I gave him my email address, but they did not arrive. I called back several times to make sure he sent them.

"It is hard here, the lines don't always work, and there are other things going on."

I wasn't sure what he meant, but I thought that he might be able to provide another clue. Perhaps there was something to Alan's fears.

1:28 P.M.

The Italian journalist's forwarded email message arrived, with the strongest piece of information so far:

```
Dear sir I'm small brether of Amir. Amir and
Michael are kidnap By AL mehdy Army in nassiriyah
13-8-2004, now we are in discussion with thes
pepels for releas them
```

This was our first real clue about who the men with the Kalashnikovs who had abducted Micah and Amir might be. Micah had been kidnapped by the Mahdi Army. If it was the Mahdi Army, that meant they were Shi'ite, and that was positive news. Unlike the extremist Sunni militants in the north, Shi'ite militants in Iraq were not known to kill foreign hostages. And they might listen to an appeal from Sadr, if we could reach him, since most Iraqi Shi'ites respected either Sadr or Grand Ayatollah Ali al-Sistani.

My concern over the Italian journalist's call faded with the concrete information from Amir's family, particularly the part about negotiations. Driven by the email, my spirits swung upward.

By the early afternoon, any Italian connection to Micah's disappearance seemed unlikely. But I worried that the theory would gain currency in the media, misleading people and hurting the effort to locate Micah.

Having heard from Alan and Sally that John Burns was writing a story about Micah's kidnapping for the Tuesday edition of *The New York Times,* I called John and he reassured me, saying he did not put much credence in an Italian plot, and wasn't including it.

Joel at CPJ also did not believe that the Italians were involved in Micah's disappearance. "Nothing's impossible," he said, "but of everything I've seen in my lifetime, that would be the most unusual and unlikely situation."

Mitch, working out of the *New York Times* office in Baghdad, was also reaching the same conclusion. He had spent most of the day confirming that the Italians weren't holding Micah. The Coalition Press Information Center (CPIC) in Baghdad checked with Italian forces in Nasiriyah. "The Coalition doesn't have him," CPIC told Mitch. A contact Joel had at the Pentagon said the same thing.

"I'm pretty sure the kidnappers are Shi'ite," Mitch said, "and somehow affiliated with the Mahdi Army. That's good news. On the downside, Sadr is busy with the siege in Najaf."

The U.S. Coalition forces had launched a massive assault on the Mahdi Army in Najaf on Friday, August 13, during which Sadr had been lightly wounded. Micah had the misfortune to be kidnapped at one of the tensest moments of postwar Iraq. There had been a brief lull in fighting on Saturday; on Sunday, fighting resumed on the outer edges of the Old City and in the sprawling cemetery where most Iraqi Shi'ite are buried, the Valley of Peace, just north of the Shrine of Imam Ali. No one was sure where Sadr was or how to reach him, and journalists had been warned, for their safety, to leave Najaf.

Around two P.M., I spoke again with the Pentagon official in Baghdad, the one who'd said he would pray for Micah. "I'm no longer on the case," he told me. My spirits sank, and I feared I had lost an ally.

"The FBI will get in touch with you. It's their jurisdiction."

"When?"

"Soon. I'll stay up until I know they have gotten in touch with you."

2:03 P.M.

Our first public statement with RSF aired and news articles reported the appeal, accompanied by the picture of Micah. Except for some minor facts, nothing new had surfaced. The appeal and the picture felt right, an accomplishment. I had moved a piece in the game and hoped it was the right one. The rules of the universe dictated that we should hear back. Every action has a reaction.

2:16 P.M.

I was back to juggling two phones and four phone lines when the door to the apartment opened and Chantal walked in.

She put down her luggage as I tossed her my ringing cell phone. She improvised, taking cues from what she heard me say to other callers. In stereo, we explained that we were thankful for their interest, that we did not have additional information at this time but would get back to them soon. She grabbed the envelope I had been using to record the names and numbers of everyone who had called, to graffiti another name, another number.

"Thank God you are here," I told her after I hung up, not sure how much longer I could handle the nonstop pressure of the swelling stream of phone calls.

"Are we going to Baghdad?" she asked. She had brought her passport, thinking that her flight, originating in Indianapolis that morning, might continue on to Baghdad, if that was what we had to do.

"We're working from here, at least for today. It's easier from here because we can reach everyone by phone. Maybe when we find out more, we'll go."

"What do you need right now?" she asked.

"Office supplies, a new phone, and can you walk Zeugma?"

Chantal ran to the drugstore, Zeugma in tow, and picked up a small, thick wire-bound notebook, posterboard, and markers. Her own cell phone rang with a call from another reporter. As she juggled the supplies, the caller, and Zeugma, the manager huffed up to her.

"You cannot have a dog in the store. You have to get out."

She ran out, pulling Zeugma by the neck, stood on the sidewalk with the shoplifted supplies, and wrote down the information: date and time of call, name and number of caller, reason of call. Page one of our Project Book had been created.

She tried to pay.

"Don't come back in!" the manager yelled, ferrying her dollars to the cashier and back.

"I need a phone, too," she requested from the doorstep.

They directed her to a nearby RadioShack.

"I need a phone." She stood on the doorstep, yelling into the store, Zeugma tugging at the leash. Everyone inside was busy. She yelled louder and the employees looked up. They assessed their inventory, listing the options, yelling over other customers.

"We have a speed dial 45 option with recordable ringtones and a vibrating handset, or a 5.8 GHz speakerphone deluxe with TeleZapper. We also have—"

"I just need a phone!" she interrupted.

They continued. There were many choices.

"Any phone will do!" she screamed.

"You can come in, you know."

Chantal returned with a new phone and office supplies for our war room.

Media requests, through calls and emails, increased throughout the day. There was mounting pressure to do an interview about Micah: from CNN, *Good Morning America,* ABC News, CBS, NBC. "It could help," friends cautiously suggested, and RSF emphasized that "it was very important." Major media coverage would keep interest alive, keep the pressure on, and reach an international audience.

But by the afternoon, there were a growing number of voices warning against going to the media, reflecting my own feeling. "My take is, you need to be really careful with the media," Joel from CPJ offered. "Publicity is always good," a public relations friend advised, "but in a kidnapping, I don't know." The range of opinions on the media was dizzying. I began to fear I had said too much already by agreeing to the RSF statement, and felt sick when I thought the information in it might possibly harm Micah.

At the risk of being too cautious, I stuck with my intuition and decided against speaking with the media. Finding the right channels on the ground in Iraq was what mattered, and major media attention could make that more difficult.

Faced with mounting pressure and difficult decisions, Joel suggested to Eva we speak with Terry Anderson—a former hostage held by Shi'ite militants for seven years in Lebanon—for advice and support.

.   .   .

I had not heard back from my email to Amir's family, so I searched again through my Iraqi contact notebook. On a page that was frayed and faded I found the number for Amir's family home in Nasiriyah. After one try— very lucky for Iraq—a man answered the phone.

"*Salaam alaikum,*" I began loudly and distinctly. "*Ana Ms. Helen, Mr. Mike's zawjat.*" Hello, and peace be with you. I am Ms. Helen, Mr. Mike's wife, which was what everyone called me, and all I could manage in Arabic.

After several tries, the man, whom I understood to be Amir's brother, answered in broken English. "Very bad," he said.

"I can help you," I said again and again.

"How? No one can help. Very bad."

"Anything," I told him. "Anything. What do you need?"

We repeated this cycle many times, until he said I should call back soon.

"Email," I said. "Send email."

I hung up, upset and frustrated by the language barrier. What is contact without communication? At least they knew I cared and wanted to help. But I was frightened by his words: "very bad."

By five P.M., already the middle of the night in Iraq, the phones and email were quieter. There was nothing to do in Iraq at this hour. It was time to focus on help from here at home.

I had not yet heard from the FBI. Eva had been in contact with FBI agents in Washington, D.C., throughout the day, and they had told her that since Micah was a New York resident, the New York FBI would be in charge. "I'll call the FBI again," Eva said, "and make sure they call you."

Chantal googled the FBI, and dialed their New York number.

"Federal Bureau of Investigation," a voice answered.

"Hello? FBI? We have a situation," she said. She explained that she wanted to talk to someone about Micah, and to someone who could advise us about the media. Chantal leaned forward, ready to write in the Project Book. She leaned back. "Excuse me?"

I tried to read the expression on her face as she pulled the phone away from her ear.

"The media person is gone for the day. She said to call back tomorrow."

"Give me the phone. I have to talk to her." I grabbed it.

"Hello? Yes. This is Marie-Hélène Carleton. I am the fiancée of Micah Garen, who has been kidnapped in Iraq." I took a deep breath, trying to stay calm. "The U.S. embassy in Baghdad said that the FBI would be calling us, and no one has called us."

"You've got to call back tomorrow, during business hours," the woman said curtly.

I paused, trying to understand.

"I want to talk to someone right now." My voice was rising and sticking in my throat, catching on anger. "This is not about business hours, this is an emergency."

"Don't speak to me that way."

I exploded. "How dare you tell me how to speak to you, how dare you focus on that when we are trying to save someone's life!"

"I don't appreciate being spoken to in that tone."

The person on the other end of the phone was obviously not a hostage negotiator.

"I don't appreciate my fiancé being kidnapped in Iraq." My anger was growing rapidly.

She tried to talk over my rising voice, then my tears. I had built a wall, as tall as I could, of self-control, but the enigma of a woman on the other end had pushed my emotions relentlessly. I lost control. Chantal came over and held my free hand.

"The FBI was supposed to contact us, and we haven't heard anything," I cried. "It is now night in Baghdad. I can't get hold of anyone over there."

"I already told you," she continued, annoyed, as if I weren't listening, "it's after five P.M."

"Someone needs to help me, someone needs to help him!" I was standing up, shouting into the phone. She hung up.

I sat down and stared at Chantal, listening to the drone of the dial tone.

Throwing the phone down in frustration, I cried on the couch, frightened that people were not doing enough to rescue Micah. Were we alone looking for him? Was he alone? Had he been separated from Amir? Was he scared? Short, terror-filled blips, bits of imagined scenes, came into my head as I thought again about the armed men with the Kalashnikovs.

5:26 P.M.

Trying to control my sobbing, I focused again on my own contacts at work in Iraq. I emailed Rita in Baghdad.

    The most helpful thing would be to get local sheiks
    and the Sadr office involved. Is that happening?

5:27 P.M.

I jumped from the sofa when I saw the next message appear in my inbox.

```
Dear Helen
Amir & Mich were kidnapped in Friday in afternoon
when they went for a walk in bazaar until now we
dont know who kidnap them but we think that they
kidnap by AL mahdee army pleas keep the media awy
for now at less, we looking for them and we told the
Iraq giverment we here some news that Mich & Amir
are fine, pleas dont try tocome to Iraq becouse it
was unwise step and the case will be begest, we will
tell you the email of Hamadani in the next message.
```

I reread the line over and over: Micah and Amir were fine. "We have good news!" I shouted to Chantal, who jumped from her seat. I called Eva on her cell phone and read it to her. I could feel her joy through the phone. She called Alan and Sally, and I called Jonathan, trying to keep the family updated.

This piece of good news helped me regain my composure. I had to trust Amir's family's assessment, though I wondered if they would know how to handle this. Certainly we had the same interests—keeping Micah and Amir alive and getting them released. But Amir was Iraqi, and Micah an American. They could have dramatically different fates. Life and death could be decided by nationality alone.

Amir's family counseled against going to the media, but I had already done so, through my RSF statement. I worried that I had made a mistake.

I knew Amir's family only a little. We were, however, united by a volatile situation that concerned the lives of people we loved. I had to believe that they would extend the concept of family—brother and son—to Micah, even though he was a foreigner. For me, Micah and Amir were a unit. They had to stay together. Their fates were intertwined, dependent on each other, and the abilities of their families and friends, radiating from Nasiriyah outward, working together. Success would take trust—trust in Amir's family, in all of our friends, in all of our colleagues, in people we did not know. We had to believe that they would do everything they could, and that Micah and Amir's lives were just as precious to them as they were to us.

Rita, emailing me from Baghdad, reassured me that journalists, photographers, fixers, and translators were working on Micah's case. The people who had helped secure James Brandon's release were helping, contacting the Sadr offices in Baghdad and Nasiriyah. "Trust that many people here are doing all they can. With everyone working together, we will work this out. Everything will be okay."

6:24 P.M.

Greg Carr called with more good news: Elizabeth Rubin, a writer for *The New York Times Magazine,* had contacted an Iraqi Shi'ite cleric whom she had interviewed, Sheik Ayad Jamal Uddin. A recently returned exile who had successfully negotiated other hostage situations, he had offered to help us. I did not know him, but Elizabeth trusted him and believed he could help. I asked them to go ahead. We recognized that it might be dangerous for him and that he was taking a risk; the kidnappers or others might react badly to an Iraqi with ties to the Americans speaking for an American.

6:30 P.M.

Chantal's phone rang.

"This is Chris from the FBI." It was after five P.M., quitting time, so Chantal was wary.

"How do I know you're from the FBI?" she asked the cheerful voice.

"That's a good question. Just call this number and they will confirm that I am with the FBI. I'll give you my badge number and they'll run it, and I'll give you a number to call me back at."

Chantal dialed the confirmation number. "I'm calling to check a badge number."

The desk officer ran the badge. "Yup, he's one of ours."

"How do I know you're the FBI?"

"Listen, honey," the desk officer answered. "This is the FBI, and the agent is with the FBI, and that's all you need to know." She hung up.

Chantal dialed Chris's number. "Well, at the number I called, they said you were with the FBI, but how do I know you're not some yahoo off the street, just trying to get information out of us?"

Chris was very patient. "I totally understand. Check it out as much as you need to. Check the number, call them back, whatever you need to do."

Chantal decided she would take something over nothing. She explained that Micah had been kidnapped and that we had been told that the case was in the FBI's jurisdiction.

"My partner and I will come over at nine P.M. to talk."

"We live at—" Chantal began, but Chris cut her off.

"Listen, I'm with the FBI—I know where you live. Don't worry about directions."

6:42 P.M.

Chantal answered the phone:

"I am so sorry to bother you, I know this is a hard time," said a French consular officer calling from New York. "We are trying to ascertain if Micah is a French citizen or not. Could you please tell me?"

"Hold on, please."

Chantal covered the mouthpiece. "What should I say?" she mouthed to me.

"Don't confirm or deny right now," I whispered back.

"Thank you for your call," Chantal responded. "We'll have to get back to you."

"Oh yes, yes, of course. I understand. Please call me back when you can."

7:02 P.M.

Jeff, another graduate school friend from SAIS, walked in the door, dropped his work bag, and opened his arms, enveloping me in a hug. Aparna and another friend showed up shortly after, bearing food and a huge pile of paper; all the press, national and international, that had come out that day about Micah. Dean and Michelle, two married friends from SAIS, came over with more bags of food they stocked in my fridge, and their printer, which I had requested. As Michelle stood in the cramped apartment trying to network the printer, Amanda, our friend and dog walker, also came by and took Zeugma out for a walk, telling me that she would come by several times a day to take care of Zeugma. Knowing how much Zeugma loved Micah, Amanda sat with her by the Hudson River and visualized herself and Zeugma swirling around Micah, creating a protective shield.

8:01 P.M.

There was a knock on the door. Jeff answered, expecting the FBI, but instead found a man holding still more food, several gourmet sandwiches. *That's strange,* Jeff thought, *I didn't know the FBI brought food with them.*

"Can I help you?" he asked.

"Yes, hi," said the man standing at our doorstep, talking quickly and looking in over Jeff's shoulder. "I've spoken to Chantal several times on the phone today, she knows me, I'm a television producer and—"

Jeff stepped out, closing the door behind him. I could hear him speaking sternly; then he reappeared, alone, with the sandwiches.

9:05 P.M.

The buzzer rang, and this time it was the FBI. Agent Chris and his partner, Agent Pat, walked in. Both of them were subdued, and they blended together, with their dark blazers and tan pants, blond hair, and pale complexions.

None of us knew what to expect, or how the FBI, as a domestic agency, could help. They gave me their cards with a gold seal. FBI: SPECIAL AGENT, and stood at length, turning in circles, searching for a place to sit in my tiny apartment. As Pat looked at me, maintaining eye contact, Chris would gaze around. After a few minutes, they switched, and Pat surveyed the crowded scene as Chris continued to listen, looking at me, nodding.

I worried that, seeing the apartment and my youth, they would not take me seriously. I didn't know if they took Micah's case seriously or were just trying to get information. They had a lot of questions. How long had Micah been in Iraq? Why was he there? When had I last heard from him?

I had a list of questions, too: What was the FBI doing? Were they our contacts? Was Micah officially listed as kidnapped? They said Micah wasn't listed as kidnapped, that he was listed only as missing. In order to move him from the missing to the kidnapped category, they needed more information, and that was why they were talking to me.

"Once we have determined that a crime has been committed against a U.S. citizen overseas, the FBI becomes involved," Pat said. "Our job is to do the legwork before your fiancé is listed as kidnapped. After that, a different team will be assigned."

I felt as if we'd just taken a step backward. We had to *prove* he'd been kidnapped?

Loren Nunley, our intern and a New York University student, walked in, nodded to the agents, and hugged me. "All right MH, let's do it! This is what we have been training for," he said. "Let's bring him home!" He had learned about the kidnapping that morning while on vacation. Unsure how best to help, he called his mother, who told him, "Marie-Hélène might be alone right now; she needs you." He immediately flew back to be with me.

Over the course of the next hour and a half, I reviewed in detail with Pat and Chris everything we had done that day. They asked me whom I thought could have taken Micah, and I listed my theories: looters unhappy at his investigative work on the looting, a criminal gang for money, the Mahdi Army, maybe for political reasons. I told them about the Italian issue briefly, but only so they were aware of it and would not be sidetracked.

I explained the differences between north and south in Iraq—Sunni versus Shi'ite—and how geography might play out in Micah's kidnapping. Because he'd been abducted in Nasiriyah, in the south, a predominately Shi'ite area, he'd probably been taken by a Shi'ite group. Though the Mahdi Army had detained journalists for several hours or more, Shi'ite militants had not killed any Western journalists. I explained that if it was a Shi'ite group, we could reach out to people who could help and that with our journalist friends we were trying to contact Sadr. The Shi'ites have a hierarchical religious structure that is headed by just a handful of religious leaders, whereas the Sunnis follow individual Imams.

My biggest fear, I told them, was the possibility that it was a criminal gang; in that case geography would not matter. Micah might be sold to Zarqawi or some other extremist group. Nothing we had heard so far pointed to that conclusion, so I continued talking about the Mahdi Army, the most likely possibility.

I told Pat and Chris about James Brandon, who had been taken from his hotel. Though Micah's time line was still a mystery, I told the FBI that if Micah had stayed at a hotel in Nasiriyah, he might have been spied on and followed from there. The only hotel in Nasiriyah Micah and I had stayed at was the Al-Janoub.

. . .

Micah and I stayed together at the Al-Janoub Hotel only once. It was in June, at the end of the first Mahdi uprising and the beginning of the hottest months.

The Al-Janoub was directly adjacent to Hamas and Hezbollah, on the street that ran along the north side of the Euphrates. The Hamas and Hezbollah building, where the Palestinian and Lebanese militant groups had opened their offices shortly after the 2003 Gulf War, was small, quiet, and worn, an old bicycle usually leaning against the front door. There had been more activity there lately. The building was pockmarked with bullet holes from recent fighting between Italian forces and Mahdi militia, which had turned the Euphrates River into a front line.

I stopped in front of their shared complex to read a U.N. poster about the elections, which cheerfully suggested that the reader should vote. Amer, one of our drivers in Baghdad who had reluctantly agreed to take us to Nasiriyah, forcefully pushed me away from the Hamas-Hezbollah front door and through the lobby of the Al-Janoub, muttering and rolling his eyes, and left me at the desk to check in. He shifted from his left foot to his right and back again, biting his nails, dropping his eyes when anyone glanced his way. The ten or so rotund men sitting on the lobby's baroquely flowered couches had stiffened as we entered. Now two men got up, only one managing a strained smile. "Welcome, welcome," he said, indicating an Iraqi soft-drink dispenser. He pulled out a cold Pepsi. Thrusting it into my hand, he broke into a limping jog to grab our large camera bags from Amer and take them out of sight. The hotelier signed us in, checking the French passport I conspicuously presented. I made a loud comment about Paris, so all the eyes and ears could pick up a French connection. "You are the first foreigners we have seen in several months," he told me. He gestured to Amer with a slight nod of his head and spoke to him in a low voice.

Later, as Micah and I settled into our room on the third floor, overlooking a large, empty cement courtyard, Amer knocked softly, whispering his name into the door.

With no eyehole, we cautiously undid the lock.

Amer stood with the limping man who had carried our bags. The limping man handed us a bar of used soap and, with a small smile, apologized that there was no other soap, then left.

"The hotel man, he say please leave tomorrow morning, very quick," Amer said. "He is scared, very scared for you, and hotel of his. By seven in the A.M., please leave, he say to me. He fear that the Jesh al-Mahdi have seen you and will say he have foreigner here and they will come and burn his hotel. They keep eyes on the hotel."

Staying here was not our choice. We had come down to film an Italian archaeological patrol, having been promised a bed at the base. On arrival, we were told that the paperwork was still being processed. In May, we had stayed overnight once at the Nasiriyah Museum, the gates double-locked with a chain, whose key Mr. Hamdani kept in his pocket; several members of Sheik Abu Fetah's tribe set up outside the door with AK-47s and cigarettes to pass the night. Two weeks later, the Mahdi Army burned and looted the Nasiriyah Museum, and Mr. Hamdani no longer felt that it was safe. We did not want to ask him if we could stay at his house. He would not refuse our request, but it would put his family in danger. The Al-Janoub was the only option that night.

"You stay here now, do not leave," Amer instructed us, chewing his nails farther down; now bleeding slightly. "I will bring chicken dinner. No worry, the guard and me is in next room," he said, pointing to a door down the hall.

I was somewhat reassured.

"What's he doing?" I asked.

"He is tired, he sleep," Amer responded.

"Does he have his gun with him?"

"No, no, we leave it in the car. It attract too much attention to bring it inside."

A sleeping, gunless guard in an empty hotel. Amer left to get *d'jaj wa timann*, chicken with rice.

We finished the two large chicken dinners while watching an Imam's Quranic lesson on the local channel, under the single naked lightbulb that hung from the ceiling. Amer stopped by one last time before retiring to his room, the guard still sleeping deeply. "Please, it is most important that we leave right away in the morning. Be ready. Jesh al-Mahdi cannot know we are here." He waved fingers raw from chewing. Feeling he needed to add a note of calm to his message, he continued, "But no worry, Mary Helen, no problem." Looking over his shoulder, he hurried to his room.

Micah and I pulled the thick satin curtains tightly closed over the windows. When we looked out, there were no other lights on in the hotel. The city was quiet. After a while, a lone man with an oil lamp appeared, pacing back and forth in the courtyard below. He smoked a cigarette, looking around, staring up at the windows. "Maybe he is a guard?" I ventured.

We heard a solitary set of footsteps in the hallway. Frozen, we listened for more. Nothing.

"What are we going to do if someone comes to our door?"

Micah turned off the lights. In the dim light from the courtyard that filtered through the green satin curtains, I hid our personal papers in the pouch I wore around my waist—our link to the West—then put on my bulletproof vest and, over it, my *abaya*. I looked hideously misshapen, as the black polyester took on every sharp angle and buttressing protrusion of the Kevlar underneath. The added protection would betray me. I looked at our equipment: five large bags full of cameras resting by the door. I packed all our film and one small camera in a single bag in case we had to run; at least we could document our escape.

Outside, the oil lamps were out, and the pacing man was gone. Micah stepped quietly onto the balcony and surveyed the distance to the ground. He pulled the sheets off our beds and tied them together, making a rope long enough to reach from our balcony to the ground, three floors down. We debated leaving it tied to the railing but thought that would make us too conspicuous. Instead, we left the bedsheet rope just inside the balcony door, to be quickly tied if we heard someone at the door. If they came in through the balcony, we'd run for the front door.

I looked out one last time into the dark courtyard. We both lay down on our respective beds, eyes open, ears open, struggling to mold our backs into the turtle casing of the bulletproof vests. Micah took the bed closest to the glass doors. He always did this so I would be farther from shattering glass if there was an explosion. For that reason, he always got the heavier blanket.

At two A.M., Micah was jolted awake by the pitch black. All the electricity in that sector of Nasiriyah had gone out. The courtyard spotlight was off. The darkness was immediately followed by a long staccato of multiple gunshots, eagerly repeating their sharp refrain. The dogs began to bark. Micah jumped to the window and peered out through the very small opening where the curtains came together. He looked right, left, up, down, but there was nothing to see. When the guns fell silent, the dogs continued to bark for a long time. Eventually, exhausted, Micah fell back asleep.

At seven A.M., Micah and I were downstairs, ready to check out. Mr. Hamdani and Amir, about whom Micah had talked often and fondly, were waiting for us in the lobby.

Amir greeted me warmly. "Mrs. Helen, I have heard so much about you. Welcome, welcome to Iraq. Are you ready for the patrol? Let's begin our work."

We told him about the past night's fears, which were quickly dissipating in the bright Iraqi morning. He laughed, dismissing them with a *tsk* that stuck in his well-trimmed mustache. "There is no worry for the Mahdi Army now in Nasiriyah," he said. I only half believed him. "Have you read Nietzsche?" he continued, directing the conversation down a philosophical road, as he always would do, each time adding his own unique translation. "According to Nietzsche," Amir continued, "you only understand the meaning of life when you stand at the edge of the volcano."

· · ·

As I talked to the FBI agents, they took notes, occasionally looking at each other. When I was done, I handed them several pounds of media reports Aparna had printed out. We all looked at the huge pile.

"Well," they said, clearly surprised. "Looks like you've got things under control."

They promised to return the next day with a hostage negotiation team to advise me on dealing with the media.

As the phones quieted late Monday night, while Iraq slept, Chantal was frightened, and thought hard about how we could keep working. She had read accounts of Daniel Pearl's kidnapping, the *Wall Street Journal* reporter taken hostage and beheaded by al-Qaeda in Pakistan in 2002. His story was one of the reasons, despite her support, that she had been worried about my trip to Iraq. She remembered that former president Bill Clinton had been helpful, so she left a message at Bill Clinton's Harlem office.

By two A.M. in New York, ten A.M. Tuesday morning in Iraq, we still weren't tired. Things were quiet, though, and we decided we were better off getting some rest. Our friends left and Chantal and I lay down in bed and turned off the light. Chantal kept talking to me, afraid of what thoughts the dark would bring.

Micah was alive, I told her. I would know if he were dead; I would feel a hurt, and an emptiness. And God wouldn't allow Micah to die, I added, but it sounded ridiculous when said out loud to Chantal. Dad had died when we were little girls. His death, which for a long time I blamed on God, left a huge, empty space, a wound that never fully healed. I reverted back to my girlhood thinking. God wouldn't take Micah away, too. My mom often quoted an old saying: "God only gives you what you can handle." Since I wouldn't be able to handle Micah's death, God would not allow Micah to die. Chantal stayed awake, my sentinel against fear, talking and listening until I fell asleep.

. . .

In Nasiriyah, on Friday, August 13, Hatem had run from the kidnapping in the market to his father's house; his father had immediately gone to the Nasiriyah Museum and told Mr. Hamdani. When Mr. Hamdani learned that Micah and Amir had been kidnapped, he immediately set to work, contacting the governor and deputy governor, giving an interview about how Micah had been made to leave the Italian base, sending pictures of Micah and Amir to Al Hurra, a U.S.-funded Arab satellite TV station, and asking the Carabinieri for help.

On Saturday, Amir's sister, watching TV in Basra, saw Mr. Hamdani's pictures of Amir and Micah and called the family in Nasiriyah.

"Where's Amir?" she asked.

"He's in Baghdad with Micah," they replied.

"No, he's not, he's on TV, he's been kidnapped."

Amir's younger brothers ran to the deputy governor's office seeking help.

Learning of Micah's disappearance, Major Frascinetto of the Italian Carabinieri sent out hundreds of flyers about Micah and Amir to his contacts in Nasiriyah to locate them, and possibly parachute in on a rescue mission with the help of the Italian air force.

Word on the street was that a gang had caught two spies—the third had escaped—and brought them to the Sadr office. With the deputy governor Adnan al-Sharifi, Mr. Hamdani rushed to the Sadr office to try to convince the officials there that Micah and Amir were not spies. No, the kidnappers insisted, they are spies and we will kill them. No, Mr. Hamdani and Adnan al-Sharifi insisted, they are journalists. No, they are spies.

Little happened that morning. Day five. It was the routine I had gotten used to. Being led into the enclosure early in the morning, sleeping for a few hours, then breakfast, the sheep moving past, clearing out Freedom's Gate a little more, then lying on my back staring up at the sky through the small opening between the palm leaves.

"What do you think, Amir?"

"I don't know."

"Do you think we will be released today?"

"Somehow."

Then everything changed.

I was sitting on my mat, Amir resting on his side, when two men came into the enclosure, keffiyehs wrapped tightly around their faces. In Arabic they commanded me to get up. I patted my pocket to make sure the shiv was still there, then stood up. It was too early for lunch.

"Amir, what's going on?"

Amir asked them, but there was no response.

They tied my hands in front with the cloth from the ground, then put my blindfold on. Something was wrong. They were not taking Amir. This was the first time since we had been kidnapped that we were going to be separated.

"Where are they taking me?"

Amir tried to ask them again.

"*Shaugla baseta.*" Small problem, we'll return him shortly, they replied in Arabic. Amir did not translate.

I dreaded separation. How would I communicate? To keep calm, I told myself they might be taking me to speak to someone in a position of authority who spoke English.

They were never good at tying my blindfold, and I could vaguely make out a hazy world over the top edge as I tilted my head forward. They led me out of the enclosure and toward the field where we slept.

The man holding me by the arm stopped for a moment a short distance beyond the entrance of the enclosure.

"Can you see?" he asked in broken English, pronouncing each word slowly.

"No," I responded, shaking my head.

"Good," he said.

As we approached the field we turned to the left, toward the house, a long, tan one-story structure possibly made of mud bricks or cement blocks. I had seen it only from a distance, from the field where we slept. My mind filled with darkening thoughts. Was I being led into a Sharia court where they would determine my innocence? As we rounded the corner I saw the hazy outlines of three or four young men standing out front, one or two with weapons. They fell silent as I approached, watching me. I stopped to take off my plastic slippers at the door, a sign of respect, then crossed the threshold.

The room was a long, open space lit by an orange glow from windows covered with cloth. Fan blades hanging from the ceiling slowly sliced through the hot air, an exhalation at each pass. A large white cloth banner with black Arabic writing hung on the wall to my right. About a dozen young men with weapons of all kinds milled around. In the middle, carefully set up on a stool, was a small video camera pointed away from me, toward a window on the far wall covered by a cloth. It seemed unreal, and yet coldly real—a scene I instantly recognized from kidnapping videos on television.

I began to wonder where my life had gone so completely wrong that I found myself walking blindfolded and tied up into a scene like this.

My dark thoughts coalesced into one: they were making a video.

Daniel Pearl, Nick Berg, Kim Sun-il—the names and the tragic footage of their videotaped beheadings flashed though my mind. I knew how these videos ended. I stopped and turned blindly in the direction of the man leading me by the arm. *"Aesh?"* What? I implored. He was the only one I could reach out to.

"Okay, okay," he said quietly in English.

Okay meant nothing. Okay, there was going to be a video? Were they planning to kill me on video? I didn't know how to ask that. The little Arabic I knew was useless, and even those words escaped me. I had my shiv, I had my strength, I had my wits about me, but I needed to know what they were planning.

They led me to the far wall, in front of the cloth that was covering the window opposite the camera. Hand pressing on my shoulder, the guard made me kneel on the ground. I went though the motions delicately. Every movement, every moment mattered. Through the haze of the blindfold, I watched the men as they prepared, making sure their faces were covered, wrapping their keffiyehs tightly, one putting on a black mask for the first time. Then a man approached, lifted my hands and undid the knots, and removed my blindfold. Strange. I didn't think they would kill me with my hands untied; they wouldn't want me to fight back. Some beheading videos came in pairs: first the unmeetable demand and deadline, then the execution. But there was no way to know what they had planned.

As my blindfold came off, the world came into focus. I looked around at the men's hands and at their waistbands, to see if anyone had a large knife, a sign to me that I was about to be beheaded. I didn't see one, but they would probably hide it. I moved my left hand down next to my pocket with the shiv, studying the room for opportunity. There were so many of them that anything I did was sure to end badly, but I would rather that than be killed at their leisure. They were passing around weapons—AKs, an RPG, rifles. Which gun could I go after? It was impossible to make a plan. If I was going to act, it would have to be spontaneously.

I recognized one of the men from his voice; he was the one who would eat with us, the one who prayed before dinner, the one who'd led me here. I caught his glance and signaled to him with my head. He walked a few feet and leaned over.

"*Aesh?*" What? I asked again in as sympathetic a voice as I could muster. Tell me what is going to happen? I was sweating and nervous but tried not to show any weakness.

"Just video," he said in English.

I wanted to believe him, but you don't tell the truth to someone you are about to kill.

I remained kneeling on the ground as young men moved around behind me, trading weapons, switching positions, and being redirected as they set up the shot.

This was not what I'd expected. It seemed like some of the younger men were being used as props. A few appeared to joke with each other as they held the guns. I was certain some were our guards, but I could not tell which ones. Then I recognized the man with the thick plastic glasses from the van—at least, I recognized the glasses sticking out from his tightly wrapped head. He said hello to me, calling me by my name; then someone handed me my *International Herald Tribune* press card.

Stunned, I took my press card, trying to understand what this meant. I last saw it in the hands of the stout man in the Sadr office in Nasiriyah. Had the Sadr office given the kidnappers my press card when I was put in the van? Had the kidnappers gone back to the Sadr office to pick it up? Was this Sadr's group? As I stared at my press card, I had a terrible realization. If they were using my press card to identify me in the video, they knew I was a journalist. They weren't checking my credentials to determine if I was innocent, as they had repeatedly assured me. They knew who I was, and it didn't matter. All that mattered was my nationality; I was an American. Numbly, I put the press card around my neck.

The small video camera sat on a stool ten feet in front of me, the most powerful weapon in the room. The man with the glasses walked behind the stool, bent down, and spent a moment adjusting the settings, looking up after each adjustment and telling the men standing behind me how to frame themselves in the picture. When he finished, he looked up a last time. I could hear the men shifting behind me, getting into their final positions, then were silent.

"Say name," the man with the glasses instructed me in English. Another man near him motioned for me to hold up my press card and keep it in the air. I realized that this video would probably be seen around the world and understood that I had to appear courageous and defiant. I wanted to represent my country with dignity. I also knew that Marie-Hélène and my family would see this video, and I wanted to send them a message. But what? And how? I thought about conveying a message in Morse code by blinking, but I didn't know Morse code.

A man holding a piece of paper in his hand knelt down directly behind me, a little to my left. He planted his bare foot just to the left of my knee. I looked at his foot through the corner of my eye. That was my plan. If something happened, if someone pulled out a knife, I would stab his foot with my shiv and in the commotion go after a gun. I slipped my fingers into the top of my pocket, ready. The man behind the camera gave me a signal with his hand that the camera was on. The room was quiet. I said a quick "I love you" in my head to Marie-Hélène and my family, and prepared myself.

"Micah Garen," I heard my voice say. Was it my voice? It was almost a questioning tone, with the inflection rising at the end, not at all what I had intended—no courage, no defiance. There was a pause and I winked twice with my right eye, the second wink because I thought someone might not see the first. That was the message, the wink. It was so little, but it was the best I could do to defuse the terror of that video. I meant for it to suggest that things might not be what they appeared to be: my captors were probably not al-Qaeda; they might be connected to Sadr, they might not. But mostly it was a message to my family, saying, "Don't be scared, it will be okay, I will be okay, whatever happens."

A sound thundered in my ear. The man behind me began to bellow, up on one knee, perched over me as if I were a captured animal, a prize trophy. Our bodies tensed as he started reading a statement in a commanding voice that filled the room. Holding my press card out in my right hand, I looked away from him toward the ground, feeling angry and humiliated, trying hard to convey defiance through my expression. I could not stop them from making the video; I could only control small details: my expression, my sense of disgust, my thoughts. I focused on every second, his voice booming behind me. Now, more than ever, I wished I could understand their Arabic. If something was going to happen, I knew it would be at the end of his speech. I pushed my fingers farther into my pocket, ready to pull out the shiv and stab it into his foot if I had to. I hoped I would stab it with such force that it would stick into the floor beneath his foot.

Then it was over.

There was silence again. I froze, not breathing, eyes straining to my left so I could see the man behind me, waiting for any sudden movement—any movement, a hand, a knife, anything. Nothing.

He rose; the men behind me relaxed and quickly dispersed. I was left kneeling, drenched in sweat, with my left hand halfway in my pocket. Like a sudden earthquake, it was over. But the shock waves were just beginning.

A man signaled for me to get up. Dazed, I stood. They took back my press card, tied my hands again, put my blindfold back on, and led me out. My body moved forward, my mind floating full of bewilderment and relief at still being alive.

I was not going to be killed that day.

Two guards led me across the field and back to the enclosure. By then
the bewilderment and relief had vanished and I was seething. What had
just happened to me was beginning to sink in. Amir could tell something
was wrong as soon as I entered.

"What happened? What did they do?" he asked quickly.

"They made a video. The ASSHOLES made a video!" I shouted at the
two who'd led me in after they left. I knelt on my mat, powerless and
empty.

"What did they say?"

"I don't know!" I yelled, frustrated that without Amir I wasn't able to
understand anything. Amir was not only my ears, he was the only person
I could express my anger to.

"ASSHOLES!" I shouted again.

Amir fell silent.

"What's wrong with him?" one of the guards called back casually
from outside the enclosure.

"He is just upset," Amir told them, covering for me.

"They didn't hurt you, did they?" Amir asked in a hushed tone, leaning
toward me.

"No, they only made a video of me to hurt my family," I replied bit-
terly, sitting back on my heels, hands in front on my mat, head hanging.
My anger grew, displacing any sense of relief at still being alive, as I tried
to make sense of this thing, this video, something so awful, churning in
its wake emotions I had never experienced before. The video of me
would soon be used to hurt others, and my powerlessness to prevent
that, a mental torture that grew more painful by the minute, com-
pounded my already intense anger.

It occurred to me that I didn't even know what the man behind me had
said, or why they had made the video.

"Ask them what they said in the video, what the demand was." I was
certain I already knew, that it was some kind of death threat, probably
demanding that America leave Iraq within twenty-four or forty-eight
hours. They were threatening me, terrorizing my family, and blackmail-
ing my country. My anguish intensified as Amir called out to the guard
sitting outside.

"He says he doesn't know, he wasn't there."

"LIAR," I said in a loud voice. "He was there. They were all there."

My mind hardened on thoughts of fighting and escape, as I remained
kneeling on the mat.

"We have to get out," I said quietly and firmly to Amir, looking into his eyes. "Tomorrow morning. And when we escape I am going to kill one of them." *How absurd,* I thought, *I am not a killer.* But the pain overwhelmed my reason.

"Be careful," Amir cautioned, "they understand English."

"I don't give a shit," I shot back, exasperated. I started punching the ground with my right hand until my knuckles were bruised, trying with each blow to release the pain, but it didn't help.

"I don't care if they take me hostage, or kill me, but it's not fucking okay if they make a video to hurt my family."

Amir tried to absorb all of this. I was still alive, that was what was important to him. A part of me was just happy to be alive as well, but I was overcome by the thought of the pain I would cause others and tortured by the fact that I couldn't protect them from it.

My mind flashed with images of how my mother and my father would react when they saw the video. I was afraid one would have a heart attack. My mother was seventy and my father seventy-eight, and both were in poor health. That my kidnapping could be the cause of their death was too much to face. I clenched my teeth, drawing air. *Please don't die,* I thought.

"But Micah, I don't understand—why are you so upset? The important thing is that you are alive." Amir was doing his best to reason with me, but not having been in the room and not being the subject of the video, he had no point of reference.

"No. That is not the important thing." I looked at Amir again. "I don't care about my life, I care about my family. Those men are going to use this video to hurt them. That is what matters to me." I wanted Amir to understand, but more than that, I wanted him to stop questioning me.

I spent the rest of the afternoon lying on my side with my back to Amir, staring at Freedom's Gate. My thoughts, like a dark pendulum, moved from depression to anger to depression. Why hadn't I seen this coming? Believing even a word the kidnappers said was foolish. It was no longer about Amir and me, a matter that could be settled quietly by Mr. Hamdani and Adnan al-Sharifi; it was now something much larger. I was a tool they would use to inflict pain on my family, people in America, friends around the world, anyone watching. I felt as if I were seeing the disaster unfold in slow motion, a glimpse of the future, and I was powerless to stop it. When these thoughts became too much to bear, I sat up and pulled away the palm leaves covering Freedom's Gate and began clearing out more leaves, breaking off more low branches. If I could escape before the video came out, I reasoned, the video would be meaningless.

Thinking about escape calmed my mind, and I sat back again, forcing myself to breath deeply.

"They humiliated me, Amir."

"How?" He jumped up, encouraged that I was speaking again.

My humiliation over being used as a weapon of terror against my will was so intense, I believed that even if I somehow lived through this I would be ostracized by everyone, like the two Japanese aid workers and one Japanese journalist taken hostage and set free in April. They returned to Japan not celebrated for their courageous work but shunned for their "irresponsible behavior." People told them and their families, "You got what you deserved."

"It was never about being innocent." I turned to Amir. "They know I am a journalist. They even gave me back my press card. They have no respect for me, or why I am out here. They pretend being a journalist means something, that you can be *innocent*, but they are just liars." I was not a combatant but I was an American, and they didn't make a distinction.

Amir listened but still did not seem to understand the depth of my anguish.

"They are liars, Amir, you know that, right? We have to escape." Everything they had told us about a "short story," about being let go was probably lies, too. "They are not going to let me go," I continued. "They are probably going to kill me."

Amir tried to remain rational for both of us. "I don't know," he said, attempting to fit the pieces together like a puzzle. For him, they somehow still added up to freedom. Our captors would release us eventually. Amir was willing to try to escape, but he didn't think it was our best option.

I knew that unless we attacked the guards, there would be no way to escape before morning. Our only chance was in the early-morning hours after they brought us back to the enclosure as the single guard dozed off, but the video would certainly be out by then. The damage would be done.

As night came, they led Amir and me out to eat. Something had changed in me; I had been betrayed, used, violated. There was no more goodwill, no trying to pretend, or to connect. We sat silently, picking at the sparse food. A guard asked me a question and I didn't respond. After the meal they brought us back to the field through the darkness. I lay down, looking up at the stars, and wondered if Marie-Hélène and my family had seen the video yet. I shut my eyes tight, trying to flush out the image of their horror. Detached, almost fatalistic, in a strange way I felt liberated. These moments were borrowed time in a life that I felt had ended that afternoon.

The Grim Reaper came again to speak to Amir, and I listened to his voice without any emotion. I was floating on whatever stream fate led me down.

I awoke with a strange feeling of dissociation. On my back, in my bed, eyes wide open, I was looking down at myself. As foggy morning sleep gave way to a clearing consciousness, the thought that Micah was still missing took the shape of a boot crushing my windpipe, and I collapsed like an accordian back into myself.

I jumped up and was soon at my computer, warming up my brain by reading email. Nothing new from James, our friend with the line to Sheik Aws. I had yet to fill out the Hostage Report Checklist; I hadn't had time to even open the document. Besides, I had told the embassy in Baghdad everything they needed and everything I knew, several times to several different people, from Micah's Social Security number down to my three possible abduction scenarios: looters, the Mahdi Army, criminals. I could barely say the fourth. Al-Qaeda, who beheaded hostages.

The phone rang, and a producer told me I had ten minutes to decide whether to go on *Good Morning America*. Many people thought I could reach a national, perhaps international, audience. My gut said it was too early, and Joel, and Mitch from CPJ and Amir's family, had said it was better to hold off. *Good Morning America* had a deadline: if I was going to go, I had to leave within the next half hour for prep, and "who knew if it could happen the next day." Agonizing, I said I couldn't do it that morning. Maybe tomorrow. They were disappointed, and I feared that I had turned down a one-time opportunity. I told every American TV morning show, Canadian Radio, Radio Monaco, and dozens of others the same thing: not today, maybe tomorrow. I held off, hoping the FBI hostage negotiators, coming by in the late morning, could advise me.

By seven A.M., I started to get some more good information. Sami, a Portuguese Iraqi journalist and fixer we knew, called his Sadr contact in Nasiriyah to vouch for Micah. The Sadr contact had a lot of information about Micah. It was a good sign, indicating that the Sadr office was taking it seriously.

APTN in Baghdad had sent their Basra stringer to Nasiriyah and were told that Micah and Amir had been taken from a barbershop next to the market. I called Imam al-Husainy in Michigan, informed him of the news, and urged him to call his contacts. He said he had spoken with Amir's family, and would try to contact Sadr's office to appeal to them as an Iraqi American.

James wrote in detail of his conversation late the previous night with Sheik Raad, head of security for Sadr's Nasiriyah office, and a member of Sheik Aws's inner circle. James said he'd told Sheik Raad three important things: he'd known Micah for more than a year; Micah was a journalist, a good guy, and a friend; and if anything could be done to secure his release, it would really be appreciated. In response, Sheik Raad had three points: they were working on Micah's release; because of James's call they would work harder; and call again tomorrow night. We are Muslims, he added, and of course we are against this kind of kidnapping.

James never suggested that the Sadr movement might be responsible for Micah and Amir's kidnapping. In return, Sadr's office offered to work to secure Micah and Amir's release. James's approach reflected his deep knowledge of Iraqi tradition, customs, and politics. The Sadr movement in Nasiriyah liked to see itself as an enforcer of Islamic law and order, and had frequently intervened to catch thieves and looters. "It may be that they are 'working on his release' because they are against crime generally," James wrote, "and this kind of kidnapping makes Nasiriyah look lawless." If some branch or sympathizer of the Sadr movement was involved, he said, Micah's chances were better because "the Sadr leadership in Nasiriyah is genuinely embarrassed by this sort of behavior."

It appeared that our local effort was beginning to pay off. The Sadr offices in Baghdad and Nasiriyah were informed and involved. Requests from people they knew, respected, and even trusted were coming in, putting pressure on them to find a solution.

It seemed even more now that shining an international spotlight through media attention that might accuse the Mahdi Army or Sadr of the kidnapping could derail the good work that was already happening.

"It's better to stay away from the media," suggested a helpful and concerned press officer in former president Bill Clinton's office, returning Chantal's call from the previous evening. He said he would try to contact a U.N. hostage negotiator who had been successful in difficult cases, and put us in touch with the family of Daniel Pearl. "Perhaps they can give you guidance."

Chantal went to the yellow-tiled bathroom, the only private room in my small, crowded apartment, and shut the door. She got through to Ruth Pearl, Daniel Pearl's mother and, while explaining why she was calling, began to cry. "It's very important to cry," Mrs. Pearl comforted her. She reinforced that we were on the right path, and agreed that we should wait on going to the media. Focus on getting heavy hitters, respected in the Islamic world, to speak on Micah's behalf, she counseled. And if they have to speak publicly, send the message through Arab media channels.

"But I can't tell you what to do," she added. "I'm only speaking from our experience. It's a benefit that Marie-Hélène has been to Iraq," Mrs. Pearl continued. "You need to focus on your contacts on the ground. Even if the FBI are involved, you should absolutely not stop your efforts.

"I'm praying for you," she said, "and thinking about you, and thinking about Micah. You need to keep positive."

At 9:26 A.M., my hope was rocked by a new message from Amir's brother.

```
Dir sir
We don't identify the terrarism or there requests
all I know about the case is Mich and Amir were
went to gun market in Nassiriyah and when Mich took
some pictures to all the guns. The seller became
angery and asked them to give him the pictures they
delet the pictures from the digital camera but the
seiler donot understand then Mich spok to him the
seller know that he was a foreign then he and other
sellers beat Mich and Amir, took the camera and the
maney, and took them to unknown Place.
```

I sank into the sofa, felled by a punch that took me down and all my hopes with it. The positive feeling from James's update evaporated. Our new day had started with good news, and now we'd learned that Micah and Amir had been beaten. The image of Micah being beaten was paralyzing, and I feared for his body. The unknown was more frightening than the known, especially the "unknown place" that Amir's brother had written about. Worse, Amir's family did not know who the kidnappers were. They could be anybody. My hope that they were Mahdi Army sympathizers came undone. The only positive news from the email was that Micah was not dead.

Like a bop doll, I was up again and called Eva, who was just getting into her old Honda to drive down to New York with Suzanne. "It's good, and bad," I told her. "The good is that we heard from the family, and have more information. The bad is that they beat Micah and Amir when they took them." Eva tried to cover up her cry so that Suzanne, getting into the passenger seat, wouldn't hear it. "Let's not tell Suzanne. She doesn't need to know stuff like this," she whispered.

The phone rang again and Bob Callahan, from the U.S. embassy in Baghdad, told me that the Americans were working closely with the Italians, and that the Iraqi police had informed the Italians of the kidnapping on Saturday. I could not imagine why they hadn't contacted the family if they'd known on Saturday. At the least, they must have told someone. What had gone on for three days before the world knew?

"Whatever you want us to do, whatever message you want to pass along, whatever you need," friends from SAIS told me. "My colleague's father was supreme allied commander of NATO. He is willing to lend an ear, and give you advice." "I will contact Paul Wolfowitz. His deputy is a friend." "I will make sure the senator I work for pushes Micah's interest at the White House." "I have interviewed insurgents, I will try to phone them," a journalist emailed me. "A well-respected sheik is my friend, I will call him immediately."

Friends came by with more office equipment, food, names of Arabic translators, and the baskets of fruit and flowers the media continued to leave downstairs. My apartment was beginning to look like a produce stand.

Loren arrived early, and I asked him to put together answers to the FBI's request from the previous night: Micah's cell phone number, bank information, a list of Iraqi phone numbers. "I'm on it," he said. In between, he made frequent trips to the front door with Chantal, together a polite but firm buffer against the flash cameras and questions—reporters often mistaking her for me—relaying that the family was not making a statement.

Nabila, an Iraqi and a close friend of Micah's mother, had been up all night making calls to Iraqis in exile in London and to her school friends who were close with Iyad Allawi, the interim Iraqi prime minister. An Iraqi friend of hers whose brother had recently been kidnapped and released suggested that we appeal to the kidnappers through Al Jazeera. He also thought we should contact the spiritual leader of Hezbollah in

Lebanon, Sheik Fadlallah, to ask that he make a public appeal for Micah's release. A public appeal from a high-level religious Shi'ite authority would be effective, he reasoned, since the people involved in Micah's kidnapping were likely Shi'ite. It would also put pressure on Sadr. Sheik Fadlallah was an ayatollah, second only to a grand ayatollah, the top of the Shi'ite religious hierarchy. More than that, he had been a militant who had recast himself as a political figure, a model that Sadr seemed eager to follow. "Do not stick to the official track only," Nabila advised. "You must take other initiatives."

On the phone with Micah's family, we decided that we would make a public appeal only when we had run out of options through other channels. Hezbollah and Lebanon didn't have much significance for me in this context. Lebanon was far from Iraq, and I did not know how strong Sheik Fadlallah's influence was among Shi'ites in Iraq. Iraqi Shi'ites looked to Grand Ayatollah Ali al-Sistani for religious leadership or, more recently, Muqtada al-Sadr for political leadership. Their influence was profound. Posters, particularly of Sadr, hung everywhere in southern Iraq, with Sadr's thick pointing finger commanding his followers from lampposts, market stalls, and the crumbling, cream-colored walls flanking city streets. Contacting Sheik Fadlallah of Lebanon might not be the best use of our time.

Eva called from the road. "I have good news," she said. She had just gotten a call from Bob Callahan. The French government had agreed neither to confirm nor deny Micah's status as a French citizen. Though they strongly disagreed on the war, the two governments were working together to protect Micah. It was another significant victory.

Five FBI agents arrived at one P.M., moving carefully through my hallway packed with books and cameras, trying not to knock over anything as they gingerly made their way forward. They looked for a place to sit in our crammed ten-by-twenty-foot studio apartment.

Two of the five men were hostage negotiators. Both radiated the same air of concern and concentration. One, Frank, explained the psychology of kidnappers, and how to influence them through words, saying it was like dealing with the Mafia. His affable personality, deeply lined face, thick mustache, and eyeglasses, hanging low on his large nose, made him look the part. His bushy eyebrows, like giant woolly caterpillars, would rise and hover above the rims of his glasses, remaining suspended for several seconds, emphasizing his main points. His colleague, Bob, a fair, middle-aged man, nodded in agreement, giving us long, concerned smiles.

"Okay, all right, so," I began again. I felt as if I was leading an odd get-to-know-you meeting between two very different groups: me, Chantal, and Loren, and the FBI team.

I recounted everything we had done in the past twenty-four hours, explaining our grassroots approach. The agents and negotiators looked at one another, surprised and relieved.

"This is good. You guys are doing great."

"And," Chantal said with emphasis, causing all heads to turn in her direction, "we are doing all of this out of this little apartment." The agents leaned back, waiting for her to finish her thought.

"What can you do for us?" she asked. "We need a room that has more space, secure international phone lines, high-speed Internet access, and privacy. Have you seen the press outside?"

"We have some places," an agent answered. "We'll get back to you."

Against the backdrop of nonstop phone calls and the front-door buzzer, we asked Frank how we should deal with the media. "Listen, we can't tell you what to do," he said. "We can give you recommendations, tell you what we think, but you have to decide. Right now, based on what we know, we think you would benefit from waiting to talk to the media. There's no upside and you run the risk of making Micah a high-value asset. But it's all up to you."

His words were empowering and awful at the same time; it would be easier if we had no choice. I began to worry that his advice not to speak to the media might be tied to the fighting in Najaf. Perhaps the government did not want a loud, messy scandal during the Najaf offensive.

But I had to trust that the FBI had Micah's safety at heart. It seemed to me there was no right answer in a hostage situation. There might be patterns, but the details make each case unique. The government, like us, was learning as well.

"Listen, the media wants to help," Frank said. "But they are also doing it for themselves. Well, I mean, you know—you're part of the media. This is a big story. Not to say they are bad or anything like that. They have good intentions and want to do what they can. But the business of their whole thing is to get the story. So, keep that in mind when you talk to them."

"But if we do talk to them, what do we say?" I asked.

Frank pulled out a yellowed two-page list.

"First, and most important, the ball's in your court. Second, it's like a trade. You want something from them; they want something from you. It's a negotiation." He looked around at us for emphasis. Chantal and Loren were carefully taking notes in our Project Book, adding big stars next to the main points.

"When and if you talk to the press, your main goal is to humanize Micah; you have to help them see his humanity. Show his captors what they should have already observed. His captors have seen and spoken to Micah. Point out that he is a gentleman, that he believes in respect and dignity, that he lives by positive values that he has passed on to all of us. Say that Micah honors life. Put him on a pedestal.

"If you make a statement, talk to Micah directly. Reach out to him. Use his name, talk about his relationship to you—he is a brother, a son, a fiancé.

"Show respect for the situation, and say that you know they are serious. Say please.

"Micah is powerless. They have the power, and taking Micah's life would do nothing more than hurt us. Because they have power, they should follow the path of dignity and respect, of doing the right thing. Empower them. If they release him, they can earn the respect of the world."

He paused after reading through the list, resting the worn pages on his knee. "Does this make sense to you?"

"Yes," I said.

"All right, I'll tell you things to avoid. . . . Most importantly, keep politics out of this—for or against anything. This is about Micah as a human being. Don't say anything about the government. And just as important, don't say anything about religion."

"Just like at Christmas dinner," I said, trying to ease the tension.

Frank looked over disapprovingly. "And no jokes.

"Let's continue," he said, throwing a cautionary look my way. "Absolutely no 'Christmas' commentary on terrorism and no criticism of any kind. Do not criticize his captors. And it's best if you use pronouns. 'They' is better than 'kidnappers.' "

"What about detailed questions?"

"Just be simple; stick to the facts," Frank continued. "Point out the obvious: 'I am not a politician. I am half a world away. I only know what I read in the papers.' "

"What if I start crying?"

"Just be natural, be you. It is natural that you should be emotional. Be emotional, be communicative, but don't be convulsive. It will be hard to get your point across and will diminish your message. Remember, say his name. 'Micah is my fiancé. Micah's family loves him. Micah's mother and father would like for him to return to his home safely. Micah is innocent and powerless.' "

Emotional, not convulsive, I repeated to myself in my mind.

Micah's brother, Jonathan, slipped into the apartment quietly, looking exhausted, and sat at the far edge of the group, taking the last available sitting space. He was trying to hold himself together, and not fall apart in front of us. He wore a dark-blue-and red-striped polo shirt that Micah had given him several months earlier. It looked slept in.

"This will help," Frank counseled. "Hesitate after a question. Take a breath. You won't blurt anything out that you can't take back. And it can help you control your emotions."

"The most important thing, and it looks like you are doing it, is to coordinate all family statements and have one point of contact."

At around three P.M. the FBI hostage team left, wishing us luck, telling us we were doing a good job, saying they could be reached anytime, day or night.

"I'm so glad you're here," I told Jonathan, who had moved to sit on the edge of the bed. "That's the shirt Micah gave you."

He nodded. "Don't worry about the media," he offered. "Let's focus on the people you're talking to on the ground."

Shortly after the FBI left, an exploratory conversation with a TV producer, building upon earlier conversations, almost turned into a disaster. She emphasized their ability to reach an international audience, and warned me of the closing media window, saying that "if I did not speak soon, the press would probably not be interested for long." Pressured and confused, and wanting to keep my options open for an appeal, I agreed to talk at my apartment. She arrived quickly with a cameraman, ready for an interview. The ringing buzzer jolted me; I didn't even want to make a statement, let alone do an interview.

Chantal called Aparna and told her we needed her help right away.

The buzzer rang again, and I asked the TV producer to wait. The buzzer continued to ring as I delayed. Finally, Aparna arrived and explained to the producer that it was not in Micah's best interest to do an interview now, thanking her for her concern, and closed the door—while at the same time keeping it open for the future.

Crisis resolved, we decided that Aparna would be our filter for the media, handling all calls and following all the news that came out.

"I'm ready to head to Baghdad," Eva said, arriving with her passport and Suzanne, who remained calm and focused.

Coming together geographically motivated us as we gathered in my small apartment, reviewing what we knew so far and updating charts that we had hung on the wall above the bed, the only free space. Aparna kicked off her shoes and stood on the bed to reach the charts, marker in hand. Chantal's cell phone rang. She grabbed it from the long line of cell phone chargers.

" . . . thanks for calling, uh-huh, uh-huh. Okay, listen, what I am telling you is at this time we are not going to give an interview. No, no, I just said . . ." Chantal covered the mouthpiece of the phone. "It's that reporter again. He says he has a right to know."

"Do you want me to handle this?" Aparna asked. Chantal gladly handed the phone to Aparna, who, at four feet eleven, towered above us on the bed.

"Have you been listening to what they are saying? That is what they want. . . . Uh-huh. Yes, listen. . . . Please stop talking. Do you think you are going to convince them to talk to you by stalking them? I don't think so. *We* will call *you*. That's how it's going to work."

Chantal's cell phone rang again.

"Hello, *bonjour,* sorry for bothering you, please, is Micah a French citizen?" the man from the French consular office asked politely.

"Thanks for calling," Chantal responded. "Can we get back to you?"

"Of course, of course. I understand. Just, please, call me back."

. . .

We settled back to work on our sheik wall chart. At around six P.M., we got more news from Iraq. James had called his Sadr contacts in Nasiriyah by satellite phone. He had reached Sheik Moyed, who reiterated that Micah was alive and said that the Nasiriyah Sadr office could help secure his release. Sheik Moyed gave no facts but indicated that they knew who was holding Micah, and might know where. "Don't worry," Sheik Moyed told James, "we know he is alive and well. We have found an open thread on the sweater. We think he will be released in two or three days." Everyone in the tiny apartment cheered.

Suddenly everything was on the right path again—the right people were saying the right things, and all sides were reporting the same good news. We had a plan that we had confidence in, and our team was working together effectively around the world.

We called Micah's father, Alan, immediately to let him know. He and Sally, still feverishly making calls, were overcome with joy.

An hour later, I called Alan again to let him know a new FBI team, including more hostage negotiators, was on its way to the apartment.

"Why are they coming over?" Alan said, his voice thickening.

"This is the new team that has been assigned to the case," I explained.

"But Micah is being released."

"Sheik Moyed says Micah is alive," I answered, carefully, realizing how easily there could be miscommunication because we were operating in different locations.

"I understood that Micah was being released. We've opened a bottle of champagne. We're getting ready to drink it."

"He hasn't been released yet," I continued. "It looks good, but it hasn't happened yet."

We were both silent. I was pained imagining the disappointment at Alan's house.

"I misunderstood," he said quietly. "I'll put the champagne away."

In Baghdad, a lot of Mitch's journalist friends had gone to Najaf to cover the fighting, and Mitch continued to put the word out: everybody contact your Sadr sources and see what they can do. After a day of meeting, talking, calling, and emailing, Mitch reckoned that it was almost certain that the kidnappers were Shi'ite, and that Micah was in Nasiriyah. Mitch's intrepid driver and fixer, Osama, grew increasingly confident that he could

negotiate Micah and Amir's release. Osama knew the son of a powerful
sheik in Nasiriyah, who he thought could open some doors.

Osama told Mitch, "I think I can get this done. I want to go down to
Nasiriyah, and I don't want you to come with me. Give me twenty-four
hours."

Osama knew he had to go on his own, and Mitch understood. "Osama
is going to get his Iraqi on," as Mitch put it. "When there's a white guy in
the room it gets more complicated. The tough work and bullying has to
look like it's in the family, not done on behalf of a white guy." Mitch approached the Committee to Protect Journalists with Osama's sugges-
tion. CPJ had never conducted a rescue operation like this; they weren't
in the hostage-retrieval business. CPJ wanted assurances that Osama
could handle the job and wouldn't get killed. Joel called us and explained
the idea, telling us that CPJ felt comfortable doing this only at the request
of the family, and that Osama would have to go as the family's representative. We discussed the risk to Osama, worried that something might
happen to him. I knew that Osama's life, and Micah's, would depend on
his skill, connections, and luck. But Osama felt confident that he could
handle this, and he was willing to try. Negotiating for a hostage was dangerous, and I was amazed and elated that he would take it on.

John Burns suggested a driver he knew who could travel down with
Osama. This driver was a "tough guy," a former officer in Saddam's
army, who knew his way around the Nasiriyah underbelly. He could also
help open doors.

Very quickly, very excitedly, we decided to do it, and gave Joel the
green light. The two "tough guys" headed south. Soon we would have
our own man on the ground.

The FBI was now working under the assumption that there had been a
kidnapping. The case had been escalated, and a new team was assigned.
At around eight P.M., a larger group of agents filed in.

Agent Kim and Agent Tom introduced themselves and said they were
taking over the investigation. Tom, a veteran agent in a dark suit with a
strong face, did not smile as he surveyed the room in a quick glance. Kim,
sharply dressed, with a thin gold bracelet around her ankle, was younger,
open, and friendly. I wondered if she had been assigned to help deal with
our group, so overwhelmingly female.

Tom, who had been standing against the wall, observing, with his large hands folded in front of him, spoke in a low baritone that got everyone's attention. He told us he had experience with kidnappings; he had worked on the Daniel Pearl case.

The room fell silent. Reminded of the horrific outcome of that kidnapping, I turned away from Tom. It was a possibility that I could not face at that moment.

Kim spoke, easing the transition. Technology could be a clue, she said; we should check email, phones, bank accounts. I hadn't thought to check Micah's emails, and was angry with myself for having overlooked this. She also suggested that they download the information on my computer. I was happy to give them anything they needed, but I did not want to jeopardize the delicate work and relationships of our friends on the ground.

"Why don't I read you the emails," I said, "and if there is something you think you need, we can take it from there."

"Okay, sounds good." Kim, efficient, wanted to make things easier, not harder.

I knew the bank information would yield nothing. Iraq is a cash society, where crisp, new dollars bills, never bent or dirty, do not leave a trace. "But sure, let's check," I offered.

All the doors were being pushed open. I'd fling them open myself if it helped, but there was a sense of the huge government elephant lumbering into the room, making itself comfortable. It could stay for a long time.

"What about Micah's cell phone? Maybe it has GPS and we can locate a position," Kim continued.

It worked only in Baghdad and probably hadn't been charged. "But, maybe," I agreed.

"Hi, this is Micah." My call went straight to voicemail. I wanted to call back again and again, to hear Micah's voice.

I hung up, closed my eyes.

"All right, let's go through his emails. I'll read them out loud," I suggested. Everyone settled into a silent circle, family sitting and FBI standing, to hear the oral history, ears sharply tuned to possible clues. Chantal moved over to sit next to me, so close I could lean on her.

I started with my emails, reading through the messages from Iraq. Thinking only of useful information, I forgot to filter for Suzanne, and read the email from Amir's brother saying that Micah and Amir had been beaten. Suzanne gasped, leaning her head back.

"Please email or contact the U.S. Consul in Baghdad. There has been concern expressed for your well-being. Thank you." The U.S. consul had emailed Micah on Monday, August 16. The time stamp read 4:57 A.M. EST.

There were several emails from the previous days, mostly from media requesting that Micah submit a photo or text for a story. Nothing else. No threat, warning, or clue.

We reread the emails, trying to re-create a time line. So far we knew that the Italians said Micah had handed in his Italian press pass for the base on Thursday, August 12. Mitch had seen Micah on Thursday night in Baghdad in his red swimming trunks, heading to the Hamra pool, and John Burns was almost certain that he had had lunch with Micah on Friday, August 13. But Micah was kidnapped on August 13. I knew that Micah would not leave for Nasiriyah on a Friday afternoon because the roads would be too dangerous; there might be unrest after Friday prayers. We planned every trip carefully, always leaving at dawn, and rarely traveled on Fridays. It didn't make sense; he must have left in the morning.

Micah had written to John Burns after arriving in Nasiriyah on Friday morning to tell him the roads were safe enough for travel. Micah had also written to Suzanne and had been unusually open about the volatile security situation, saying that there had been a lot of action with the Mahdi Army "but what can you do, that's Iraq. I am sure it's just a passing murmur."

In his last email, at 11:30 A.M., Friday, August 13, Micah wrote to Lauren Sandler, a journalist friend who had also worked with the Carr Foundation as a journalist in Iraq, telling her of his plans. "I am still, yes, still in Iraq, but should be leaving next week. I hope my dog remembers me."

I choked. Micah was usually reserved about his emotions, and his concern about Zeugma remembering him was unexpected. Unable to catch the feelings that forced their way out, I started crying in the center of our circle, my first public breakdown. No one moved. I cried for Micah, alone and in danger, and because I couldn't be next to him to help him and comfort him. I cried for us, our hands reaching out to him in a darkness so deep and so frightening. I cried for the families of other hostages who had waited and worked in days of suspended animation. We were now among them, filled with a deep longing for Micah. And yet, there was emptiness where he was supposed to be.

. . .

The FBI team left at around ten P.M., promising to be in touch early the next morning. They would be spending a large part of the day down at the courthouse. Suzanne and Eva headed back to Jonathan and Nieves's house to get a few hours of sleep.

After everyone but Chantal had left, with no more emails to send, I filled out the Hostage Report Checklist. It was a simple document that asked for basic information, easy enough until I hit question E: "Distinguishing physical characteristics." I couldn't think of any scars or birthmarks, and Micah had no tattoos. What else would distinguish a person to a forensic eye? I thought about how one knows a body, intimately. Its smell, how it curves, how it reacts to touch. This wasn't the information they were looking for. I could think of nothing, but it was important to have something on record.

I called Suzanne to ask if she knew of something, maybe a childhood fall that had left a scar.

She paused, and we both filled the silence with unspoken thoughts of Micah's body.

"He's perfect," she concluded, laughing. "Perfect except, of course, for his big feet."

In the blank next to "Distinguishing physical characteristics," I wrote: "According to his mother, he is perfect other than his big feet."

That offered nothing useful for identification purposes. A detective would find it superfluous; it wasn't even a hard fact. It was an important fact to me, though, because it gave Micah dimensionality on paper that the other answers did not. It showed his individuality. He wasn't just an American hostage with blood type O and salt-and-pepper hair.

He was our Micah whom we loved, with big feet that we teased him about.

Micah, Wednesday, August 18

By the time I awoke, my depression had receded, leaving behind grim determination. Amir was right. The video didn't matter; my humiliation didn't matter. What mattered was getting back to my family alive, and the more I thought about it, getting back alive meant escaping. Today would be the day to plan.

We were led back to our enclosure through the field. I followed the guard who held Amir by the arm, almost sleepwalking. He had made sure Amir's blindfold was secure but hadn't bothered to blindfold me or see that my hands were tied. As we walked, I silently positioned myself two steps behind him, my mat tucked under my arm, my fists tightly clenching the cloth. Raising my hands to my waist, elbows by my side, I pulled the cloth taut. I could easily slip it around his neck. Should I? The course of our lives would change in an instant, but toward what end? As I teetered on the edge of that life-or-death decision, the guard cocked his head halfway in my direction. I dropped my hands and moved off to the side, where he could see me. Freedom's Gate was a better plan.

Back in the enclosure, sitting in the pale light, I asked Amir what the Grim Reaper had spoken to him about the previous evening.

"He said they have been to my home." Amir looked at the ground. It was an indirect threat against his family; our captors were smart enough to know how to control us. As the eldest son, head of the family now that his father was an old man, Amir was responsible for protecting them.

Our lives were in danger, my parents might die from grief, and now Amir's family was in danger as well.

But we couldn't make decisions based on implied threats. We had to stay focused on our only remaining option: escaping with our lives. It was a gamble.

The boy came to guard us that morning, changing places with the guard who walked us from the field. He squatted at the entrance and again pointed the AK squarely at my chest, eyeing me through the sight as I sat on my mat.

"*Aesh?*" What? I said, staring at him blankly, masking my anger. *You aren't going to shoot me, you are just a child,* I thought to myself. *I should come over there and kick the shit out of you.*

After a minute he lowered the gun and went back out.

"I don't like that kid," I told Amir. "He's going to kill me by accident."

As the sun rose, the enclosure warmed. The single wasp had become three wasps. They silently passed through the small spaces between the palm leaves, entering our somber sanctuary with long legs that dangled lifelessly from their thick abdomens, like Apache helicopters, settling on the ground to scout the remains of our meal with probing antennae, then taking off to circle the enclosure. First one, then two, then three, then two, then one. All day long, in and out. Growing up, I'd been allergic to wasps. Out here, I didn't have that luxury. I sat still as they moved about at will.

Amir attempted to kill one with his hand as it walked stealthily across the floor, but I stopped him.

"If you kill it, it sends a signal to the others and they come." This was something I had learned as a child. I didn't know if it was true, but best to make peace and not to attack those who could easily do you harm, unless absolutely necessary. Though I was uncertain if that idea applied here, in a place like this.

A few hours later, another guard relieved the boy. He sat down in the entrance, leaning on his elbow with the AK resting beside him. Pulling out a small book, he began to read.

"Any news?" Amir asked him.

"No."

Amir tried again: "Do you know what the demand was in the video?"

"I was not there," the guard responded in Arabic without looking up.

"He is lying," I said to Amir.

The guard paused for a moment, then looked at me and said, "You are not married. You have a fiancée." Amir translated his words.

A fiancée? Marie-Hélène! Hearing the word *fiancée* was the first indication I'd had from the outside world. We had been completely cut off from any information, except a few half-truths we could pry out of the guards. It must have been reported somewhere that I was engaged. I tried to contain my smile. But why fiancée and not wife? Marie-Hélène and I had told people we didn't know well in Iraq that we were married. Maybe Marie-Hélène had said fiancée because she was afraid people could discover that we were not actually married. I had a vision of her working hard to free us. What if she was on a plane to Iraq? She might show up at Sadr's office demanding to be taken to see me, and soon all three of us would be stuck in the enclosure together.

Or worse, she wouldn't make it to Nasiriyah. Would I go free only to have to turn around and search for her? I tried to coordinate our stories.

"Well, in America things are different," I said casually. "We are together, sort of a civil marriage." I didn't know how Amir would translate my words; they didn't even make sense to me.

"No," the man replied. "You are a liar." He wrapped his head tightly and continued reading. His words struck hard. Amir stroked his jaw, looking at the ground. The enclosure felt smaller and our options fewer. Amir was right: they would find out the truth anyway.

The guard was replaced by the large guard with the soft voice who brought us food and water. He lay his AK down, squatted at the entrance, and held up a set of silver handcuffs. My heart stalled, only to start again at a frantic pace. He held only one pair, so I assumed he was planning to handcuff Amir and me together, making escape impossible.

"Believe me," Amir pleaded with the guard, "we respect you, we would never escape. The handcuffs are not necessary—the cloth is enough." Whenever they brought me back to the enclosure, I would untie my hands. Sometimes a guard would retie them, but mostly they didn't bother. Occasionally I would tie them again myself when a new guard appeared. Amir kept his hands tied the whole time, and held them up to show the guard. The guard nodded his head as he thought about it, adjusted his dishdasha, and lay the handcuffs down in the dirt.

"Amir," I said earnestly, "please tell him that if they are planning to kill me I would like to know so that I can make peace." This was a genuine sentiment. I wanted to know if I was going to be killed so that I could prepare, could send good thoughts to my family, "Don't worry about me, I love you and want you to continue your life and be happy."

But it was also a calculated effort to get information to help us plan our escape. Any clues about their exact intentions and timing were critical.

"Don't worry, they will not kill you," the guard with the soft voice said. He left, taking the handcuffs with him. He stood outside for a moment, speaking in hushed tones with the other guard, then disappeared.

"Can you hear what they are saying?" I whispered.

Amir strained to listen, then shook his head no.

"What do you think, Amir?"

"I don't know. I know they are liars, but somehow I believe him. What do you think?"

"I think it's fifty-fifty."

I reached into my shirt pocket and pulled out the Rosemans cover where I had written MH, ZEUG, LOVE, and looked over at Amir.

"If something happens to me, Amir, can you make sure Marie-Hélène gets this?"

Amir paused.

"Yes. But believe me, you will give it to her yourself."

I put it back in my pocket.

The other guard settled back down in the entrance with a radio. Time was passing and I was getting anxious. We tried asking him questions.

"Have you heard any news about our situation?" Amir asked.

"No," he said. "It takes time. You are innocent, they will release you."

"What did they say in the video? What was the demand?"

"I wasn't there."

"There were many guards there," I said angrily.

"We have nothing to do with what happens to you in the future or yesterday; we are just guards. Another group comes to make the video. Each has their different role."

"Why did they make the video?"

"They send it out to see what comes back. If the response is from your family, we know you are innocent. If it is from the government, we know you work for the army."

"What has come back?"

"Your family. We know you are a journalist. But your situation has created a schism."

Amir pressed him on this new complication.

"Your situation has divided the group. Half feel one way, half feel another. But you will be released. *Insha Allah.*"

Amir explained to me that there were two brothers who disagreed about what to do with us. One might be the large man with the quiet voice, who seemed genuinely concerned about us; perhaps the other was the Grim Reaper. A schism spelled trouble. It confirmed my prediction: our chances were literally fifty-fifty. Even if the large one with the soft voice wanted us to go free, who was to say that would be the outcome?

"The fighting has stopped in Najaf," the guard added.

"Alhamdulillah." Thank God, I said, trying to show my concern.

Again the news was both heartening and troubling. The lull in fighting might be good for us, but if they thought my video had anything to do with it, then it meant I had value. I felt that the only way I would get out alive was if the press didn't make a big deal of my story and the American government didn't negotiate.

After we finished eating, the guard motioned to the top of the six foot date palm tree, from which hung a bunch of ripe dates.

"Have some," he said.

I stood up, pulled down several, and handed him a few. They were sweet and overly ripe. *"Shokran,"* I said. Thank you. He smiled back. I knew by now that his sympathy had no impact on my fate, but at least I might be able to get information.

"Do you think there will ever be peace in Iraq?" I asked.

"No." He smiled. "We have been fighting for thousands of years. We have been fighting Saddam for the last fifteen years. All we know is war."

"Are you thankful that America got rid of Saddam Hussein?"

The guard thought carefully before answering. "Yes, we are thankful the Americans got rid of Saddam Hussein, but they must leave."

"Are people angry at America for not supporting the Shi'ite uprising after the 1991 Gulf War?" Immediately following the 1991 war, the United States had encouraged Shi'ites to rise up in the south and over-throw Saddam. Behind the scenes, there were clear signals that America would support their efforts, and in March 1991, the Shi'ites rebelled. The United States established a no-fly zone in southern Iraq, but did nothing to support the uprising. Saddam Hussein brutally suppressed the rebel-lion, starting a thirteen-year persecution of the Shi'ite population. The marshes were drained, wells poisoned, and hundreds of thousands of Shi'ites went missing, many executed. It surprised me that I rarely heard people in Nasiriyah talk about this.

"No. It is not to do with America. Our misery is because of Saddam Hussein."

"Do you believe America will leave Iraq?" I asked.

"*Insha Allah,*" he replied. Then he asked me the same question.

"I don't know," I responded. "Half of America does not think America should be in Iraq, and thinks this war is bad for both Iraq and America."

"Ahhh." He nodded his head slowly, looking at me.

"Amir, ask them if they are part of the Mahdi Army?"

"No," the guard responded. Being secretive about political affiliations was a reality in Iraq because of Saddam. It was the expected response; they probably would not admit to being members of the Mahdi Army even if they were.

"But you are followers of Muqtada al-Sadr?"

"Sayed Muqtada stood up to the Americans; that is why we respect him."

"What do you do when you are not guarding us? Are you fighting?"

"No. When we are not guarding you, we work as civil servants in town."

Amir laughed. "They have desk jobs. They are clerks."

"Some are in school, but it is summer, school is out," the guard added. Then, looking over at me approvingly, he asked, "Where did you get your hair cut?"

The conversation wasn't going anywhere; I needed useful information to plan our escape. "Amir," I said quietly, "let's see if we can figure out where we are."

Before Saddam drained the marshes in southern Iraq, the biblical Garden of Eden, they covered almost twenty thousand square kilometers, stretching from Nasiriyah southeast to Basra and northeast to Amarah, running into the border with Iran. Now, there was less than one thousand square kilometers of marshland left, the rest a dry, salty wasteland. The area, traditionally home to the Marsh Arabs, had become a refuge for Shi'ite rebels fighting Saddam. Amir thought we were being held somewhere near Suq ash Shuyukh, a small town and Mahdi stronghold in the marshes just south of Nasiriyah. Southeast of Nasiriyah, where the Euphrates and Tigris meet, lies the town of Al Qurnah. If we could roughly figure out where we were, we would know how to make it back to Nasiriyah. I tried to think of a way to tease out the information.

"Do you play soccer?" I asked, trying to strike up a more casual conversation.

"Yes."

"I like soccer," I said.

"Zidane good," he said in English, looking directly at me, putting his thumb in the air, and smiling from behind his keffiyeh. Zinedine Zidane, the most famous soccer player in France. originally from Algeria, was a hero to most young boys in the Arab world.

"*Nam, Zidane zane kathir,*" I said. Yes, Zidane is very good. I smiled and put my thumb up, too.

"Where do you play?" I continued to probe. "Around here?" Amir had no interest in a casual conversation about sports. I reminded him that the point was not to discuss the merits of Zidane but to find out where we were so we could escape. He repeated my question in Arabic.

"No, this area is too rough," the guard replied.

"Is there a field you play on?"

"Yes, there is a field."

"Is it far?"

"Three kilometers," he said, yawning. A field three kilometers away—not much use.

"Near the river?" I asked, taking a guess at the geography.

"Yes, across the river." A river. The Euphrates? Good, we were getting somewhere.

"You have a soccer ball?" Amir asked.

"Yes."

"Can you buy soccer balls around here, or do you have to go into Nasiriyah?"

"We go into town."

"You drive?"

"No. I ride my bicycle."

"I saw a bicycle once with mirrors all over it. Do you have mirrors?"

"Yes, a few."

"How long does it take you to ride to town?"

"Fifteen minutes." Fifteen minutes, about ten kilometers. There was a town ten kilometers away and a river between.

It was his turn.

"Is it true you can have sex with any woman you meet on the street in your country?" he asked me.

"No," I laughed. Amir was annoyed by his question.

"Ahh." The guard sounded disappointed.

"I am married," I added, then quickly corrected myself: "I have a fiancée."

"Baby?" he continued in English.

"*Nam, wahid.*" Yes, one.

"Good," he said, again in English. "Boy?"

"*Bint.*" Girl, I replied, referring to Zeugma.

"Ahhhh," he said, disappointed again.

"Are you married?" I asked.

"No. Not yet."

"Do you know who you are going to marry?"

"Yes. I have already picked a wife."

"Is she beautiful?" I thought this might provoke him in some way.

"Yes, of course."

"From another tribe?"

"No. From my tribe."

"Why not another tribe?"

"It's better if she is from your tribe. You know who she is, you know her family."

"How big is your tribe?"

"About seventy families."

"Do you all live together?"

"No, but in this area."

"Do you get along with the other tribes? Your neighbors?"

"No, they think we are thieves." That was the clue I was looking for. That would explain why they'd made us get on the ground when they'd heard a car passing the night we were brought to the enclosure. If we could make it off their land, their neighbors might have sympathy for us. But their tribe was spread out all around. The town was ten kilometers down the road. Where, exactly?

"Do you ever travel to Qurnah?" Amir asked.

"No, Amarah is closer," he said slowly. Amir didn't believe we were near Amarah, and gave me a look that said, "He is on to us, he is lying." The guard stopped answering our questions. Soon, another guard replaced him, sitting outside the enclosure.

"So, if we can make it through the field to the road, and we walk to town, then what?" I asked Amir in a low voice. He leaned his head toward me.

"We hire a car."

"Okay." I thought carefully, picturing the walk at the edge of the road. By the time the guards brought tea and *khubz*, they would know we were gone. That would give us a two-hour headstart at most. I pictured a carload of angry guards with AKs driving down the road searching for us. It would be critical to spot them before they saw us. I thought about Amir's glasses, which had also disappeared in the market. They were thick, and he normally wore them all the time.

"You're farsighted, right?" I asked, double-checking.

"Yes."

"That means you can see things at a distance."

"No."

"What? You cannot see far away without your glasses?"

"No. I am nearsighted." He had misunderstood my question. We were both blind.

The chances that two groping, dirty, shoeless men with no money wandering the marshes would flag down a ride to Nasiriyah before a band of AK-toting kidnappers caught up with us was much less than fifty-fifty.

But the following morning would be our last opportunity to escape. If there was a death threat, the deadline was usually forty-eight hours. I looked over at Freedom's Gate. Sitting upright in the middle where I had cleared the brush, on its haunches with its paws straight in front, tail wagging, looking directly at me, was Zeugma. Well, not Zeugma, but a black dog with wavy fur that looked like Zeugma.

"Amir, it's Zeugma," I said, checking that he too could see the dog, and I wasn't going crazy. "Yes, there is a dog," he replied, unmoved. Most dogs in Iraq were brown and scruffy; a black dog with wavy fur was unusual. *It must be some kind of a message*, I thought, *but what exactly?*

Despite my joy at seeing the dog, I became worried that her presence in Freedom's Gate would alert the guards to our escape plan.

"Hi," I said quietly to the dog. "Now go!" I waved my hand.

She wagged her tail.

"Go! Shoo," I said. She wagged her tail again. I told Amir to ask the guard if I could urinate, and went out, taking the red plastic jug of water. Outside the enclosure, as the guard watched, I whistled the two-tone whistle I used with Zeugma. I heard a rustling; then the dog came bounding over, away from Freedom's Gate. I bent down and looked into her eyes. "I love you," I whispered in her ear and gave her a kiss on the head. Then I said, "Please go."

The dog lay down next to the guard for a while, outside our enclosure, then disappeared.

I lay back on my mat, tormented by that vision. Was it a message from home? Was this dog, this vision, warning me that I was about to be killed and that I should escape through Freedom's Gate as quickly as possible? Could I return to my life and to Marie-Hélène and Zeugma through that passageway? Did it mean, instead, that Freedom's Gate was a terrible idea and escape would end badly? Or did it mean that I was simply going mad after six days in captivity?

Escaping was a desperate idea. My gut told me that the vision meant we should *not* attempt escape. Marie-Hélène was smart and would find a way. But waiting meant putting all our faith in others, and I was not willing to do that, and not ready to give up on Freedom's Gate. Convinced that Marie-Hélène and Zeugma were trying to communicate with me but unable to decipher the message, I grew discouraged.

As the day slowly transformed into evening, my desperation increased. At dusk, two guards blindfolded us and led us to the field to eat. Sitting in the dark, we again asked one of them about our future.

"Do you think we will be released?" Amir began.

"*Insha Allah,*" a guard replied. "But when you are released they may put conditions on it," he added.

"What sort of conditions?" Amir pressed him.

"They may say you cannot return to Iraq."

My heart bounded at hearing him allude to possible terms of my release. Had the demand been met, I wondered, or was this just idle talk? His words became the stepping-stone for my next concern: my potential banishment from Iraq. Amir conveyed my disappointment. The absurdity of being banned from Iraq by an outlaw group of kidnappers didn't occur to me. In Nasiriyah, power was evenly divided between the Mahdi Army and the government. During a recent Mahdi uprising, the Mahdi Army agreed to leave Nasiriyah only if the city council publicly denounced the interim Iraqi government attacks on the Mahdi Army, which they did in a page-long statement handed out in Habubi Square. If militants told you to stay away, you were wise to stay away.

"Don't worry, they will send someone to replace you," the guard said indifferently.

After we ate I told Amir to ask again about what the demand was in the video and if there had been any threat.

"They said the U.S. must stop fighting in Najaf and pull out in forty-eight hours," one of the guards replied.

"Or what?" I asked.

"They will kill you." I stared, not breathing. "It's just a threat," he added.

When I heard the unmeetable demand my hope was destroyed. Sickened, I thought about the simple, familiar pattern: video threat, then execution.

"Why did they say that?" I asked the guard, struggling to maintain my composure. "Why couldn't they ask for something more reasonable? The U.S. won't pull out of Najaf."

"I know," he replied without emotion. "I told them they should ask for something more reasonable."

"But they are going to have to kill me now or it will look like a hollow threat," I continued. He didn't answer.

His words had forced my decision. I couldn't take the chance that it was not a hollow threat, and I had been given the warning. I had to act. Turning to Amir, I said in a hushed voice, "We are leaving tomorrow morning through Freedom's Gate."

Amir nodded in agreement, accepting this path as our only solution.

"Bingo," I said for emphasis.

In the darkness we were led through the thorns back to sleep in the field. I lay down, carefully planning our escape in my mind. We would wait a half hour, until the guard dozed off, quietly remove the date palm fronds in front of Freedom's Gate, slip through—me first, then Amir—on our stomachs, walk silently down the field toward the road, then turn left on the road toward freedom. Somehow we would reappear at the Nasiriyah Museum triumphantly having escaped from six days in captivity.

I thought again about Marie-Hélène and my family, trying to imagine their reactions to the news, and everything that must have happened since the video, but I couldn't. I tried picturing them in my mind: faces, hair, eyes, hands. It was difficult, but the thought comforted me. All the thoughts and memories I recalled of my family and Marie-Hélène were good ones, as if there had never been any bad ones. Only the good ones remained.

The voice of the Grim Reaper jolted me awake. Something in his tone was more disturbing than usual. It wasn't the severe questioning and dour condemnation I had come to expect. It was upbeat, almost cheerful. Something wasn't right.

"Micah," Amir said excitedly at the end of their long conversation.

"Yes?" I replied without moving, my back to Amir.

"This man assures me we will be released soon. He says, 'Absolutely I give you my word you will be free.' He said that at first he did not believe the story of the ambulance, but now he knows we are telling the truth." Amir was excited, believing the words of the Grim Reaper, to me just another lie to keep us in check. The Grim Reaper was certainly clever enough to know that we were thinking of escaping, and he was just anticipating our next move.

"Okay, let's discuss it in the morning," I said grudgingly. We couldn't talk in front of the guards, and I was worried. We had made a decision, and with one false promise, everything was now in jeopardy. Was Amir afraid? Was concern for his family clouding his judgment or was he doing what he thought was in our best interest? I wasn't sure; perhaps it was a little of each. I pulled the wool blanket up around my ears—it didn't even offer protection against the mosquitoes—and lay on my back, unable to sleep.

Chantal and I woke up early, groggy after four hours of sleep. As my thoughts cleared, my main concern was hearing news from Amir's family and Osama, who would have arrived in Nasiriyah by now. He had a cell phone that worked in the south, and called Mitch every few hours. Mitch then relayed the information to Joel, who called Eva, who told us.

There was news. Suzanne and Eva arrived early, followed by Loren, and I relayed that Micah and Amir were alive and healthy and that the Sadr office was working on getting them released. James and his translator, who risked traveling after curfew, called every night by satellite phone from the rooftop of James's hotel in Erbil. They had finally been able to reach Sheik Aws. As James put it, because of the siege in Najaf, Aws was concerned with other matters besides freeing Western journalists. The tricky part was getting him to devote some of his energy on Micah's behalf at a time when it was politically difficult for him to be publicly seen as doing so. James wrote up a list of bullet points explaining why it would be to Aws's political advantage to play a role in freeing Micah, and had his Assyrian Christian translator sweet-talk them into his ear, using all of the most religious Arabic he could muster. Because his translator had learned his Arabic while serving twelve years in the Iraqi army, James was always afraid he would slide off the script into a stream of orders and expletives.

Sheik Aws thought the situation would be resolved soon. The good news was a wave that lifted us all up and carried us forward.

"And that's not all," I added. "Sheik Aws asked James, joking, 'If I arrange for your friend's release, can I marry your sister?' "

His humor belied the difficulties he faced. Sheik Aws sounded tired and sad on the phone, James wrote, from all the fighting with the Italians the previous week. Taking hostages was not the style of the Sadr inner circle, he continued, but was well within the range of some in the Mahdi Army, as we had seen with the James Brandon experience. Sheik Aws had given James his Thuraya satellite-phone number, which signaled to me a real desire to help.

We added the number to our sheik chart, which hung on the wall, slowly filling with additional names of sheiks, journalists who could reach them, and phone numbers. We added the positions and tribes of the different sheiks, and drew arrows between them to show their relationships.

Working constantly in New Haven, Alan and Sally had heard back from an international relief agency that told them they could possibly contact different leaders of criminal gangs in Nasiriyah, a valuable connection if the Mahdi Army was ruled out.

On the time-line chart, we still had only a few facts and many overlapping possibilities. Since we knew from Mitch that Micah had been in Baghdad on Thursday evening, this meant that Micah must have left on Friday morning for Nasiriyah, which meant he had not stayed at the Al-Janoub Hotel Thursday night. The time line was clearer, but it provided no more clues as to who might be holding him.

Tom Carpenter, a photographer friend of Micah's, arrived with his silver briefcase and a bag of technology. He sat at the edge of the couch, plugging in wires, trying to get the printer to print. Another friend arrived with plates of sushi and several long pages of notes. She had spoken to a retired army colonel and another government official she knew, asking them to call their contacts and give us advice. She read her notes to us: "Lay low. Keep things quiet, and really push any contacts you might have on the ground." She never said what else they had told her—that both men held out little hope for Micah. They believed that Micah would become a casualty of the war.

Since none of us spoke Arabic, Nabila, Suzanne's Iraqi friend, had taken the bus down from Boston to help us communicate with Amir's family. She walked in around noon, leaning on her cane. Many brothers, husbands, and sons of her friends had disappeared during Saddam's regime. Her eyes, framed by large glasses, shone full of concern.

We must speak to Amir's family right away, we told her, having just received another email.

> Dear
> The last news is that Mich and Amir are alive,
> please understand that I can't tell you more
> becouse that a dangerous of there life.

"Salaam alaikum," she began her conversation with Amir's sister, introducing herself and stressing our concern for Amir. She thrust the phone at me.

"You should say hello, say your name. They need to know it is you who is calling, so they can trust us." Though we couldn't communicate more than a few hellos, Amir's sister's voice was warm and loving on the phone. Nabila began a long conversation with her, frustrating for us who did not understand Arabic. Nabila talked passionately and listened intently, writing notes quickly in Arabic that grew in looping calligraphy on the page, overtaking the various names and numbers we had written down.

"What, what did she say?" we asked anxiously after she hung up.

"They are very worried about Micah and Amir," she said, tears spilling down her face.

Fearful, hearts beating, we pressed her for more. "What else, what else?"

"The family says there is no one there with any authority to help. The government has no authority. They told me, quoting an old Iraqi proverb, 'They cannot tie or untie a knot.' Find a solution, they begged you, because they are totally handicapped."

"Do they know who has them?"

"The family says that they were taken by a criminal gang, and might be selling him or trading him."

Oh no, no, please no. After the earlier good news from Sheik Aws, I couldn't take another reversal, but I knew I had to listen. My ears were buzzing, ringing, deaf, after I heard that Micah could have been taken by a criminal gang. A market in hostages would mean he could easily end up in the hands of people like Zarqawi.

"But rumor is, from the boys on the street who saw it, that they have been sold or traded to Sadr," Nabila continued. "If we know that, then we can reach whoever is in control of Micah and Amir. There is a way to reach them—through Sadr. This is better, girls, better. If it were the criminal element, we could never reach them. And what do they want? They want money. They will sell him. Or if it is the smuggling market—of arms and antiquities—it will be even more complex because they do not want to be exposed and have their toes stepped on."

"What did Amir's family think about talking to the media?"

"Amir's sister told me that, in the first, when they took him, that these people are away from civilization, that they don't even know what an international channel is, or TV news, that they are just out in the wilderness. She did not think they were going to watch TV or see anything like that.

"A coin has been flipped," Nabila said, referring to Micah's possible transfer from a criminal gang to a Sadr group. "We have to reach out on a humane level, on a spiritual level, that Sadr cannot ignore."

If Micah had somehow ended up with a Sadr militia, then we should continue the path that we were on, reaching out to Sadr and Sadr's clerics. Sadr had called for the release of James Brandon, and he had been released. The taking and killing of hostages is un-Islamic, Sadr had said.

Nabila called Amir's family again. She asked, listened, talked. She wiped her eyes and blew her nose. We held her knee and stroked her back, trying to comfort her through the conversation. When she hung up, we were all as drained as Nabila from the emotion of what we were learning.

"They do not think that Micah has been taken to Najaf. The roads would be too dangerous, and they think that Micah and Amir are still in Nasiriyah. For this reason, they said, you must go to Sheik Aws and appeal through him. He will have the power and the authority to help. That is what they say."

This was our plan; James and many others were working on that. Their words reinforced our belief that we were on the right path.

"It is the tradition in Iraq," Nabila continued, "that if you go to a friend and ask for something, he is morally obliged to do all that he can, and to reach out to his friends, and his friends' friends, to help you. That is why I have reached out to my friends, and why we should reach out to Aws and to Sadr. If you ask for help, they must help you."

We decided to work on a statement for Sheik Aws and for Sadr that we could send to them, either through James or Osama. Not a media statement, but a private plea to add emotional weight to their negotiations.

"It should come from the women of the family," Nabila advised. "They will respond to your plea for mercy. A male member of the family would be an affront and a challenge to their masculinity. They will listen to you and can show how merciful they are."

"And we must work now, it is important," Nabila continued. "Seven is an important number in Islam." She counted on her fingers from Friday, August 13. "Seven days will be Friday. The kidnappers will have to do or say something by then."

.   .   .

Suzanne, Eva, and I worked on a statement, incorporating Nabila's advice and the guidance of the FBI hostage team as Chantal and Loren answered the ringing phones and apartment buzzer.

> *Micah and Amir are innocent men, are journalists, and we respectfully ask that you please show them mercy and allow them to return home to their families where their mothers, sisters and family love them and wait for them.*
>
> *We are appealing to you who are holding Micah and Amir that you please release them. As you have seen, Micah and Amir are both gentle and kind people and believe as you do in compassion and mercy. Micah respects and loves Iraq and Iraqi culture and he is truly your friend. Please, we beg and trust that you will have mercy on Micah and Amir and please let them go and return them to us.*
>
> *Micah, we love you and are anxiously awaiting your return.*
>
> *Amir, your sister and your family love you and are waiting to see you home soon.*

Nabila wiped her tear-stained face and called Amir's family again.

"You must call Al Jazeera," she said urgently, her chair pushed backward as she held the phone away from her mouth. "Amir's brother says it is time to go to the media. They have heard some news, and you must act."

Her words shocked us, provoking a chorus of questions. "What was the news? How should we act?" "Why, why, what did he say?"

"You must go to the media now, they say, don't delay."

Someone in Amir's family had told Nabila that things had changed; Micah and Amir's condition was now much more dangerous and we should take a drastic step. We had discussed a public plea with them, and we had all agreed that we would take it only as a last step. Though Amir's sister had dismissed TV because she did not think the kidnappers would see it, TV was our most powerful public platform. I was certain that TV news would reach the kidnappers, particularly Al Jazeera.

"Are you sure?" I asked Nabila.

"That is what this man is telling me," Nabila responded.

Not knowing how or why things were now so desperate, we became desperate, our plans and our reasoning suspended. We reacted, scrambling, looking for our statements and Al Jazeera's phone number. Should I call Mitch or Joel to check? Time seemed to be the most urgent factor, and I stopped weighing my options, succumbing to the advice from Nasiriyah.

I called Al Jazeera's New York office.

"This is the family of Micah Garen, and we'd like to make a statement on his behalf."

Not interested, a producer said.

"But it is important to air a statement now. We think it could save his life!" I told her, barely able to control my voice.

She would call her superiors and get back to me.

We spent the next several minutes rewriting our statements in large, clear letters and changing into appropriate clothing; the apartment now hot and suffocating.

The Al Jazeera producer said that she would send over a cameraman, but they only had one and he would be working overtime.

"Al Jazeera's on their way," I told everyone, more concerned than relieved. We practiced reading our statements to one another, not certain who would end up on television.

"I want to make sure this is the right thing to do; I'm not sure about this," Eva told Nabila. "Can you call Amir's family again, and make sure?"

We got through, and after several frantic exchanges in Arabic, Nabila began to wave her hands in the air. "Stop! Stop!" she shouted, telling us to find a cell phone immediately. "You must call Al Jazeera back. We cannot go to the media!"

The chaos expanded and filled the small, hot room, knocking against bodies. "Why not?" we yelled back.

"The older brother has just gotten home. I was talking to the younger brother before. The older brother has reached some people, and he says no media at all. You must not go to the media, it will be dangerous."

I frantically dialed Al Jazeera on the cell phone as Nabila continued to talk to the older brother.

"We have just gotten new information," I told the producer. "We are very sorry, but it would endanger Micah to make a statement at this time. We are going to have to wait."

Annoyed, her cameraman already on his way, she hung up. We had probably lost an opportunity, but we had to trust the new information from Nasiriyah, though I couldn't understand it. Nabila hadn't learned from the family why Micah and Amir were in more danger, but she thought that one brother stayed at home, perhaps protecting his family, while another went outside to get news from the boys in the street, and other intermediaries.

As quickly as we had been pressured to go to the media, we had been advised against it. I covered my face with my hands, horrified at how close we had come to making a wrong move. We had almost lost control; it could not happen again.

Maybe we should film our own statement, I thought. We could send it to TV stations for broadcast if necessary. It would be our backup, and remove some of the pressure allowing us to focus on our contacts in Iraq.

Justin, a friend and filmmaker, arrived immediately, slipping past the line of large satellite trucks parked outside the building with his small video camera, which he quickly set up in our friend Leslie's apartment upstairs.

The phone rang and Chantal jumped to grab it.

"Hello again." It was the French consular officer. "Please, just *oui ou non*, that is all I need to know: Is Micah French?"

"You know, this is not a good time at all," she told him.

He sighed. "Please, call me very soon."

Nabila suggested a walk; we were not in the best frame of mind to film a statement. After changing back into our loose, comfortable work clothes, we headed out for a quick break before making our self-produced video statement.

Nabila, Suzanne, Eva, and I looked around for reporters before stepping outside. The steady stream of reporters was for the moment a trickle. We walked around the block, talking quietly. The Palestinian American man who ran the pet store downstairs from our apartment greeted me sadly.

"I can't believe this happened to such a good guy. I hope he'll come home."

As we walked slowly, turning down leafy, sunny blocks, talking of other things, the tense muscle that my mind had become began to relax and my breathing deepened, refreshed by a steady breeze blowing in from the Hudson River. We stopped at a small garden, the plants muffling the noise of cars and strangers on the street. Outside for the first time in more than two days, I felt hopeful. We were all working hard, and working together.

We turned the corner onto Hudson Street, then back to Christopher, when Eva's cell phone rang. It was Chantal.

"Eva, you've got to come back. Now."

Amir's brother must have called back, I thought to myself. Eva and I quickened our pace back to the apartment.

I was second up the stairs, looking up at my sister, who was looking down at me, both hands resting on the railing. Eva moved past her into the apartment. Chantal stood in the doorway. I tried to get by her, but she would not let me. She held me firmly.

Pushing past her, I entered the hallway into the apartment and was surrounded by noise—disorienting, strangled, sharp, loud. The noise melded with the air. I looked into the kitchen as I walked by. The sound was clearly coming from there. Eva was lying on the kitchen floor next to the dog bowl screaming.

Standing now in the middle of the room, I looked toward the big computer screen, but Loren blocked my view, and Tom rose to join him. No one spoke.

"What's going on?" I asked.

Chantal held my arms. "There's a video."

Micah had reappeared. He was one-dimensional, on a screen. For the past days, we had searched, craved, asked for information. Here it was.

Forcing myself forward, I tried to get by Loren and Tom. "I have to see it." They moved closer together. "No, you can't," Tom said firmly.

"I have to see it! Let me see it!" I pushed my way toward the computer and leaned in to the screen.

I began to scream. Suzanne came in, and I wanted to be strong for her. She was followed by Nabila.

There was a video.

My thoughts separated from my body, and I struggled to breathe. Chantal moved closer to hold down my arms, which had begun to move on their own. I was drowning, every breath a struggle, raspy and pained, as I listened to them.

Micah was in a video.

The ziggurat of Ur, now in the heart of Tallil Air Base, west of Nasiriyah. Ur is one of the most famous and culturally rich archaeological sites in Iraq, and the purported birthplace of Abraham. *(Micah Garen)*

Micah films an Italian Carabinieri patrol at a looted site in the Dhi Qar province. Micah often accompanied such patrols; on the day of his kidnapping, he was scheduled to go with an Iraqi civil guard patrol to film their first day protecting Umma, one of Iraq's most important archaeological sites. *(Abdul-Amir Hamdani)*

U.S. Marines detain looters found at the archaeological site Isin, an important Sumerian site in Qadissiya province. Up to several hundred looters would work through the night digging for statues, jewelry, and cuneiform tablets, destroying the site. *(Micah Garen)*

Lance Corporal Troy Merrell, a U.S. Marine from Pennsylvania, holds an inscribed Sumerian brick he recovered from the looted site at Girsu, in southern Iraq, and returned to the Nasiriyah Museum. *(Micah Garen)*

(Right) Marie-Hélène films from an Italian helicopter during a survey of looted sites in the Dhi Qar province. *(Micah Garen)*

(Below) Looters running from a helicopter at Isin. Simply having helicopters fly over the sites would deter looters from plundering them for days, although helicopters rarely flew on such missions. *(John Russell)*

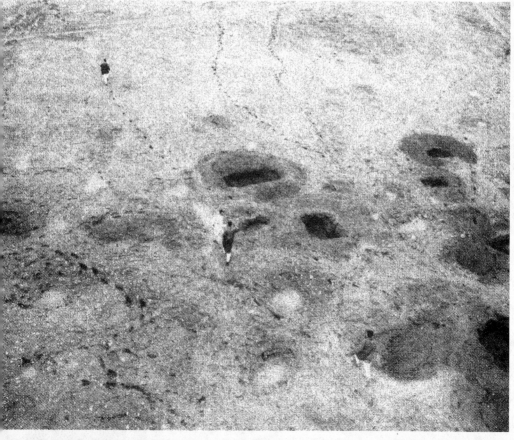

The Iraqi police recovered many artifacts stolen from the archaeological sites, including this cuneiform tablet, during a raid in Baghdad. *(Marie-Hélène Carleton)*

Micah films Mr. Hamdani and the Iraqi police on a patrol to an archaeological site. Mr. Hamdani struggled to organize patrols with either the Coalition forces or the Iraqi security forces to protect the sites and prevent looters from completely destroying them. *(Kais Berzan)*

Marie-Hélène and Amir
film inside the burned
Nasiriyah Museum.
(Micah Garen)

The Nasiriyah Museum, looted and burned by militants in May 2004.
(Micah Garen and Marie-Hélène Carleton)

Marie-Hélène, dressed in traditional Iraqi garb, and Micah, in an Iraqi shirt, had their photos taken at an Iraqi portrait photographer's studio in Baghdad.

Amir Doshi's office in Nasiriyah, the Sinbad Translation Bureau, is piled high with books and papered with pictures of Sartre, Don Quixote, and works by local artists. *(Marie-Hélène Carleton)*

Marie-Hélène dresses in a traditional *hijab* during a patrol to an archaeological site. *(Micah Garen)*

Amir holds Micah's hand in a traditional Iraqi show of friendship in July 2004, a few weeks before the kidnapping. *(Marie-Hélène Carleton)*

Iraqi Shi'ite supporters of cleric Muqtada al-Sadr after Friday prayers in Basra on August 6, 2004, protest U.S. attacks on Sadr's militia (known as the Mahdi Army) only days before Micah and Amir were captured. *(Atef Hassan / Reuters / Corbis)*

Micah photographed the remains of an ambulance in Nasiriyah reportedly fired upon by the Italian Coalition forces during fighting with the Mahdi Army. A woman in labor, her baby, and three of her family members were killed. *(Micah Garen)*

Sabah Khazal Kareem, the driver of the ambulance destroyed by Italian forces, holds a thank-you letter from Pfc. Jessica Lynch, whom he had driven to safety. *(Micah Garen)*

An Iraqi man wears a keffiyeh and dishdasha in the marshes of southern Iraq with a date palm tree in the background. Under the rule of Saddam Hussein, most of the Iraqi marshes were drained of water and marsh Arabs were forced to leave their homes. *(Damir Sagolj/Reuters/Corbis)*

Micah scratched a message to Marie-Hélène and Zeugma on this cigarette case, just in case. *(Micah Garen)*

(Right) This is the blindfold Micah wore throughout his kidnapping. *(Micah Garen)*

(Far right) Micah shaped a palm frond spike from the enclosure where he and Amir were held into a weapon. *(Micah Garen)*

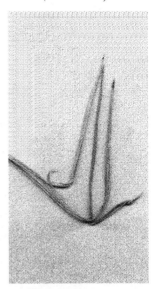

A still from the video made by the Martyrs Brigade on August 17 and aired on Al Jazeera on August 18 shows the captors threatening to kill Micah in forty-eight hours if U.S. forces didn't pull out of Najaf.

The FBI transferred Marie-Hélène and Micah's close family to a secure location hotel room, where Zeugma stayed by the makeshift shrine. (Leslie Bakke)

The media camped out in front of Micah and Marie-Hélène's apartment on Christopher Street. *(Robert Stolarik)*

Chantal, Marie-Hélène's sister, takes a break from constant phone calls in the hotel room. *(Leslie Bakke)*

(From left) Ayatollah Ali al-Sistani; the shrine of Imam Ali in Najaf; Muqtada al-Sadr. *(Getty Images)*

Sheik Aws al-Khafaji. *(James Longley)*

Marie-Hélène and Eva, Micah's sister, were on the phone constantly as they worked for Micah's release. *(Leslie Bakke)*

A video still shows Micah moments after his release at the Sadr office in Nasiriyah on August 22, 2004, the same spot where he and Amir had first been brought after they were kidnapped in the market. *(APTN)*

Marie-Hélène and Chantal celebrate Micah's release while Aparna Mohan still makes calls in the background. *(Eva Garen)*

Jonathan, Micah's brother, talks to Micah for the first time since his release as Eva listens. *(Marie-Hélène Carleton)*

Family and friends celebrate Micah's release: *(from left)* Jonathan, Eva, Suzanne (Micah's mother), Chantal, Marie-Hélène, Loren Nunley, Nieves holding Tomas, Aparna Mohan with Zeugma. *(Amanda Harmon)*

Micah and his mom hug for the first time upon his return home. *(Marie-Hélène Carleton)*

Micah and Eva reunited. *(Marie-Hélène Carleton)*

The new Iraqi archaeological civil guards pose for a photo at Umma, two weeks after Micah's release. *(Amir Doshi)*

Marie-Hélène and Micah enjoy Micah's freedom and each other, after getting officially engaged in fall 2004. *(Micah Garen and Marie-Hélène Carleton)*

Suzanne, standing in the hall, was driven backward by the screams toward the bed. She lay down and covered her face with her hands.

I could no longer stand. My knees, my legs were soft and could no longer support me. I heard strangled sounds. They were getting louder. My throat began to hurt. I was screaming, an unearthly scream that everyone in the room would later describe as the worst sound they had ever heard.

"Is he wearing an orange jumpsuit?"

No one answered. I shouted again.

"Is he wearing an orange jumpsuit?"

I looked at Chantal instead of the computer screen. Micah must have been sold to Zarqawi. Our greatest fear, what Amir's family had feared: the criminal gang had passed him on. I filled the space where her answer should have been with sounds that ripped my throat, burning objects fighting to escape my mouth.

"Is he?" I shrieked and choked and clawed her arms.

Chantal spoke quietly, trying to hold me. "No, no, he's not."

She turned me away from the screen, determined that I not look at it.

I grabbed Chantal's hands and looked into her face. Clutching her shirt as I slid to the floor, I begged her, "Please help me. Please, please help me." I gulped air, letting go of her shirt, and grabbed my hair with both hands, pulling. No physical pain could diminish the pain of the video.

Chantal would do anything to help me, yet she could do nothing. The screaming drove Justin out of the room and into the bathroom, the only place in the apartment where he could separate himself from it. He closed the door and sat on the floor.

My body was moving involuntarily, in different directions at once. Loren tried to hold me up. Chantal tried to move me to the couch. I was falling to the floor, conscious of nothing but the video.

I knew what a video meant. Micah and I had seen them together in Baghdad, in May, then June. We had stared at the TV screen and begged, silently, for the lives of Nick Berg, of Kim Sun-il, but they had been beheaded; no amount of pleading could save them.

Tom got me to the couch, grabbing my torso and pining my arms down, afraid that I was going to have a seizure. Chantal sat on me, to keep my body still. I freed myself from them. I could not think.

"Is it him?" Eva was screaming at Loren. "Is it him?"

"I think so." He held her hand, and spoke as calmly as he could.

"Look at the screen! Are you one hundred percent sure?"

"I'll look," he said. No one wanted to go near the screen again. We were in the other corner of the small room.

"I'm pretty sure it's him," Loren ventured, staring deep into the picture. "I'm sixty-five percent sure."

Suzanne, lying down, the bright light on the nightstand bearing down on her face, answered her cell phone, "There is a video. They are going to kill him."

I tried to gather myself, but hearing a mother say this about her son made me collapse again, and I crawled on the floor, not knowing where to turn.

Eva, the first to grab a phone, called Bob Callahan at the U.S. embassy in Baghdad, waking him in the middle of the night. She yelled, "Are you in bed? Do you know what is going on? Get out of bed! Get out of bed!" Then, screaming and crying as she shook the phone: "Please, promise me you will save him!"

As she scrambled for a phone, Chantal was shouting at everyone: "Call someone!" We had six cell phones and one land phone. Eva was talking on two phones as Nabila grabbed a third. Chantal began dialing another.

Chantal yelled at Justin, who was watching us, unmoving, having emerged from the refuge of the bathroom. "Call someone!"

"Who?"

She forced a phone into his hand. He stood still, holding it.

"Anyone!"

Chantal grabbed the phone back from Justin. It was covered with sweat.

I moved back to the couch, then back across the floor. I pulled myself up on my knees. I was trying to think. I had to do something.

I lifted my eyes, my hands upward.

"Please God, save him. . . . God! . . . Please, please."

Anything. I will do anything. From now until eternity. Just save him.

I began to chant, "Nam myo ho renge kyo, nam myo ho renge kyo." Buddhism, Christianity. Anyone. I dragged Chantal and her phone and Loren to kneel beside me. Chant. Imagine him alive. Pray for his life.

Get up and do something. Get up and call. I got up, weaving, and began dialing a number in Baghdad. Dear God, save Micah.

Suzanne, lying alone on the bed, turned onto her right side, away from the noise in the room. "Tom!" I yelled. "Go to her. Hold her!" She could not be alone. Someone had to connect her to life. She had to feel warmth, not the video. Tom got back on the bed and began stroking her head.

Eva was on the phone to Hillary Clinton's office. No one picked up. She cried into a machine. "I'm his sister. There's a video. They're going to kill Micah. Please help us."

Chantal called the FBI. The first number, the second number, a third. All went to voicemail. They returned her call in several seconds.

"We'll be there in five minutes," someone said.

Infuriated by our limitations, her voice filled the room: "Five minutes is not fast enough! Get here now!" All we had were phones. We had to use them to help us move beyond this moment.

What could I give God? Could this be an exchange? A life for a promise? I had to cleanse any wrongdoing, to be in such a bargaining position.

"Forgive me, I am sorry. Micah is sorry. For anything, for everything."

Chantal called Noble. "Do something. Do something," she shouted at him, handing the phone to me. I stared at the handset. I was talking to God.

"Tell him we need ten million dollars!" I yelled. Anything.

"We need ten million dollars," Chantal repeated flatly into the phone.

She hung up. "He said yes." Noble didn't have ten million dollars, and his wife was due to give birth in two days, the day Micah would be killed.

Eva spoke to Bob Callahan again. "You don't know who the group is? Find out who it is!" Then, to Joel at CPJ: "They're going to kill him!" she screamed.

"Oh my God," he responded. "Calm, calm calm," he tried to reassure her. "Let me get Mitch on the phone."

Taking over from Tom, who moved over to comfort me, Eva sat on the bed, trying to protect Suzanne, trying to calm her with words neither thought were true. "Don't worry, he'll be okay. It's not al-Qaeda." Suzanne lay silently on the bed, ordering her body not to give up. "Do not have a heart attack, do not have a heart attack," she kept repeating to herself.

Amanda reappeared from her walk with Zeugma. "What's going on?" Bodies moved up, down, arms flying, voices screaming. She pulled Zeugma closer.

"What can I do?" Amanda asked me.

"Get down on your knees and pray," I told her.

. . .

In Baghdad, Mitch was just learning of the video, which had first come out on Al Jazeera. "We've lost him," Mitch told a contact at *The New York Times*, believing the video was the sign of an extremist group that couldn't be negotiated with.

. . .

Eva sat in the hallway holding Zeugma. "Micah, Micah. Listen to me. You will be okay. We are here," she said into Zeugma's fur. Zeugma sat still, not moving. "Don't let it be painful. Don't let it hurt. If he has to die, please let him be shot, please don't let him be beheaded."

Agent Tom entered the room, stepping over Eva and Zeugma, forehead to forehead. I jumped up from my kneeling position, ran to him, grabbed the lapels of his suit, and hung from them, screaming into his chest. "Save him! Save him! Promise me you will save him."

He held on to my elbows, not sure whether to hold me up or pull me off. He looked past me into the room. My face was wet and I struck it against his chest. *"Please."*

Other FBI agents made their way in, stepping over Amanda, who was kneeling on the floor, trying to avoid my anguish. Some pushed far enough in to reach the computer screen; others were still blocked in the hallway in a long, cramped line.

Agent Kim answered her phone. "Believe me," she told the caller, "you don't want to be here."

Aparna rushed up the stairs, forcing her way past the large group of FBI agents in the outside hallway, and pushed open the door to the apartment. Someone inside pushed it shut on her. She tried again and got in. At first she couldn't find me among the movement and the noise. When I heard her voice behind me, I pulled her down next to me. Aparna moved closer, and held me tightly.

Agents walked up to the computer screen, looking closely at the still video image of Micah kneeling in front of his captors. They wanted to know when, and how, we had found out.

. . .

While we were on our walk, Chantal had gotten a phone call from a reporter at CBS.

"I'm really sorry about the deadline," he had said.

"Listen, we'll talk to you when we are ready, thanks for calling," thinking he meant a news deadline.

"What do you mean?" he said.

"What do *you* mean?" she responded.

"You haven't heard the news?" he continued gently.

Chantal was quiet as he emailed the link to the video threat, remaining on the line for support.

· · ·

"What are you doing?" I yelled to Agent Kim, then Agent Tom. "What's your plan?"

"Calm down, we'll work this out. You have to trust us." Agent Tom spoke loudly, trying to be heard among the voices and the ringing phones.

"We have all got to calm down," Kim announced loudly to the more than fifteen people crammed in the apartment.

"I will calm down," I yelled. "Forget about us. What are you doing for Micah?"

"Let's thin out this room," Kim said. "There are way too many people and computers in here," casting a glance at Tom, busy plugging in another computer.

She pulled me aside. "Let's go upstairs to talk together."

"She's not going alone," Chantal said.

Upstairs in Leslie's apartment, Kim sat close, opposite me and Chantal. I had to pull myself together, she told me. The FBI was working on the case. They would do whatever they could. They would help me.

I was still hyperventilating and tried to look at Kim through eyes swollen shut from crying. "We have ten million dollars," I said between breaths.

Kim responded simply and kindly, "Well, that's something. But it's important to remember that they haven't asked for money. We need to keep money out of it, and not mention it."

I was certain that if it was a criminal gang, money was the answer. Then another thought struck me. Maybe it wasn't a criminal gang, and the kidnappers were motivated by political reasons, by a hatred whose price wasn't money. I realized what a dirty game it was. The kidnappers had put me in a mind-set to think of trading money for a human life. Money was not an answer. They would use money to buy weapons, kidnap more people, kill more people.

Rich, a hostage negotiator, asked me questions, the same questions we had all gone over for the past three days, and repeated my answers into his phone, mispronouncing Sadr's name.

"What is our next step?" Chantal asked.

Rich jumped in. "You should understand it is good there is a video." Chantal and I stared at him. He continued: "We have proof of life."

For the FBI, a video confirmed that a crime had been committed and provided a source for clues. There was something to work from.

For me, proof of life seemed like an old paradigm applied to a new situation I was not sure they understood. Extremists in Iraq didn't use videos as proof of life; they were a prelude to an execution.

When Hezbollah and Islamic Jihad began kidnapping in Lebanon in the 1980s, a video was a method for conveying demands and messages: a proof of life. In those years, hostage taking involved using civilians as bargaining chips, to be traded for prisoners or to extract a specific political demand. A video could be a hopeful sign, although the resolution could take months or even years.

In Iraq, a video was something else entirely. It was a weapon in itself, often the second act of a three-act play: kidnap, broadcast, then kill. And kill publicly and inhumanely, in a way that causes suffering to the hostage, their family, and anyone watching. It was a proof of death.

I was uncertain whether the FBI understood the situation or what we had to do, and angry at my own limitations.

Kim took my hand. "We'll get through this together."

The video had thrown everyone into high gear. Nabila was downstairs working the phones, calling friends and friends of friends; classmates of Allawi's; contacts in Ayatollah al-Hakim's party, the Supreme Council for Islamic Revolution in Iraq (SCIRI); Sistani and Sadr groups; even Fadlallah associates, asking for help and mercy.

"Go! Look at his website," she urged a friend who could reach Sheik Fadlallah. "Iraq needs people like Micah who care."

"The government is out of commission," contacts with Allawi commiserated. Most told her there was nothing they could do.

Kim, Chantal, and I went downstairs to my apartment and found a new email from Amir's family.

dear

~~Almahdy army~~ showed by ALIRAQIA channel and they
said if the U.S. army didnot leave ALNAJAF during
48 hours they will kill Mich and Amir

I asked Kim about the name of the group claiming to be holding Micah, Martyrs Brigade.

"We don't know it," she told me. "We're searching our databases, but it's not a name we know. There are some Palestinian groups with similar names, but we don't know if there is a connection. We're looking into it."

Eva was on the phone with Joel and Mitch, trying to reach Osama in Nasiriyah.

I called Imam al-Husainy in Michigan to tell him about the video. He called me back with an idea. "I will get a group together," he suggested, "and we can go to Iraq. Me, a Catholic priest, and Jesse Jackson."

"Let's wait on that," I told him, thanking him for the offer.

Greg Carr phoned me with the news that Sheik Jamal Uddin was heading down to Nasiriyah. At two o'clock in the morning in Iraq, he would soon be boarding a flight, and would try to make contact with the kidnappers. Flights of any kind between Baghdad and Nasiriyah were rare, a flight at two A.M. was exceptional.

The kidnapper's demands were unmeetable: "The U.S. should pull its troops out of the holy Najaf in forty-eight hours or we will execute the American."

The fighting in Najaf continued. "Can't the fighting be stopped?" I asked Kim, anticipating her response. "I mean, even for a day or so?" I looked at Tom and Kim. They gave me a smile and didn't say anything.

Sitting on the couch next to Kim, in a room full of family, friends, and agents on the phone, my throat raw and my body dehydrated, I began, very slowly, with effort, to piece together what I had learned.

Micah was not in an orange jumpsuit, an al-Qaeda signature; he was wearing his own clothes, his own beige plaid Iraqi shirt.

The name Martyrs Brigade didn't mean anything to me. The word *martyr* was a dark, fearful word, but it could be a reference to the Shi'ite history of martyrdom and oppression. The Martyrs Brigade wanted the United States to pull out in Najaf—the holiest Shi'ite city, where the Mahdi Army was fighting the U.S. forces and the Iraqi army. The few clues continued to point to a Shi'ite group aligned with the Mahdi Army. It was unlikely that a Sunni extremist group or al-Qaeda would make a video demanding that the United States pull out of Najaf.

But videotaped threats and beheadings were the tools of terrorists, and of Sunni extremists, not the Mahdi Army or Shi'ite militants in Iraq. The threat against Micah was unusual, a strange confluence of Shi'ite interests and jihadist methods.

I focused on the demand about Najaf, hoping that the Martyrs Brigade was a Shi'ite group sympathetic with the Mahdi Army, and that therefore an appeal to Sadr might be effective. But no one seemed to know where Sadr was. Perhaps trapped inside the mosque in Najaf, possibly in hiding in Kufa, or on the run. Because Sadr was under siege, he might not hear our appeal, or even be willing to help.

Our only hope was to reach out to him through Sheik Aws. The only way to Sheik Aws was through James. "I need to get ahold of you," I wrote to James. "I need a number for Sheik Aws."

The more pressure on Sheik Aws, the greater the chance that he would respond. I emailed Rory Stewart, a British friend and former CPA official in Nasiriyah, asking him to call Salah Rumaiath, the Dhi Qar governor, so he could lean on Sheik Aws, either through his political position or his tribal connections.

"We need a grassroots effort," Agent Tom said. "Keep working your network."

Again I thought of James Brandon's case. More than one sheik had spoken on his behalf. Our plan became a plan of many pressure points. I reached out to our network, already in high gear after the video threat. Journalists and friends pressured their Sadr and Mahdi Army contacts, who in turn could pressure Sadr. The network continued to grow. Natasha Lunn, a photo editor at *The New Yorker*, emailed Jon Lee Anderson, a staff writer for *The New Yorker* who had spent a year in Iraq, to ask for his help getting through to sheiks. He had many sources and he began to contact them.

Through Lauren Sandler, a *Boston Globe* reporter had sent his entire Iraq Rolodex, one year's worth of work and contact names. "Here's my list," he'd said. "Look through it for what you need." We added the names and phone numbers to our sheik chart.

There was another possible path. If the Martyrs Brigade was indeed a Shi'ite group, they might listen to Sistani. Getting hold of Sistani would not be easy either. He was in London, undergoing heart and eye surgery.

Traditionally, he did not grant interviews, so few journalists knew how to reach him.

More difficult than reaching Sistani would be soliciting his help. From the "silent" Hawza, a school of Shi'ite Islam that maintains a separation between religious and political activity, as a spiritual leader he distanced himself from politics, and it might be difficult to convince him to take an interest. Sadr, intent on establishing an Islamic state in Iraq, hails from the "speaking" Hawza, combining religious sermons with fiery political rhetoric.

"We know a guy who can get a message to Sistani," Agent Tom offered. "I'll call him."

"Even though Sistani is in the hospital in London, maybe dying of heart failure?"

"He'll get our message through," Tom assured me, reaching for his phone.

Upstairs in Leslie's apartment, a refuge from our apartment, with food, candles, and quiet, I sat with a close friend and ex-boyfriend of many years whom my sister had called after the video. He had immediately come over, and waited for several hours in the hallway filled with FBI agents. He and Chantal tried to convince me to eat. I hadn't eaten in three days, but the food felt like wood in my mouth and I couldn't. Numb, I talked to him about my fears of Micah's death, and we prayed together. He took my hand, comforting me.

Thinking I had seen the ring on his finger, he told me he had recently gotten married, something he'd wanted to share with Micah and me, but we had been in Iraq.

My sister's eyes widened at the timing of the revelation.

But he was always honest and straightforward, and his news of love and life continuing brought me calm. "I really believe Micah will be okay," he assured me.

Spiritual focus had salvaged me from the earlier despair, and now I wanted to direct it toward Micah. Leslie, Chantal, Aparna, Amanda, Loren, and I sat quietly together by the small Buddhist shrine. I tried to imagine Micah safe and healthy, to imagine him rising from his kneeling position in the video and moving away, unharmed, from his captors. To imagine the hearts of his captors softened, them putting down their guns, and Micah walking toward us, free.

But no matter how much I tried, how much I forced my mind, I could not imagine Micah rising from his kneeling position. In my mind, he remained still, his gaze downward, the scene fixed and static.

"Don't be dissuaded from your work, don't stop working your channels," Ruth Pearl urged Chantal over the phone. "The video is a sign of life. You know he is not dead, and you need to focus on that. It is crucial you stay positive. Micah can sense it."

At Chantal's insistence, echoed by everyone in the apartment, the FBI found us a new, larger, and "secure, undisclosed" location.

I had only one condition: "The dog comes with us."

"I already thought of that," Kim told me, smiling. "The dog is coming."

Jonathan, who had learned about the video while on the phone with David Bloom—who'd said, "It doesn't look good"—had rushed over to be with Suzanne and Eva. Deciding it was best that Suzanne come back to his house, at ten P.M. he stepped outside with Suzanne and Leslie, into a flood of media truck lights and journalists waiting for an image, a comment. Cameras followed the slow-moving trio down the street—in front, behind—as they silently walked several blocks to the parked car, Jonathan and Leslie trying to shield Suzanne from the cameras.

"Let's get ready to go," Kim said, directing the remaining part of the group. Aparna suggested that we wait until the media left to file their stories for the eleven o'clock news.

I was reluctant to go; this was Micah's and my home, full of happy memories, a place that he might be thinking of. I feared that if I left, I might return to something very different.

We began to pack—computer equipment, spiritual items, clothes, papers, the Project Book, my Iraqi contact notebook, the sheik chart, time line, and supplies. I packed two of Micah's old shirts that had his smell on them—one for me, one for Zeugma. At the bottom of my bag, I placed a few things for Micah that he might want when he got home.

After midnight Eva, Aparna, Chantal, Loren, and I left the apartment. The media had dispersed. Several new black FBI SUVs with smoked windows idled outside the door. Doors opened and closed with a velvet click. With a slight flash of the roof light, we cruised through red lights. New York suddenly soundless through the thick glass, we glided easily to our secure, undisclosed location, a hotel somewhere downtown that was fully set up for us to work in.

The night check-in crew at the long front desk did not lift an eyebrow at the ten exhausted people and one dog that filled their bright, shiny lobby carrying too many bags. No one had followed us; we wouldn't have to worry about the media for now.

We were joined at the hotel by Pete, a new addition to the FBI team, who introduced himself as the "go-to guy." Go-To Pete, short, tough, and unsmiling, dressed casually in khakis and a baseball cap that he wore backward, embroidered with a waving American flag, a proud eagle, and the words GITMO, then HONOR FIRST.

Under a friend's name, the FBI had reserved four rooms: one for our group to work in, one to rest in, one for the FBI, and an extra.

Loren set up our new office, plugging in the router, cables, and trying to get the printer to print. Three computers were connected and began downloading emails. Cell phones were charged and checked for reception. We put up our sheik and time-line charts, now expanded to include everyone who was working for Micah's release. Chantal set up the transplanted shrine: pictures of Micah, his favorite objects, candles, and different spiritual items that we had brought—Leslie's Buddhas, my grandmother's crucifix, Aparna's Ganesh, the Indian deity of safe passage. Everyone could pray in a way that made sense to them.

My body felt pummeled and my mind was numb. The move helped my recovery, and we filled the spacious, impeccably clean, and otherwise cold room with our energy.

It was two A.M. when we got back to work, drafting a letter a relief agency would distribute Thursday morning in both Baghdad and Najaf to sheiks and tribal leaders on behalf of the family, saying Micah was only a journalist and asking for their help. The FBI brought food, reminding us to be careful of what we said on the phones: "You never know who is listening." When on the phone, we began to refer to Micah as "the package" and the kidnappers as "the men."

Aparna searched the Internet all night for new stories. She called the FBI at two, three, four A.M., each time she found something to ask, "Have you heard about this?"

"Yep, we know all about it," they would reply, always awake.

Aparna's cell phone rang constantly with requests from the media. "Here's a funny story," Aparna said. "I got a voicemail today from Andrea Koppel, of CNN. She had a logistical question regarding your engagement." Aparna smiled at me. "She said they had been looking at the red door of your apartment building all day, and wanted to get the facts straight. She knew you lived there and wanted to know if you lived there with your fiancé. I haven't called her back yet. Let me know!"

While Aparna stayed up to monitor the news and Chantal stayed up to answer phones and chant, taking Micah's shirt and Zeugma with me, I finally slept.

Eva had fallen asleep with her cell phone on her stomach, the volume turned up all the way, jumping up every hour or so to answer after the first half ring, as Mitch updated us from Baghdad.

. . .

Early Thursday morning in New York, afternoon in Iraq, Mitch called. He was worried, though he carefully masked it when talking with us. He feared that the kidnappers were a radical offshoot of the Mahdi Army. In Mitch's view, it was only a matter of time before Shi'ite militants in Iraq began using the techniques of Sunni extremists—videotaped executions. Would Micah be the first? Like Islamic Jihad before them, it was possible that this group was an extremist offshoot of a less radical Shi'ite movement. Angry at Sadr's political maneuvering that demanded compromises, angry that Sadr was not militant enough, the Martyrs Brigade could use this video to signal the further radicalization of the movement. In that case, Sadr would not be able to help, because the group would not listen to Sadr. But Sadr and Sheik Aws were still our best options.

Mitch talked often with Osama, who met with Sheik Aws, Sadr's top cleric in Nasiriyah. Sheik Aws was generally committed to helping, but Osama felt he needed more encouragement and perhaps an incentive. He also knew that Sadr, under siege in Najaf, probably couldn't release a statement. With Sadr trapped in Najaf, Osama saw a way to help.

"Since Sadr is trapped, we can release a statement through the media," Osama told Sheik Aws, "and it will reflect well on Sadr, on you, and on the Sadr movement."

Sheik Aws thought it over.

"No one else will be mentioned, only you and Sadr," Osama offered. "It will show how much you have done to release an American hostage."

Sheik Aws agreed. "But I want the newscaster to read the information. I don't want it to be on the scrawl at the bottom. People who don't read will not get the message."

"No problem," Osama told him. "Consider it done."

I watched the first light of dawn appear, the day the forty-eight-hour dead-line was up. The guard sleepily led us back, blindfolded and bound, to the enclosure. As we laid out our mats, I looked at Amir in the dim light.

"Let's go," I said. It was our moment of truth. There was a long pause.

"I think we should wait," Amir responded. Because of the Grim Reaper's assurances the night before, I'd been afraid he would say this, and I didn't know what I could say to change his mind.

"This is our only chance," I pleaded.

"Yes, but the man last night assured me we would go free," he said, leaning toward me.

We both knew they couldn't be trusted, but Amir, perhaps afraid for his family, perhaps afraid for himself, put his faith in the words of the Grim Reaper.

"If I am a coward, I am a coward; but believe me, if we escape it will bring disaster," Amir reasoned. "People will see that our faces have hair on them, our clothes are dirty and they will know there is an American here. If they capture us again, it will be even harder to release us."

Amir would not leave, and I couldn't escape without his help. Ex-hausted and hopeless, I lay down on my side, looking out through Freedom's Gate.

I awoke again a few hours later, when a guard entered with tea and *khubz*. The sun was up and the day was in motion. Our moment had passed and I lay still on my back, contemplating our fate. I had tried to stay awake thinking of options, but after seven days of almost no sleep, it was impossible. Taking a deep breath, I steeled myself for what the day might bring. My anger and disappointment at myself for not escaping was softened only slightly by a thought of Marie-Hélène and my family, that whatever decision I had made, right or wrong, was okay. They would not be upset with me for not having tried to escape.

The animals walked by as they usually did, cows stopping to chew at the outside of our enclosure. They ripped and tore at the leaves until the small palm trees shook with the force of their teeth. Then we heard a loud rustling noise at the mouth of the enclosure. Certain it was a guard coming to check on the commotion, I was surprised to see a sheep bound through the entrance. Ignoring us, the sheep began eating our food. We watched it for a moment, then Amir made a noise to scare it away. Grabbing our *khubz*, it ran out.

"Look," I said angrily. "Even the farm animals have come to mock us. The cows are chewing at our pen. A sheep can walk out of here, but we can't."

"The animals are mocking us?" Amir didn't understand. "Micah, what's wrong?"

"What's wrong? I'll tell you what's wrong. We've been kidnapped. They made a video threatening to kill me in forty-eight hours if the U.S. doesn't pull out of Najaf. We both know that won't happen, and the deadline is almost up. We had an opportunity to escape, and we didn't take it. That's what's wrong." Teetering on the edge of despair I continued, "I don't even know if my parents survived seeing the video."

"But I am in the same position as you," Amir said earnestly.

"Don't say you are in the same position as me!" I whispered loudly, staring at Amir, my rage escaping uncontrolled in that moment. "You are not in the same position! They didn't make a video of you." I pointed at him for emphasis. "Your family is not being held hostage."

Amir grew quiet. This wasn't fair, and I felt ashamed at my outburst. The kidnappers knew where Amir's family lived. If we escaped, I would be back on a plane to America, and who knew what Amir would return to. We were trapped. As much as I dreamed about our opportunities to escape, in reality we had none. If our escape could cause harm to Amir's family, I could not fault him for staying. We had no options. There was nothing left to do but wait and see what would happen. I had lost control completely.

I lay back on my mat, still angry but no longer sure whom to be angry at.

"What are you talking about?" the young guard outside the enclosure asked.

"The sheep," Amir said.

"You want to see a baby sheep?" he asked.

"Yes," I said, lying on my back. "Can you bring one in here?" Perhaps I could jump him and take his gun. If not, it would be nice to just pet a sheep.

"No, it is with its mother, but you can see it when it comes back in the afternoon."

"Can I go out and work on the farm?" I asked. "I need some exercise."

He laughed at my feeble attempt at freedom. "No."

The only thing I could do was meditate and try to calm my mind. I sat up, took off my shirt, closed my eyes, folded my legs, rested my hands on my knees, and started to breathe deeply. Amir lay on his back on his mat, looking the other way. *When your world is turned on its head, why not turn yourself on your head?* I thought. Things might start to make sense. I knelt on my mat, put my head and arms in front of me, and, for the first time, carefully rose into a perfect headstand, lifting my legs high up through the small opening between the palm leaves. Amir said nothing, not wanting to trigger another angry outburst. I remained upside down for at least a minute, then lowered my legs to the mat, breathing hard. My headstand gave me a strange sense of accomplishment. Perhaps if I could control my body, I was more in control than I thought. Perhaps control meant restraint—not fighting, not escaping, but having the strength to wait and not act in desperation.

In the afternoon, a new guard came to sit in the mouth of the enclosure.

"What is the situation in Najaf?" we asked.

"Quiet."

"Alhamdulillah," I replied. Thank God. "You know, America won't stop fighting because of me. The American government doesn't care about a journalist," I said, wanting the guard to believe that I was of no value to anyone.

"I know," he said. "America would eat its children before changing its policies." Oddly, his blunt assessment gave me comfort. If the kidnappers didn't believe that America cared about me, their expectations might be more reasonable.

Then he thanked me for making the video, the worst experience of my life, one that had filled me with homicidal thoughts toward them. And yet the guard, sincere in his gratitude, spoke as though the video were some gesture of goodwill on my part. As much as I despised what they had done, I felt sad that they were so desperate that they had to threaten me and my family to try to stop the fighting. I didn't reply.

In the late afternoon a man wearing a long white dishdasha, who looked like he could have been the Grim Reaper, appeared outside the enclosure. Though I could not see him clearly through the palm leaves, I could see that he was holding something in his hand. The guard went out to talk with him and for several minutes they spoke in hushed voices.

"The man has a shovel," I said to Amir, recognizing the object in his hand, convinced that he was preparing our graves.

Amir thought for a moment. "Never mind. It means nothing."

The man with the shovel left, heading down the field.

"Fuck," I said to myself as I lay back on my mat. They were going to dump my body in a shallow grave in some remote marsh in southern Iraq. My family would never find peace.

As the enclosure took on a yellow glow from the fading light, we heard the sheep returning up the gentle slope. The young guard told us that if we looked out between the palm leaves we could see the baby. I heard the soft, high-pitched bleating of a lamb as it passed with its mother, and I strained to look but couldn't see anything. The noisy sheep soon passed, replaced by silence.

They came for us when the sun was setting. I knew they were not there to take us to eat, and I glanced at Amir. We shared a look, what we both feared could be a last look, as they put the blindfolds on. At least we were together.

This time they tied my blindfold tightly and led us across the field, back into the house where the video had been made. We were taken to the long wall on the right, and I knelt down, my thoughts suspended, sounds of movement and hushed voices, then, a bright light visible through the blindfold.

They untied my hands and removed my blindfold.

The room looked nothing like it had two days before. A strong light in the otherwise darkened room illuminated us, a patterned green cloth backdrop hung behind us, and a single camera again sat on a stool facing me. There were a number of men in the room with AKs, but the scene didn't have the same sinister quality I had experienced on Tuesday. The Grim Reaper appeared and spoke to Amir, handing him a pen and a small piece of paper. He asked Amir to translate his words into English. Amir listened and wrote carefully, in a large, childlike script, then handed me the paper. I was astonished to see his handwriting, normally small and el-egant, transformed into large, shaky squiggles that bespoke a fear hidden beneath his quiet demeanor.

"He wants you to read this message on camera."

"Amir," I said, becoming bolder. "Tell him I don't want to make an-other video."

Amir repeated my protest. "He says you have no choice."

I looked down and read the words written on the paper: ". . . stop the massacre in Najaf . . ." The word *massacre* jumped out at me; it was a loaded term.

"Amir, tell him these are not my words and I won't read them. No one will believe me if they are not my own words."

The Grim Reaper raised his voice, warning that I had better read the paper. It would take incredible courage to refuse, and even if I had the courage, what was the point? No one would believe that these were my words. My appearance on television would not affect anything, anyway. There was no point in getting killed over this. I could find another way to resist, and at least the video would be a message to my family: I was alive. The kidnappers in the room probably didn't know English if they were asking Amir to translate, so I would simply change the words a bit.

I wanted to look strong and confident but clearly under someone else's control. Seeing that I was strong would help my family be strong. I brushed my hair with my hands and sat up. One of the kidnappers came over and straightened my shirt. They wanted me to look well cared for.

"My name is Micah Garen—"

"Stop," the Grim Reaper said. I was holding the paper and reading from it. He instructed me to memorize the text and say it as if they were my own words. I told him I couldn't remember it, so he told me to put it on the ground in front of me but not to look down. I started again.

"My name is Micah Garen, I am an American journalist in Iraq. *I have been asked to deliver a message,"* I added to the script. No one stopped me, I had gotten my message across without their noticing; these were not my words. I tilted my head forward, deliberately looking down at the paper in front of me. "America should stop the massacre in Najaf."

Forty-eight hours had passed and I was alive. I felt a sudden rush of euphoria. The second video was not threatening; they were not going to kill me tonight. We had made it this far without risking escape.

They tied our hands and led us out. A car was waiting outside with its engine running. Something wasn't right; it didn't make sense that they would release us immediately after making a video.

"Are they taking us to Nasiriyah?"

Amir tried to ask them several times, but they did not respond, pushing us instead into the back of the car. The Grim Reaper got in the front on the passenger side and the car started off. Amir tried again and the driver responded, "We are taking you to a better place."

A better place? This was not good. I understood that to be a euphemism for heaven in Islam, where seventy-two virgins awaited martyrs, and worse things lurked for nonbelievers like me. Better than their life here certainly, but not better than mine with Marie-Hélène and Zeugma. My hope began to collapse under the grinding wheels. They were not releasing us. We were headed for either a longer story or death. Had we been sold off? After two videos, I didn't know what they needed me for. I started to break down. It was our seventh day of captivity, I had been thrust at gunpoint onto the world's stage, Freedom's Gate was gone, and our circumstances seemed to be going from bad to worse. Feeling helpless, I put my elbow on the open car window, rested my head on my forearm, and started to moan—a muffled, hopeless sound. For the first time since being kidnapped, I felt as if I was going to cry.

"Get ahold of yourself," the Grim Reaper said sternly. His words and tone pulled me back from the brink. *Never show weakness.*

"I am fine, just tired," I said, transforming my expression instantly from desperation to grim seriousness.

As the car slowly climbed the darkened roads, Amir turned to me.

"Micah, I have one question," Amir said, leaning closer. "Was it fair to say you hate me?"

"What?" I asked, startled by his words, which made no sense. "I never said I hate you. When did I say I hate you?"

"Yes, you did. Was it fair to say that? Do you really hate me?"

"No, I never said that. Why do you think I said that?"

"You said it just now. You said, 'Amir, I hate you.' "

"No, I never said that." I thought hard. Impossible—I'd never thought that; Amir was a close friend. Perhaps I had said, "Amir, I don't like you." Had I said that on our way to the car? If I did, it was a joke, my usual irreverent humor. Or was I unconsciously blaming Amir for our kidnapping?

"Do you hate me, Micah?" he said, taking hold of my hand. Amir needed to make peace as we headed toward the unknown.

"No, of course not," I tried to reassure him. "I may have said 'I don't like you,' but that was a joke, it was sarcasm."

My sarcasm was lost in translation, but I thought he believed me when I said that I did not hate him, and that I did not blame him. I didn't. It was the opposite. Amir had done so much to help us with our story, risking his own life. But after everything we'd been through, I didn't understand why he suddenly needed to make peace. Did he suspect that this was really the end?

The car stopped by an empty field and two guards brought us out. They instructed me to hold Amir with my right arm as one guard led me forward. Together Amir and I began to walk slowly, arm in arm, blindfolded, in the darkness.

I leaned toward Amir and whispered, "Thanks for inviting me to the prom." Might as well die laughing.

We walked for several hundred yards, then were told to stop. The guards removed our blindfolds and instructed us to climb over an eight-foot mud-brick wall. We struggled to climb, raising ourselves with our elbows and bound hands. After making it over, we sat breathing hard in a darkened courtyard. One guard left, telling us to remain silent.

For the first time since our journey began, Amir thought we would be killed. Our captors' demands had not been met.

For the first time, I didn't agree. There were just two guards and no video camera. If they were going to kill us they would film it. Instead, it seemed to me they were looking for a place to put us.

"Amir, ask him why they took us from the other place," I whispered.

"He says they moved us for our safety. One of the sons of the farm owner was killed in the fighting in Najaf and the family is coming for the funeral. If they found an American there, they would kill you." The man with the shovel made sense now. He was probably digging a grave for the son.

"How long does the funeral last?"

"Two or three days. The family comes and they prepare a large meal and gather for several days and sit together and remember him."

Half an hour passed before the other guard returned.

"We can't stay here," he told us. "The house was supposed to be empty but there are people here." We struggled back over the wall and to the car, then drove another hour deeper into the marshes. The two guards led us out, through a field, and into a thicket under a moonless sky. With our hands tied in front of us, I followed the faint flash of the guard's white dishdasha as we hacked our way through thick brambles, stumbling through the mud and water up to our knees, branches grabbing at our skin. Exhausted and bleeding after about an hour of wading through the marsh, we finally came upon a clearing. One of the guards went ahead, crouching with his gun.

Across the open plain I could make out the distant silhouette of a large *madhif*, a communal building. To the right of the *madhif* was a mud-brick house with a single light on. The guard moved silently toward the house with his gun, entered through the front door, then came back after a few minutes with two straw mats and two wool blankets.

"We will sleep here tonight, but we must leave by morning," he said. "The owner does not want anyone to know an American was here. He is worried that if the Americans find out they will come and destroy his house."

We laid out our mats and sat down in the open field, near tall reeds, whose dry, conspiratorial whispers were encouraged by the evening wind.

"They didn't even bring us food," Amir remarked as we lay down.

"Well, at least we are alive," I said. Now I was the optimist.

A forgotten netherworld, a land between two worlds in a place no one could possibly find us. All connections we had made with our captors, details we had gathered about our location, escape routes we had planned were lost.

Early Thursday morning, Agent Kim came into our hotel room carrying the day's papers and laid them on the table. HER HOPES CRUSHED, read one headline next to a smiling picture of me pulled off our website; LEAVE OR WE KILL YANK read another. Chantal and Aparna sprang forward in a single movement to remove the papers, but I grabbed them.

"I have to see them."

I had no memory of seeing the video the day before, and forced myself to look at the grainy newspaper picture of Micah kneeling in front of men with guns.

"Well, I couldn't really recognize him," Tante Olivia, in Orlando, had told Chantal on the phone the previous night. Micah had grown a mustache, the image was fuzzy, and perhaps she didn't want to believe it. Although in my heart I knew it was Micah, I had to look at the image to know what Micah was experiencing. If I looked closely, perhaps I could see something, maybe a clue. The shape, the clothes, the presence. It was, without a doubt, Micah. Something else made me look longer, and I could see why someone might not recognize him. Micah was looking down. It could be anything, maybe because he had been told to, but I read it differently, feeling that it was a deliberate action—either defiance or a message. His ability to deliver a message of any sort was infinitely limited, and in our hunger to understand what he was going through, it was possible that we might interpret any thing in any way.

Micah was always calm and self-possessed, even more so under pressure. He looked calm, but I wanted to know what he was thinking.

"I won't let them do that to me," Micah had said once after we'd seen a video execution threat on TV in our Baghdad hotel. If he thought he would be beheaded, he might fight back or kill himself first. But if he fought back, he would probably be killed.

What was he thinking now?

I wanted, desperately, for Micah to know we were fighting for him on this end. Sometimes I felt that everything depended on us. Sometimes I felt that he was the only one who could save himself. *Be strong, Micah,* I repeated over and over in my head. *Be strong.*

. . .

Plato wrote that love is the search for completeness through another person. We had once been whole creatures, and the gods, angered by our arrogance, had split us into parts. We were always searching for our other. The union of the two is love. It also meant, perhaps, that the kernel of the other was already in us. If I could connect to that—to that kernel of Micah—I could know what he was thinking. We had always believed that maintaining our individuality while being in love was a sign of a successful, healthy, creative relationship.

Plato also wrote that yearning is only half of love. Goodness is the other; we yearn for the other half only if it is good. We seek to possess goodness in the other. Most importantly, we seek it not temporarily but permanently, and so Plato added the idea of immortality to love. "Love is the desire for the perpetual possession of the good," he wrote. I had to focus on the good. The more I focused on the good, the more I was able in my mind to see Micah get up and move away from his kidnappers. It was a small movement, but it was in the right direction.

I had never really thought about Micah's mortality. Even though we had worked in dangerous places, it wasn't something I focused on. Now all I could think about—the reason I felt I was alive at that moment—was to save Micah from death.

Eva spoke to Terry Anderson about his experiences in captivity. A former hostage, he had been held for seven years in Lebanon by pro-Iranian Shi'ite militants. He often worked with CPJ and was taking time out from his campaign for the Ohio state senate to work on Micah's case.

He understood our grief. Not knowing what was happening to Micah was incredibly painful, and he wanted to reassure us by talking about his experience.

"Micah is probably in survival mode," he said. "When you get into these situations you just go moment by moment and try to figure out how to survive. So don't worry about him. He's probably fine, given the circumstances."

He also told Eva not to focus too much on the deadline, not to worry too much about the forty-eight hours. Kidnappers were known to make deadlines and change them all the time.

"The waiting is torture for you, I know," he continued. "This is horrible. Whatever you're feeling, you're not crazy—this is the worst possible thing imaginable. You're probably suffering more than he is right now. This is terrible for you because you just don't know right now, there is so much uncertainty."

"You've got to find out which group has Micah," he told Eva. "That's the most important thing." He explained the difference between Sunni and Shi'ite, Eva writing furiously.

"If it's a Shi'ite group, then there is a chance you will see Micah again." He paused. "If it's a Sunni group, you should prepare to say good-bye."

Eva paused too. "But it's a Shi'ite group, right?"

"It may be. If it is, we've got a chance." He continued: "I'm sorry, but if it's a Sunni group, that's it."

Eva thanked Terry for his honesty. She relayed the first part of the message, a comfort to us, and did not tell anyone the second part, absorbing the harder truth herself.

Our network of journalists and friends continued to work around the clock. A documentary filmmaker who had been in Iraq sent Sheryl a list of several powerful Iraqi Shi'ites he knew who were well connected to Nasiriyah tribes and known in Najaf. Sheryl started calling.

"Hello?" she said to the first person on the list.

"Yes?"

She asked for his help with Micah.

He hesitated. "I'm just a musician."

"I know," she told him, "but these two people say you can help."

"Who says I can help?" he asked, tentatively.

She told him the names. It opened the door.

"This man is a cousin. I will call him," he told her.

Sheryl called an Iraqi driver she knew, currently on his way to Jordan. She had had a brainstorm. "What's your last name?" she asked.

"Muhammed."

"No, your *last* last name."

"Al-Khafaji."

"That's what I remembered. Can you reach out to Sheik Aws al-Khafaji, in Nasiriyah, and ask for his help?"

"He is in my tribe. I will try," he assured Sheryl.

. . .

Sitting at the desk in front of three vanilla-colored hotel phones, I managed to reach Rory on his cell phone and he promised to call the Dhi Qar governor again, to ask him to pressure Sheik Aws. "Do like the prophet Abraham," Rory had warned with a wink as he headed from Ur to a helicopter following the June 28 transition to Iraqi sovereignty, "run like hell and don't look back."

From the Scottish hilltop where he was hiking, mobile phone in hand, he called in many personal favors with local Dhi Qar tribal leaders, saying that Micah was a relative. The governor was finally reachable, just returning from a three-day funeral for his brother, who had been killed in a car accident. Sheik Aws had also been at the funeral and the two had spoken about Micah.

"Yes, Mr. Rory, I have made contact," the governor said.

I spent most of the morning struggling to maintain a single point of contact with the media. Many friends, colleagues, and even people we didn't know wanted to speak publicly on Micah's behalf, and I worked tirelessly to contact those I could, telling them we were working through backdoor channels, and asking that they not talk to the press.

Because of the execution deadline, media interest mounted, the river of calls now a raging torrent. A reporter called Joel at CPJ, asking to line up an interview. Joel said it would have to wait, but he would check in with her later. "Well," she told him, "I only *really* want a statement from you if he is killed. You understand, right?"

Media trucks kept a vigil outside our apartment in New York, reporters waiting in lawn chairs, producers leaving messages on the answering machines of almost all my neighbors. Media trucks camped outside Alan's house in New Haven and Suzanne and Giovanni's house in Newton. Flowers and fruit baskets arrived at Jonathan and Nieves's house in New Jersey, and several press cars waited for hours. Some journalists and news stations called to simply express sympathy and solidarity, several newspapers passing along names and lists of contacts in hopes of helping. Many others called and passed along letters to anyone entering my building, anxious to get the first interview, or any interview. In Boston, Giovanni, Micah's stepfather, cleared the answering machine several times a day. "We know you're in there," he heard a producer's voice say over the machine as he remained in the house.

No one should come directly to the hotel, the FBI had instructed us, if we wanted the hotel to remain secure, undisclosed, and a sanctuary where we could work. To throw off the press, Nieves and Suzanne made three stops over a two-hour period, waiting at a crowded McDonald's in midtown on their way to the hotel. Leslie, who brought us healthy food, accompanied by Nabila, made a half dozen stops, leaving separately from my apartment.

Nabila brought positive news: she had heard back from her friend who knew how to reach Sheik Fadlallah. "Contact has been made," he assured her.

Being together in the same location helped us maintain our concentration, and not think of the passing minutes. I spoke often on the phone to Tante Olivia and my mom, who, as she battled the chaos of two consecutive hurricanes in Florida, was praying for Micah and that Sadr would release a statement. Nieves brought Micah's newborn nephew, Tomas, to cheer everyone, and we took turns holding him. Together, Jonathan and Nieves spent time looking after Suzanne, who in turn looked after the rest of us.

The tension was steadily building. The FBI had brought in their own Arabic translator, a middle-aged Lebanese woman in a light-blue suit, who tried reaching Amir's family. We knew they trusted Nabila, and worried that their trust would be lost if different people began contacting them.

Loren checked Micah's email throughout the morning to see if there was anything new. As Go-To Pete walked by he commanded Loren in a gravelly voice, "Don't delete anything!"

"No worries," Loren replied, attempting a smile.

"And don't smile at me. It's not over till someone's in handcuffs," Go-To Pete growled, giving us a backward glance, and slamming the door.

While we were making another round of calls, our hotel door burst open onto a vista of FBI agents.

"People, family, listen up!" Rich yelled, as agents streamed in. "It's time to move. NOW! We're making a statement."

I knew we would make a statement only as a last resort, when all options had failed.

Suddenly everyone was frantic. Tom asked Eva and me to join him and Kim in the bedroom. He shut the door.

• • •

In Baghdad, Mitch had decided it was time to make a move but not the one we'd been expecting. Despite everything we had all heard from colleagues with experience in hostage situations about speaking to the media—"keep your mouth shut"—Mitch felt that the fighting in Najaf was preventing Sadr from helping, and that his Sadr contacts were too busy, distracted, upset, or in hiding. While journalists who had made it into the Shrine of Imam Ali under siege in Najaf indicated that Sadr wanted to help, they said it was very difficult to get a message out. In Nasiriyah, Osama felt that Sheik Aws needed some additional motivation. It was in Sadr's interest, he promised Sheik Aws. If they helped get Micah released, they could take credit and show the world that they weren't the terrorists the Americans were calling them. If Al Jazeera and Al Arabiya report that we're helping, then we'll help, Osama was told.

A plan was hatched. It was simple: the family would thank Sadr for helping, and this statement would initiate action. Mitch informed the Hostage Working Group at the U.S. embassy in Baghdad, then called Joel, who called Eva. It was time to make a statement.

• • •

"This is the plan from your people on the ground in Iraq," Tom told Eva and me. "We will release a press statement from the family to the Arab media, saying that Sadr has called for Micah's release. A family member has to make a statement on television."

"Eva or I should read the statement," I said.

Tom moved quickly. "Eva, you should do it."

"I'll do it as long as it doesn't hurt him," Eva responded. She thought for a second. "Tom, didn't you say that in previous hostage cases, going to the media got people killed?"

"Eva, listen to me," Kim responded gently and firmly. "You make a decision based on the best information you have available at the time. Right now, this is the best thing for Micah."

"Do you think it's the best thing for Micah?" Eva asked me.

I took her hand, holding it tightly. *"Yes."*

She squeezed back. "Oh my God, what if we hurt Micah, what if something happens to him? I'll have to live with this for the rest of my life."

"Eva, we're all making this decision," Kim said. "If it's a mistake, it's not your mistake. It's everybody's mistake."

Eva turned to face me. "I want all the family members to agree. We're taking a risk, and everyone needs to agree."

She talked to Jonathan, Suzanne, and Nieves in the next room. They agreed. There was one more person to talk to.

"I need to call Dad," Eva said. "I want to make sure he understands what this means." She talked to her father on the phone; he agreed.

Making a statement was a risk, but it was our best option according to our sources on the ground in Iraq.

The phone rang and Eva answered. She listened for a moment to a family friend who, after consulting a relief agency, had just talked to Alan. Looking up, Eva said, "She really doesn't think we should do this. She says it could harm Micah—she says it could be a huge mistake."

Afraid, Eva insisted, "I need to talk to Dad again. I need to make sure he understands and agrees."

Again, Alan said he understood what the plan meant, and he agreed.

The phone rang again. It was the family friend. Eva's face collapsed.

Tom intervened. "Let me talk." He leaned in and took the phone. He pulled up to his full height, his face set and red. "This is Agent Tom from the FBI," he said, his voice loud, the first time we had seen him angry. "You have no idea what is going on here. Whatever you are doing, it has got to stop. Do you understand me? It will stop."

He flipped the phone off.

We worked on the statement with Joel and the FBI, writing several drafts, including what Eva would say to Al Jazeera when she called to tell them she wanted to make a statement; everything had to be scripted. The message had to be simple, no more than one or two sentences. By saying that Sadr had called for Micah's release, we might be able to set Micah's release in motion. The plan was a gamble to overcome the many impediments that prevented Sadr from intervening on Micah's behalf. Because of the intense fighting in Najaf, Sadr wasn't able to speak for Micah, or get his message out, and we were fighting against time. The videotaped execution threat with a forty-eight-hour deadline had been broadcast at five P.M. on Wednesday—we had only twenty-five hours left, though we weren't exactly sure when the clock had started ticking, and what time zone applied.

"Let's start with Al Jazeera," Tom said.

"This is Eva Garen." There was silence in the room as she spoke to the Al Jazeera bureau in New York. "I am Micah Garen's sister, the American hostage threatened with death in Iraq. We are reaching out to you because our family received information regarding Micah and we know that you have the ability to get information to those who need to hear it."

"Uh-huh. Uh-huh." We listened as Eva fluttered her hands in frustration. Her voice remained calm. She looked up, worried. "They are saying they don't know if they'll run it."

Media from around the world were desperate to talk to us, but the one outlet we needed wasn't interested.

"They said we said we would do a statement yesterday, and then changed our minds," she continued.

"Tell her it is important for Micah's life! Why is she even hesitating?" This wasn't a favor to us. I leaned over and yelled into the phone. "This *is* news!"

"Hello?" Eva calmly continued her conversation. "This is very important. This is about somebody's life, and we need your help."

"She said I should call D.C.," Eva repeated to us.

The Al Jazeera bureau in Washington told us that many people had called claiming to be the family, and they wanted proof that Eva was Eva. They wanted Eva to come to D.C. to make the statement. We faxed them a copy of her passport, and Joel called to vouch for her.

"I heard that Al Jazeera might be blocked from broadcasting in parts of Iraq, because of the fighting in Najaf," I told Tom. "Our statement may not even get through. Maybe we should call someone else."

"Fine, find the Al Arabiya number!" Rich said. "We'll call them and give them the story, an exclusive! See if we can't convince them with some good ol' competition."

We called Al Jazeera to tell them we would give the story to Al Arabiya, a Dubai-based TV station founded after the 2003 Gulf War.

"Fine, go to Al Arabiya," the Al Jazeera producer responded.

Chantal got through to Al Arabiya on the hotel phone line. The connection was staticky, the woman on the other end barely audible as Chantal handed the phone to Eva.

"Hi, this is Eva Garen, calling on behalf of Micah Garen, the American hostage. I'm his sister."

Interested in the story, the producer at Al Arabiya agreed to meet Eva and film her statement. The only trouble was, their cameraman didn't have a camera. As we scrambled to find a camera, the FBI agents called their office. An agent brought over an out-of-date camera that no one could find a tape for. Finally, after more searching, Al Arabiya found a tape.

Jonathan accompanied Eva in the back of the black FBI car as they drove with Tom, Kim, Rich, and Go-To Pete to Battery Park. The site at the southernmost tip of Manhattan had been chosen beforehand as a neutral location, with nothing that stood out in the background and nothing that would carry any sort of message, like a flag or a monument.

"Your first public appearance in the Arab world." Kim smiled at Eva. "You'll be great."

Eva's cell phone rang. "It's Al Jazeera," she told the team in the car. "They said they will do a live radio piece where I read the statement and it's translated into Arabic. In ten seconds."

"Do it," Kim said.

"Okay," Eva agreed, looking for the carefully worded statement.

"Ten, nine, eight . . ."

Rustling among her papers, she could not find the statement.

"Seven, six, five . . ."

Where was the paper? She began to panic.

"Four, three, two . . ."

Here!

"One."

Eva heard Arabic, then Micah's name, then "Eva Garen," followed by silence. "Hello?" she said. Her voice echoed. More silence. Eva realized it was her moment to speak.

"My name is Eva and I am Micah Garen's sister and I am speaking on behalf of my family. I am reaching out to you because our family received information regarding Micah and we know that you have the ability to get the information to those who need to hear it. We were told that Muqtada al-Sadr and the Mahdi Army have ordered Micah's immediate release. We, the family, are hopeful for a positive outcome."

As she spoke, Eva heard a big echo, and a voice speaking in Arabic over her words. Then it was over.

Once she had read it, she was taken off the air, and the producer came on the line.

"That was great," he said. "Thank you."

Our statement was out.

There was still the statement to film for Al Arabiya. The FBI car pulled up to the park. Eva, Jonathan, and the FBI team got out, one agent holding the out-of-date camera. The day was bright and clear, the park full of tourists oblivious to the small group that had assembled off to the side, ready to make a hostage plea video. Not sure whom to look for, they stood waiting for someone who looked like they were waiting for someone. After fifteen minutes, the tall, blond Al Arabiya producer arrived, saying how sorry she was for what the family was going through. In less than thirty seconds, Eva read the short statement, the camera focusing only on her face. The two groups parted, the producer hurrying back to her office with the tape.

The FBI stopped to buy everyone ice cream to celebrate the statement on the way to pick up Alan and Sally, who were arriving at Penn Station.

It was important that Alan and Sally be with us in New York. With negotiations now so focused and delicate, it was paramount we have only a single point of contact and one locus of action. And we did not want them to be alone if Micah was killed. Alan and Sally joined us in our hotel war room, exhausted from four days of continuous work and little sleep.

When I was in motion, I rarely had time to think about the specifics of what might happen to Micah. The captors had not threatened beheading, but had said Micah would be killed. Yet the image of beheading had entered my mind and would not leave. That was how many videos, just like Micah's, ended.

Sometimes, during quiet moments or a routine act, like recharging the phone or looking for paper, I was vulnerable to an assault of imagination that burned like acid. And then: blackness. It was better to keep moving. Those thoughts would destroy my heart, and I needed all of it for Micah.

When I thought of Micah's possible death, I hoped for small things. That it would be quick, that it would not hurt too much. That he would have thoughts of us, that he wouldn't feel alone. Yet I did not want to hope for these things, because I didn't want to think of them at all.

It couldn't be that all I would have of Micah was memories. It couldn't be that the one-dimensional Micah in the photographs that filled our hotel room would be all that remained. That the still, grainy video image would be the last time I would see him alive.

A terrible thought wound its way in the back of my mind, a memory, stubborn and persistent, of a fight that Micah and I had had at the Italian base just before I left. During a helicopter survey of the archaeological sites, in the fading light as dusk gave way to night, we managed to surprise looters at Umma. They ran from the low-flying Italian helicopter as it repeatedly swung over hundreds of craters in tight figure eights to avoid possible enemy gunfire. The intensity of shooting frame after frame had jammed our sand-tired digital camera, and we ended up with only a handful of blurry photos. Dust from our footsteps followed our conversation, which was filled with disappointment, and ended in angry words toward each other. Now one of my greatest fears was that Micah might die with those words in his mind. Over and over I repeated, "I love you, I love you," hoping that those words would somehow reach Micah. Micah had to know, to feel, to be filled with the intensity of my love for him.

Back at the hotel, Eva locked herself into the bathroom, dreading that the TV, always on in the hotel room, would announce Micah's execution. She said out loud to Micah that we had done what we thought was best and that she was sorry if she had messed up. Would Micah ever forgive her, she wondered, or could she ever forgive herself if Micah was killed?

As we waited for the impact of Eva's appeal, with Joel's help we drew up a short statement on behalf of the family, which journalists and others in Baghdad and Najaf began distributing to their Sadr contacts, in addition to the written statement handed out through the International Rescue Committee. With telephone and broadcast communication almost nonexistent because of the fighting, our words were passed from hand to hand.

The FBI thought Micah might have been moved to Najaf. "We have people in the shrine," Kim tried to reassure Suzanne, making the motion of holding a machine gun. "I don't want any shooting," Suzanne replied, feeling anything but reassured.

Mitch and others continued to head to Sadr offices in Sadr City—"I'm back, what have you heard now?"—but their Sadr contacts were fully preoccupied with the fighting in Najaf. Hezbollah's Sheik Fadlallah, a man I was learning had strong influence in Iraq, agreed to release a state-ment on Micah's behalf but also said, "If this man is really held by Shi'ites, no harm will come to him." Mitch also sent a letter to Sistani, in London for medical treatment, and received an email that said the letter had been received, but it wasn't clear if it had been read by Sistani. I tried imagining Sistani being briefed on the email request in his hospital room. "With Sadr in Najaf and Sistani in London, it's a terrible time to get kid-napped," Mitch told us.

We reviewed our now fully filled charts with the FBI, reading aloud the names of people whom we had contacted and whom we knew were working on Micah's behalf in Iraq. We also added the names of people in the U.S. government who had been contacted, and those who had ex-pressed concern. The list stretched from Paul Wolfowitz at the Penta-gon, to Congress, to the State Department, to the army, to the Special Forces. The State Department's "must-call" list for updates about Micah's case, spurred by the urgent calls of friends, family, and journal-ists, was the longest in recent memory.

"We want your Rolodex," Kim joked to all of us gathered in the room. "How about coming to work for us? We could use a tough musicologist with an organized project book," she added, winking at Chantal.

Eva dubbed our far-flung team "the blob," a group drawn together by a common purpose: bringing Micah home safely. Together we gained strength and courage. We answered one another's phones, read one another's emails, called out all news, knew every piece of information that came in, pooled our contacts, and coordinated our actions. Since the hotel was a secret, undisclosed location, many friends who wanted to be with us could not. But they called constantly, and were also part of the blob. The blob was powerful and comforting, a buffer against despair and an engine for action.

The blob included people we did not know. Our phones and emails overflowed with messages from strangers. "We love you! Be strong!" At our apartment on Christopher Street, beyond the four-layers-deep media waiting in the street, behind the red door, our neighbors had erected a small makeshift shrine in the lobby. They had put up Micah's picture, flowers, candles, a picture of Gandhi, and a huge heart drawn by our neighbors' kids. "We are waiting for your safe return," they had written, and they had included a poem that ended with the words "God waits where love is."

When friends and colleagues heard about Micah's kidnapping, everyone offered to help. But not everyone had the same outlook. Most were positive and hopeful. "If I know Micah," a friend said, "he's probably playing cards with the kidnappers." Another friend told me not to worry; Micah was smart and would get out of this. Micah's aunt had written me, "I'm very proud of your commitment to cultural history . . . you two have risked everything to stand up for what you believe." A few others were not as hopeful, the situation too political and the players too extreme. They didn't think Micah would make it.

Many people—friends, family, strangers—offered their support and prayers, and many found themselves praying for the first time. Individuals, churches, and prayer groups prayed for Micah: that he be protected, for his family; for the kidnappers; for Sadr, that he be found and release a statement. By request, or spontaneously, prayer chains formed in different countries, and several monasteries focused on Micah. Friends at a Buddhist center in New York chanted twenty-four hours a day for Micah's safety and release. More than one person called upon the Catholic patron saint of hopeless cases. "I can't say I'm religious," Sheryl said, "but I'm burning up the lines to Saint Jude."

As Thursday afternoon darkened, we sat in our war room and waited, family filling the long, beige couches in front of the large TV. Waiting was much harder than acting.

As the deadline neared, people gathered together. In New York, friends held a vigil and others gathered in Washington, D.C. Still others boarded planes and trains to New York to be with us at zero hour.

Late on Thursday, we heard hopeful news. Sheik Jamal Uddin had flown to Nasiriyah in the middle of the night and had made contact with the Mahdi Army. His contacts said they did not have Micah but knew who did. They said Micah was "good," and promised Sheik Jamal Uddin that they would do everything to get Micah released.

Then our gamble paid off.

Eva's cell phone rang. Mitch told us that Sheik Aws had released a statement against kidnapping and had called for Micah's release. Once the word was out that Sadr had spoken first, Sheik Aws spoke out, a tremendous accomplishment. We all hugged in one giant lump, Kim joining in the mix.

But I guarded myself against too much optimism. Micah was still being held, and we weren't sure that the Martyrs Brigade would respond to the call.

Sheik Aws's statement was soon on the news, reported as DEATH THREAT LIFTED. "Sadr is against kidnapping," Sheik Aws said, "especially this journalist who rendered Nasiriyah a great service. We call upon the kidnappers to set him free and have tried many times to contact many groups to help us find out about his condition. Since the day he was kidnapped, we have been calling upon the kidnappers through mosque prayers to free him."

The condemnation against kidnapping found momentum. Not only Sheik Aws but also Sheik Basri, located in Basra, who had been instrumental in James Brandon's release, spoke out.

I was confident that these statements would buy us time, wedging a powerful gap between threat and hope, and that Micah would not be killed on Friday.

With a red marker, I drew a thick heart around Sheik Aws's name on our chart on the wall, and also one around Sheik Basri's name.

"Anyone who speaks publicly for Micah gets a heart," I said.

I stepped back to look at our chart. We had two hearts. We needed more. I looked up to the top of the chart, where Sadr's name dominated all the others, all arrows pointing to it. I still wanted him to speak out directly; then I would draw a heart around his name. The more hearts, the better for Micah.

I had only managed to get a few hours of half sleep, after another night mauled by mosquitoes. The guards woke us just before daybreak, instructing Amir and me to take our mats and follow them.

We walked for several hundred yards toward a thicket of scrub trees about six feet tall. I watched the larger guard as he ambled along. He was out of shape and walked with ponderous movements, breathing heavily. If it came to it, he would be the easier one to go after.

The guards told us to move twenty feet into the thicket so we could not be seen.

"They don't like foreigners around here. If the locals know an American is here, they will kill you." Now, in an ironic twist of fate, our kidnappers were also our protectors. We entered the thicket and laid out our mats under the low branches.

As the morning unfolded, I couldn't stop thinking about the two videos.

"Am I betraying Marie-Hélène when I appear on TV?" I asked Amir, upset at how I had been used, and filled with shame and remorse for not resisting more.

"No," Amir said firmly. "You are not the first to appear on TV. It is false heroism to refuse. You have no choice. You may have lost the battle, but you have not yet lost the war. You are alive. People will understand." His words comforted me; I needed to hear them.

The morning passed slowly. Around noon, one of the guards returned with food, water, and news.

"It has been announced on the radio that Sheik Aws al-Khafaji made a plea at the Friday prayer that the hostages should be released."

The guards said it had been one of the largest prayer gatherings in Nasiriyah. Thousands of people had come to show support for Amir and me and demand our release. The guard brought a small radio with him so we could listen. Amir and I were ecstatic.

"I guess you are free," the two guards said with smiles. *Free* was the sweet word I had been thirsting, dreaming, hoping for, but still several hours into the marshes with our kidnappers, I felt anything but free. We knew nothing of the efforts going on in the outside world. What had compelled Sheik Aws al-Khafaji's sermon, I wondered.

"What now?" I asked Amir as our euphoria subsided. "Do we just walk to Nasiriyah?"

"No, we wait. They will come to take us."

By midafternoon, it seemed that no one was coming. I knew these situations were volatile and could change quickly. Sheik Aws al-Khafaji had called for our release. Two guards thought we were free, but what about the Grim Reaper, and the disagreement between the brothers? Would they agree to let us go? I began thinking again about escape. We were in a much more remote part of the marsh, making escape far more difficult. And we were surrounded by people who hated Americans so much that even my kidnappers were worried for my safety, and theirs.

We spoke to one of the guards about how important it was for us to get a message to our families to tell them we were alive. I recognized his voice; he was the same guard from the first night who had asked for seventy thousand dollars. He now spied another opportunity to make money, suggesting that he could bring us a satellite phone. If he brings us a phone, I thought, someone might be able to trace the signal and locate us. I would call Marie-Hélène and tell her to trace the call without the guards figuring it out. She would find a way to send help, and an hour later a helicopter would descend into the marshes. The guards would look over in awe, without firing a shot, as Amir and I would climb on.

We agreed to pay the guard five hundred dollars if he could get a phone from Mr. Hamdani and bring it to us: three hundred for the phone and two hundred for him. Mr. Hamdani would give him the money.

"How do I know Mr. Hamdani won't capture me and turn me over to the police?" the guard asked.

We told him that we would write a note saying not to harm him, and he could give it to Mr. Hamdani. Mr. Hamdani would do nothing to him if he saw that note. After agreeing on the details, we decided to wait to see what happened that day. If we were not released by the evening, we would arrange with him to get the phone the following day.

We sat for a while thinking about this plan and everything that could go wrong. The Grim Reaper could find the satellite phone. Mr. Hamdani could have the guard followed or arrested. Or the guard might take the money and never return.

The guard interrupted my thoughts.

"How can I go to America?" he asked. Most Iraqis would jump at the chance to go to America, but that my kidnapper would want to go to the land of his enemy surprised me.

"It's difficult now. It's hard to get a visa," I said. "Why would you want to go to America?"

"There is nothing here for me. Can you help me?"

I tried to imagine what I would put on the visa sponsorship application. "Relationship of applicant to sponsor: kidnapper."

He looked down, fiddling with the strap on his gun, realizing the hopelessness of his request.

In the late afternoon, a guard returned with more water and told us the fighting had resumed in Najaf. I closed my eyes; terrible news. We were still captive, and even though they said we would be released, I knew there were no guarantees. It seemed our fate was linked with Najaf and our story was not yet over. As the sun set, the guards led us back to the field in front of the *madhif*. Amir and I laid out our mats and sat down.

A young man came from the house carrying a metal tray covered in rice on which there were three cooked chickens. The family that owned the house had prepared a large meal, a dinner to celebrate our freedom. "You are our guests," a young man said from behind his keffiyeh as he set the tray in front of us. He brought out a pail of water and a bar of soap for us to wash our hands. The two guards, Amir, and I sat together eagerly digging into the chickens with our fingers, our first real meal in eight days.

After we ate, I listened as Amir spoke to the guards about our work as filmmakers, suggesting that we would come back with Marie-Hélène to make a film about the marshes. Carried away by the thought of freedom, he said that the guards could even be our guides. The guards smiled, happily offering their services.

"What are you talking about?" I said to Amir under my breath. "These men are kidnappers." Perhaps, knowing we were still not free, his promise of future work was another way of befriending them.

As a red sun hung at the edge of the marshes, bats flew overhead, looping small, dark forms cutting the still night air, picking off the mosquitoes that had come to dine as well.

"Shhhh." One of the guards held a finger in the air. Faint, desperate cries like those of a child grew in the distance, first one, then many. The sounds became louder and louder, growing into a wild cacophony of howls and screams that rose from the marshes.

"Jackals," he said as the sounds faded into the distance. "They come at night. The marshes are full of animals. There is a large turquoise snake that lives in the *madhif.* If you see her, don't be alarmed."

"The snake bit a woman last week and she had to be taken to the hospital," the other guard added as he lay on his side, picking his teeth with a stick. His AK was resting on the blanket next to me. He had set it down while getting up to adjust his dishdasha and had forgotten to pick it up. The simple black gun with a wooden handle and tape around the bullet clip was just a few inches from my hand. I looked at Amir, then back at the gun. Amir thought for a moment, then gave a slight shake of his head. Wait.

We sat with the two guards listening to the sounds of the marshes and watching the night sky as it turned from deep blue to black. In the distance I could see small lights from airplanes moving low on the horizon, passing slowly from left to right about every half hour. I thought about who was in those planes, and how different our realities were at that moment. "They are American planes patrolling the Iranian border," the guard said, but Amir didn't believe him; he didn't believe we were that close to the border.

Then the guards pointed up at a large, fiery white object with a long tail moving slowly between the stars. I had seen meteors before. They were small, usually only a pinpoint and moved so quickly they covered the arc of the constellations in seconds. If you blinked you missed it. This was different, more like a comet, a glowing smudge across the sky. We marveled at it for a few minutes, until it faded from view. The two guards speculated on the strange sign from the heavens.

"He thinks it's the Mahdi spaceship," Amir said, laughing.

The larger guard turned to me.

"What do you think it is? Do you think it's the Mahdi spaceship?" he asked.

"Yes," I replied, "it could be the Mahdi spaceship." Why not?

I took it to be a sign that the cosmos was celebrating our impending freedom. Amir saw it as simply a comet.

. . .

In Shi'ite theology, al-Mahdi, Abu'l-Qasim Muhammad ibn Hasan, the Twelfth Imam, born in the ninth century A.D., vanished at the age of five. Known as the "divinely guided one," he will one day return to Earth to lead the forces of righteousness against injustice, tyranny, and the forces of evil. The Mahdi will prevail and the Day of Judgment will follow with the return of Christ and the other eleven Imams. The texts say nothing about returning by spaceship.

Wisely, Muqtada al-Sadr assumed the mantel of the divine Mahdi, not for himself but for the legions of poor, uneducated young men who flocked to his cause. They rallied under the black banner, a widely recognized apocalyptic sign in Shi'a Islam that the Mahdi is coming, envisioning themselves as the army of "the divinely guided one," who would bring justice for the underserved and rid Iraq of the tyranny of foreign domination. Sadr's approach angered many Shi'ites we knew in Nasiriyah, who told us that Sadr's militia was not Mahdi's army. They did not believe al-Mahdi was coming, at least not anytime soon.

I heard the grinding of a car engine; then two white lights emerged from the darkness. The headlights cut a trail across the field, drawing a swift line from the scrub, across our blankets, to the taller palms in the distance. The old car swung around in a wide arc and stopped near where we were sitting. Two men got out and walked toward us, talking and laughing. They were in a good mood. One was the Grim Reaper.

"Are we going to Nasiriyah?" Amir asked.

"Yes." He repeated his usual refrain: "Soon. It's too late tonight. Tomorrow."

I lay down again. Another night in the marshes. The Grim Reaper sat talking to the others as I tried to sleep.

Sleeping was impossible. The mosquitoes attacked incessantly, but the wool blanket, my only protection, was too hot to sleep under. For a time I would lie under the blanket, completely covered except for a small hole to breathe through. Every few minutes a mosquito would find its way in through that hole and I would slap my face, closing the opening until I could no longer hold my breath. When the heat became too intense, I would throw off the blanket and lie there, allowing the mosquitoes to attack at will. Then I would shake off the blanket of mosquitoes, pull the wool blanket over me, and repeat the process.

During this period of half sleep while under the blanket, I heard voices in the distance; people were approaching. I lay absolutely still, holding my breath. The Grim Reaper and his companion got up to meet them, but within an instant they were upon us. Immediately there was shouting, and the metallic draw of several AKs being loaded. The Grim Reaper was doing most of the talking, replying to the shouts of the leader of the unknown group. They must have heard there was a foreigner here and come to kill me. My heart beat quickly as I lay motionless, pretending to be asleep under the blanket.

The shouting went on for at least half an hour. I couldn't understand what was said but could clearly understand the nature of it. The Grim Reaper was doing his best to calm them, and finally managed to negotiate the conversation into a normal banter. There was no more shouting, just boisterous talk. The Grim Reaper said something to Amir, who immediately sprang up.

"Micah, get up. Everything is okay," Amir said in English.

This seemed like a bad idea. What possible good could getting up do? I slowly pushed the heavy wool blanket away. Drenched in sweat, I felt a sudden coolness on my skin as it evaporated in the dry night air.

"Aesh?" What? I said in a low whisper, doing my best to blend into the night, and avoid the stares of four unknown men with AKs sitting near us.

"It's okay," Amir said, laughing. "These men came here tonight because they say someone poisoned their pond, killing all the fish. They came here to have a gun battle. When they saw you they said, 'Is the sleeping man the one who poisoned the fish?' pointing their guns at you. They were going to shoot you!"

Fishermen in the marshes sometimes used poison to explode the lungs of fish and collect them as they floated to the surface. The situation was absurd, and under other circumstances I might have found it amusing. But out in the marshes in the middle of the night, knowing that I had narrowly avoided an accidental execution as a fish poisoner by the chance arrival of the Grim Reaper, it was not the least bit funny.

"Where is he from?" one of the men asked the Grim Reaper.

"Amreeka."

"Ahhhh," he said.

One of the four men walked over and bent down to look at me. "Amerekee."

He squatted squarely in front to examine me closer. A broken pair of glasses with tape sat at an awkward angle on his face. He put his face right up against mine and tilted his head from side to side, looking me over. I sat motionless, staring back at him, trying not to show any expression. He locked onto my gaze about four inches from my nose. After an uncomfortably long silence, he leaned in closer and shouted, "Boo!"

I remained still, coolly looking at him. He stood back up, laughing. There was laughter all around as I thought about the internationally accepted use of the interjection *boo*. The four men left, walking into the darkness, satisfied that we hadn't poisoned their fish and having satisfied their curiosity about the captive American.

"Great, now they know there is an American here," I said to Amir, pulling the thick wool blanket back over my head.

"Never mind." Amir was still laughing to himself about the encounter. "They were going to shoot us over poisoned fish," he said incredulously.

A while later the Grim Reaper left as well, the old car retracing the arc back over the small hill and out of sight.

Early Friday morning, as I awoke, I felt more hopeful. The flurry of diplomatic negotiations between James and Sheik Aws, between Osama and Sheik Aws, with Jamal Uddin, with others seemed to be going well. James had spoken to both Sheik Aws and Sheik Raad, on Thursday, thanking them for issuing the statement against Micah's kidnapping. I wanted to contact Sheik Aws directly if things did not move by the end of the day. Sheik Aws agreed to talk, and gave James the number of a safe house he stayed at during the night. We wrote the number on our wall chart, and waited to hear more news.

At nine A.M., Amir's brother emailed me again, a short message full of hope:

```
Dear Helene
Call me soon there are a very good news about the
situation Mich will be free today or tomorrow
```

Sheik Aws had preached the noon sermon at Friday prayers in Nasiriyah. People in Nasiriyah knew that the topic would involve the journalist hostage and their neighbor Amir Doshi. The mosque filled, more than usual. People flowed through the doors, in one of the largest turnouts. Sheik Aws called for Micah and Amir's release.

Amir's brother must have gone to the mosque, or heard from people on the street. His message did not mention Amir, but given his enthusiasm, I suspected they would be released together.

In calling for Micah's release, Sheik Aws was following a tradition. When Sheik Aws had been imprisoned by Saddam's security forces in the 1990s, Muqtada al-Sadr's father, Mohammed Sadeq al-Sadr, had called for the release of Sheik Aws and other prisoners. When Muqtada al-Sadr's uncle Mohammed Baqir al-Sadr was imprisoned by Saddam in 1980, Mohammed Baqir's sister, Amina al-Sadr, a respected writer known also as Bint al-Huda, delivered a fiery appeal from the Imam Ali

Mosque in Najaf calling for his release. She was also imprisoned, tortured, and killed. The women of Sheik Aws's family and Sheik Aws himself held a great admiration for Bint al-Huda. Having Eva deliver the statement for her brother fit with that tradition.

In the late morning, an AP story hit. Sheik Aws said the kidnappers had promised to set Micah free. "The kidnappers have put the journalist in a safe place, and expressed their readiness to release the journalist after Friday prayers," the story said. My heart soared. It was already evening in Nasiriyah, and perhaps the logistics were being worked out.

Sheik Aws said the Mahdi Army was against kidnapping, "especially this journalist who rendered Nasiriyah a great service." I wasn't sure if he was referring to the archaeology or the ambulance story. Regardless, Micah's stories trumped the fact that he was American, which meant that they understood and valued his work. It also showed how media savvy Sadr was. Sadr could use the call for Micah's release to further his political goals.

But like so much that week, my hope was jolted by a reversal.

Farther down in the article, another official in Sadr's office was quoted as saying that Micah would only be released "after the crisis in Najaf is defused." It wasn't clear whether this statement came from the Nasiriyah or the Najaf office, who the official was, or whether this was part of a political tango to keep pressure on the United States until the last minute.

Chantal had received an email from Ruth Pearl, who said she was encouraged by Sadr's aide's statement, though she hadn't seen the video of Micah—it would be too hard to watch. "Stay strong," she wrote.

At around one P.M., Agent Tom knocked on our door. With a big smile on his face, he opened his arms wide and said, "Draw a heart for the governor!" After much prompting and Rory's request, the governor of Dhi Qar province was helping, something Tom had learned from the FBI team in Baghdad.

"Here, you do it," I told Tom, handing him our red marker.

Tom positioned himself in front of the poster and drew a large heart around the governor's name. Standing back and surveying his work, he leaned in for a final touch, adding a cupid's arrow that pointed down.

"Usually heart arrows point up," I said, approaching the sheik chart.

Tom stepped back with a laugh, giving me a look that warned me not to jump on him again. Then he opened his arms and I gave him a hug. After several twenty-four-hour days, Tom had given up the dark suit for a T-shirt, jeans, and flip-flops. We felt like one team, one blob, working together.

Aparna returned to the hotel at around two P.M.

"I have a surprise for you!" she told us as she opened a large bag with items from our friends' vigil the previous night: pictures of Micah, messages for us, and a small video camera.

"Press play," the instructions read, the tape in the camera from our friends Dean and Michelle's engagement party a year earlier. Micah came to life on the screen. Dancing around the table to the beat of the SugarHill Gang's "Rapper's Delight," Micah sang the words to the song:

i said a hip, hop, a hippie to the hippie
to the hip hip hop, you don't stop

I turned up the volume. "Everyone!" Eva, Suzanne, Chantal, Jonathan, Nieves, Loren, Nabila, Leslie, Alan, and Sally gathered round as Micah continued:

and guess what America, we love you
cause ya rock and ya roll with so much soul

We pressed rewind. We couldn't get enough of this new video, a much-needed suspension from the exhausting cycle of emotions.

Kim and Tom arrived immediately after I phoned them.

"Wow," Tom said as the last "hip, hop, a hippie to the hop" faded into the background. "Well, just send this to the kidnappers and they'll let him go right away," he added with a wink.

A couple of hours later our hotel phone rang. From the FBI room, Kim told us to turn on the TV. "There's another video."

We all ran into the room, our gaze unraveling to the television.

Micah, Micah! We stared, stretching our hands out to the screen. Micah was alive.

"I am an American journalist in Iraq. I have been asked to deliver a message."

Micah had been looking into the camera, and suddenly his head bobbed forward slightly. He looked up again. "I am in captivity and being treated well."

The reporter presenting the segment came back on, saying that the tape continued, and that Micah said he had been asked to call for an end to the massacre in Najaf. There was no mention of a deadline.

My cell phone rang. The woman assigned to our case at the State Department spoke. "We'd like to let you know that we are in possession of another videotape of Micah."

Before I could say that I was watching it as it was being broadcast around the world, she continued.

"It was dropped off at CBS this morning. The guy dropping it off asked for money. Can you believe that? Of course they said no. Anyway, it shows Micah. He is drinking tea with his kidnappers and says he is being treated well." Tea? I didn't know what she meant by that. It wasn't a tea party. It was a proof of life.

"I'm watching it right now."

The door burst open and Nabila walked in as quickly as her cane would allow. "Look, look," she said, motioning with her eyes to the TV. She lifted her arms to the sky, dropping her cane. Her smile was wet, covered by the tears that fell down her face.

"Oh God, thank you. *Alhamdulillah.*"

The CNN reporter was hazy behind everyone's kiss marks on the screen.

"The wallpaper, oh the wallpaper!" Nabila continued.

"What about the wallpaper?" I asked.

"The wallpaper has replaced the men. The wallpaper—and it's a nice wallpaper at that. He is being treated as a guest. He is not being threatened with death. This is different, now. The situation, it has changed. Completely."

We looked more closely at the screen. The wallpaper was cream colored with some sort of spiral design. Wallpaper gave the sense of affluence and a residence, not of a hiding place. Someone's house.

Aparna wiped the kiss marks from the screen so we could see the TV image better. "There he is!" she said.

"He looks strong," Eva remarked, staring at the screen without blinking, not wanting to miss an instant.

We began to deconstruct the scene, sitting on the floor, leaning against the wall. Much in the video was obvious, yet much had to be interpreted.

"Obviously, he is being forced to say this," I said. "He would never say it otherwise."

"People will understand he said it under duress," Chantal said.

It played again. We continued to analyze it.

"He's wearing the same shirt."

"His face looks good. I don't see any marks."

"He hasn't shaved."

"Look at those dark circles under his eyes."

"Why is he bobbing his head?"

"I didn't see the bob."

"Maybe he is drugged?"

"He's probably really tired, and hasn't slept."

"Maybe he fell asleep."

"But he is choosing his words carefully."

His words might save his life, if he was being used as a mouthpiece. But maybe they were just being wrung out of him, and then he wouldn't be worth anything anymore. I worried, focusing on the good but not losing sight of all possibilities.

Though I was more and more hopeful, the future was still uncertain. CNN repeated what we had been hearing for a few hours: that an al-Sadr aide had been "assured" that French-American journalist Micah Garen would be released by his kidnappers either Friday or Saturday.

If he was going to be released, this video did not make much sense. He couldn't repeat a demand—"stop the massacre in Najaf"—that could not be met and then be released. The fighting had slowed in Najaf, it seemed to be a standoff, and no one knew where Sadr was.

"Mitch is really worried about Najaf," I said, "He thinks it's the wild card. We can't control that."

Rumors were circulating that Sadr wanted to end the fighting and hand over the keys to the Shrine of Imam Ali, but claimed he could find no higher religious authority to whom he could give the keys.

"Dad called a CNN journalist who was in Najaf and spoke about Micah," Eva said. "I don't know how he found her, or got through. He could hear the fighting in the background. He said he was as worried for her as she was about Micah. But she said she was going to try to get into the mosque and deliver the message about Micah to Sadr people she knew."

Three things seemed important for Micah's safety: that the fighting stop in Najaf, that the Iraqi army not attack the mosque, and that Sadr hand the keys to the mosque over to Sistani. But realities on the ground and negotiations for Micah's release might or might not converge.

Increased fighting in Najaf would likely end the positive momentum. Our appeals to Sadr and Sadr clerics would be useless if the shrine was destroyed or Sadr killed. Under the headline TAKE THAT, KOOKY MOOKIE, the New York Post ran a photo of Muqtada al-Sadr and a large explosion in Najaf, next to a picture of Micah with the caption LIFE AND DEATH SITUATION.

A single bomb could end days of negotiation.

I continued to try to visualize Micah moving away from his kidnappers. In my mind, the hardest part had already happened: he had been able to get up from his kneeling position in the video. But he stood still, not moving forward, not moving toward me.

In my mind I also saw the kidnappers. I focused on them, too. Listen to Sadr, listen to Sheik Aws. Then, please, have compassion, have pity, have mercy. I prayed that their hearts be softened, that they think of Micah as a person, that their ears be opened and they hear our calls, especially the calls of Sheik Aws. Suddenly, as I visualized them, one kidnapper began to move. He dropped his gun to his side and began to turn away. After five days of praying and visualizing the static scene, the scene had begun to change.

By five P.M., there was still no news of Micah's release. I tried not to worry; after all, we were focused now on Micah's release, not Micah's execution. Momentum was critical: pulling in the right people, connecting them, creating a spirit of interest and action, and exerting enough pressure until Micah was released. I was afraid that the longer Micah remained in captivity, the more momentum was lost. The kidnappers could change their minds, or there could be another attack on Najaf, or he could be sold. Anything was still possible.

A strange news report appeared in the Italian newspaper Corriere della Sera, saying that an Italian special ops unit had attempted to find Micah somewhere near Nasiriyah. The unit was apparently headed to where they thought Micah was being held, and there was gunfire. An Italian soldier was wounded, but not seriously, and the mission continued. There was no other information. We were so close to Micah's release, I hoped this report wasn't true. Surely we would have heard about this through the FBI, and they hadn't mentioned anything to us.

Eva got a frantic call from Sally. Alan had to be rushed to the hospital; stress and lack of sleep complicating an existing medical condition. Agent Tom ran from his room to help Alan to the ambulance, but Alan insisted on walking. Distraught, but afraid to stop working, Eva called Jonathan so he could meet the ambulance at the hospital.

"I don't know how you're handling all this," Kim told Eva, as they watched Alan and Tom disappear behind the closing elevator doors.

By late Friday evening, we were getting encouraging reports from Iraq. Wendell Steavenson, a British writer working on a book about Iraq and a friend of Micah's from the Dulaimi, wrote to send good news from Najaf. Her fiancé, Gaith Abdul-Ahad, an Iraqi photographer shooting for Getty Images, had been in Najaf for the last month. He had been reporting from inside the Shrine of Imam Ali since Monday, and had access to a lot of Sadr and Mahdi Army people. He had been asking them daily about Micah, pushing for their involvement and help. With the fighting raging, Gaith seemed to them "a man from the desert" asking such questions about an American hostage. Because they were under constant bombardment and lines of communication were "not the best," he dialed the Nasiriyah Sadr office on a satellite phone and got through. He ran up to his Sadr contact in the Imam Ali Mosque, as the Mahdi Army fought outside in the streets, and put the phone to his contact's ear.

"Tell him I know Micah is a journalist," he said. "Please ask for his help."

Mitch emailed that while still in hiding, Sadr had released a written statement about Micah on his letterhead. It said, "From the lips of Sheik Muqtada himself, let him go within 48 hours and do not harm him."

The statement was delivered by hand, and by word of mouth to journalists in the shrine, and the message quickly made its way around the world.

It was time for a big red heart around Sadr's name.

Micah, Saturday, August 21

We awoke just as dawn was breaking. There was a strange, still, desolate beauty to the place: an abandoned marshy plateau hidden in a remote corner of the world. The two guards told us to gather our mats and follow them back to the thicket. As the sun rose, the heat and the stifling humidity soon enveloped us. There was no wind, as if nature, too, were holding its breath.

The younger guard went back to the house, leaving us alone with the larger one. We sat under the low trees, trying to avoid the sun filtering through in fiery patches. Our one plastic bottle, full of cloudy water, was empty within an hour.

"Don't worry," the guard said, "he will come back with water."

Amir took the plastic bottle and went to the canal to fill it. He returned with even cloudier water, and proceeded to drink it in gulps. He offered me the bottle. I was parched but declined, and warned Amir not to drink the dirty salt water; it would make him even thirstier. But Amir's throat was burning, and he continued to drink.

By noon the heat had become unbearable. I sat with my shirt off, a layer of sweat coating my body. Amir, his body now burning with heat, stripped to his underwear and went to cool himself in the canal. The guard would only let us go one at a time. When he returned, I crawled through the thicket to wash myself. The water was a small, yellowish-green stagnant pool, a boil in a long, serpentine canal. Salt crystals encrusted the earthen walls, and a large pungent pile of human excrement sat perched at the side. I would rather suffer the heat.

"It's hot," Amir would say as he excused himself, returning again and again to bathe in the water, more like a baptism in anticipation of our liberation than salvation from the fiery air.

By midafternoon there were no sounds other than the incessant buzzing insects, possibly cicadas, whose pitch increased steadily as the temperature continued to climb. Then I heard movement in the distance. The guard was lying on his side, propped up on one arm, picking away the bark on a small stick. The AK was equidistant between us. I looked at Amir, then down at the AK. He looked at the gun, then back at me. I could read it in his eyes: "Maybe, but wait."

I motioned with my hand to get the guard's attention, pointing toward the sound. The guard lifted his head casually. Then we heard it again, louder, a stick cracking. Footsteps. His head jerked. He looked out toward where the sound was. I pointed to the gun. *Pick up the gun,* I thought to myself, trying to communicate with my eyes. He picked it up reluctantly and sat up, listening.

I knew he couldn't defend us against anyone who came, nor would he want to. I would be better off with the gun myself. The three of us sat there, motionless, ears tuned for any movement outside our hideout. Nothing.

We heard a man singing in the distance: *Abudiyya,* "father of pain," a lament often sung in southern Iraq. Then the splashing of water, and a child's voice. After a while the guard relaxed a bit and settled back on the mat, the AK close to his side.

"A man is fishing with his son," he said. "This area used to be under ten meters of water. It was a beautiful marsh, full of fish. Saddam drained it ten years ago. A few areas have not been drained, and men still fish there."

"Do people farm?"

"No, the soil is poisoned with salt. Most people have left."

Then we heard it again, definitely a stick breaking. In an instant the guard was on his feet, crouched, pointing the gun toward the sound. He whistled. Nothing. I crouched behind him. He couldn't be trusted to defend us. If anyone appeared I was going to grab the gun from him. Then we heard a whistle through the thicket. He lowered his gun. We heard footsteps, and the other guard appeared, the one who had offered to bring us the satellite phone, with a new bottle of cloudy water.

We would be free tonight, he said; they would take us to Nasiriyah. We told him that we had almost shot him because we thought he was a local coming to kill us. He laughed and pulled back his pant leg to show a clean circular red mark on the side of his knee where he had accidentally shot himself while cleaning his pistol a month earlier. The bullet had gone straight through.

After dropping off the water, the guard with the bullet hole in his knee left again. Amir and I quickly finished the bottle of cloudy water. When it was empty, Amir showed me the bottle cap. It was from a common brand of Iranian soda, Zam Zam, named after a holy well.

"They are under the thumb of Iran," Amir said quietly. "The radio stations they listen to are Iranian. Their weapons, the new black RPGs, come from Iran as well."

By sunset no one had returned. None of us wanted to remain in the thicket after dark, and we walked slowly back to the field, the large guard breathing heavily, adjusting his keffiyeh, and looking around cautiously as we made our way along the edge of the thicket. In the distance we heard the lonely cries of the jackals as the pack moved closer, then away again.

We stopped about one hundred yards from the house and knelt as the guard proceeded a bit farther, then returned. No one was there. We headed out straight toward a dirt road, keeping our distance from the house, and sat down in the ditch beside it.

"We will see them when they approach," he assured us. The day disappeared and the still, cool night emerged as we sat on our mats by the edge of the road. Leaving his AK near me, the guard knelt by the road to pray.

I could not take another night out there. I had not slept at all the previous night, and I was beginning to feel the severe tension of sleep deprivation, like a rope pulled taut.

An engine sputtered, then two headlights appeared, and in a moment an old Russian Volga was upon us. The guard rose to meet the car. The Grim Reaper had arrived and it was time to leave. Again Amir and I were blindfolded, our hands bound in front of us, and put in the back seat of the car.

Excited by the thought of freedom, Amir spoke constantly during the ride. At one point, I understood his words, as he told the kidnappers about our work on the archaeology, and the looting, mentioning Fajr and Rafa'i.

"Amir," I said quietly, "don't talk about the looting. These men are criminals. We don't know what connections they have."

Amir fell silent. After a while, I could tell something was wrong. The ride was too long. Though I couldn't see anything, I knew we were not approaching a city, since I could not hear other cars on the road.

"They aren't taking us to Nasiriyah," I said quietly to Amir. He made a noise of acknowledgment.

. . .

The car finally stopped. From the sounds ahead I judged that we were near some sort of wooden bridge. I had managed to nudge my blindfold up a bit and could vaguely make out a river and a bridge, a row of planks, dip low across the water, probably two hundred feet across, and rise on the other side. There were lights, and what looked like a small house on the opposite bank.

"What's going on? Where are we?" Amir asked the Grim Reaper.

"There is a police checkpoint ahead," he replied.

The guards ordered us out, moved us behind the car, and removed my blindfold. The Grim Reaper stood with the AK in his right hand while the others went ahead. After about a half hour they returned; it was too dangerous to cross with us in the back seat. The Grim Reaper opened the trunk, his eyes fixed on the other side of the river, where the police checkpoint was supposed to be.

Amir turned to me. "They want us to get in the trunk."

"I am not getting in a trunk," I protested.

"It's just for a little way," Amir said.

"There is no way I am getting in a trunk," I repeated. "You can tell him that. He can shoot me now, but I am not getting in that trunk." Nothing would make me get in that trunk; I hadn't survived nine days of captivity just to die of asphyxiation.

The Grim Reaper shut the trunk.

"It is too late to go to Nasiriyah. We are headed to another place to sleep tonight."

"Just let us go here and we will walk," I said. The Grim Reaper didn't respond.

He led us to the other side of the road, down a ten-foot ditch, instructing me to hold Amir's arm and follow him into a field. Amir was still blindfolded and I had to walk him slowly through another field of thorns, at least one hundred yards, illuminated by the faint blue sliver of moonlight. As the occasional lights of a car would pass in the distance, the Grim Reaper would force us to the ground, then crouch, with his gun pointed to the road, watching. When we were far enough out, he told us to sit. He remained low to the ground with his gaze fixed on the road, never moving unless it was to stand up and look farther into the distance, then crouch down again.

I watched him closely, studying his profile, without a keffiyeh for the first time. He was at least six feet, about thirty, thin, and muscular, wearing a black T-shirt. A fighter solidly in his element, he assiduously observed the movements of his enemy from a distance.

After nearly two hours, the Grim Reaper directed us to follow him back toward the car. Two guards had returned and they spoke for a moment, then ordered us to get into the back seat and held our heads down as the car headed across the bridge. I could feel the wheels bumping along the wood planks, then up the other side. There was a bright light, then darkness. What had happened to the checkpoint, I wondered. A few minutes later, the car stopped again and we were led quickly into a house.

We found ourselves alone in a large, cold, empty communal room with light blue walls and fluorescent lighting; again our situation appeared to have gotten much worse. Amir had difficulty focusing on my questions—his torn feet felt like fire as he rubbed them in pain.

Then the man with the large plastic glasses—the one from the van on the first day, the one who had directed the first video—appeared from another room.

"Welcome, Mike," he announced. "Don't worry, tomorrow you will be free."

I didn't believe him.

"What do you think?" I asked Amir.

He tilted his head as if to say "Maybe."

"I saw your sister on television," the man with the glasses continued, handing me my watch, the one that had been taken at the Sadr office.

I could tell by the wrinkled corners of his eyes that he was smiling under his keffiyeh. My sister? On international television? Making a plea to millions of people around the world? With that strange image, a gap of time, space, and emotional distance had been bridged. The thought of my sister made me light up inside, but I was stunned at the momentousness of it: my sister seen all across the world, pleading for my life.

"My sister?" I said to Amir, still trying to imagine it. I worried about where Marie-Hélène might be. Had she come to Iraq?

"Would you like to watch TV?" the man with the glasses asked. Eagerly, we both said yes.

A guard brought in a large TV and turned on the news. Amir read the text in Arabic crawling across the bottom on Al Arabiya, following it joyfully with his eyes; the hostages would soon be released.

I was slowly coming to accept that we were going to be set free. As nine days of tension and fear receded, the news of our release felt like a warm wave washing over me. Amir asked why we weren't being released that night. The guard told him that another group had made a statement on the Internet that we would be set free that day. They were keeping us another day so the other group couldn't claim credit.

The guards brought us two scratchy wool blankets and two hard pillows, and in that room we slept soundly on the concrete floor for the first time in nine days.

I awoke, exhausted, just after the sun came up. We watched, hawklike, for more news.

Worried about the slowdown in momentum, and worried that the kidnappers might not heed Sadr's call, I spoke to friends about new avenues for action. Sheryl lined up an Iranian journalist friend, one of the few to have interviewed Sistani. "But we should wait," she cautioned. "We don't want to step on Sadr's toes."

A message about Micah appeared on an Islamist website and was quickly picked up. An Al Jazeera article online reported that a group calling itself the Secret Action Group of al-Mahdi Army had issued a statement that said, "As for the American journalist we have, we will release him tomorrow, Saturday, in the afternoon, because he disagrees very much with the American administration." The captive was not named, but Micah was the only American known to be held.

Three other journalists were now missing, two French and one Italian. I imagined families like ours going through the same horrible process. All three had stayed at the Dulaimi, and all had been en route to Najaf to cover the fighting. The two French journalists, Georges Malbrunot and Christian Chesnot, whom Micah and I knew from the Dulaimi, were said to have disappeared in Mahmudiyah, just south of Baghdad. Italian freelance journalist Enzo Baldoni was also missing, his driver apparently killed. At the Dulaimi a handwritten sign appeared in the elevator, FOR YOUR OWN SAFETY HERE, PLEASE LET US KNOW AT THE DESK IF YOU WILL NOT BE RETURNING AT NIGHT.

Mitch was still staying at the Dulaimi. Georges and Christian had been in Room 8, James Brandon had been in Room 9, and Micah and I had stayed in Room 10. Mitch was in Room 11. The logic of room numbers and journalists taken hostage was not good news for Mitch.

"I am the cursed man of the Dulaimi," Mitch told Abu Noor at the front desk, thinking of the three now-empty rooms in ascending order. "Please move me to Room 7."

. . .

The Al Jazeera article ended with Sheik Aws's quote about what he said was Micah's position against the war, but did not include the rest of the statement made by the Secret Action Group of al-Mahdi Army. Reuters did, reporting that the group had also threatened to destroy 75 percent of the oil facilities in southern Iraq if U.S. troops and Iraqi forces did not leave Najaf by eleven P.M. on Saturday, Baghdad time.

While that was troubling, there was also a bright side that fit into the kidnappers' shift in approach toward Micah. Again in the name of Najaf, the kidnappers, having taken another name, or perhaps another group entirely, were no longer threatening Micah directly but the oil pipelines. They were targeting economic interests and the ultimate symbol of the war, rather than an American citizen.

Suzanne, busy caring for us, came by with bottles of water, a large Tupperware container full of vitamins, and nasal spray so we wouldn't get sick. Alan, insisting on returning as soon as he could, had been released from the hospital and was feeling better. The family gathered in the war room to share news and update one another on our work.

Alan stared at our makeshift shrine, pictures of Micah in the center. "What have you done to Micah?" he laughed, shaking his head, scientific rationalism colliding with our syncretic spiritualism.

"On your way out, please take a Buddha," Jonathan added with a smile.

Chantal, Eva, Aparna, and I took another quick hallway break to work off the tension, and our now steady room-service diet of Ooey Gooeys—a brownie sundae deluxe. Stockinged feet running up and down the anonymous, carpeted corridors, Zeugma at our heels, we returned to our room out of breath, locking the door behind us.

By the afternoon, it seemed from the lack of news that the negotiations were breaking down; the kidnappers had different ideas of what to do with Micah, and were beginning to split into factions. James, Rita, and several Iraqi drivers began planning a trip down to Nasiriyah to speak directly to Sheik Aws if Micah wasn't released soon. Mitch continued instant messaging with Joel:

> *Mitch:* hey . . . osama just called, he says no progress, but Sheik Aws is still working. . . . I'm starting to get more worried, we also

have a missing Italian and maybe two missing French journos
around najaf.

Joel: any details on what's holding things up?

Mitch: Sounds like the kidnappers are being belligerent with Aws
now and might have some splits within their own camp . . . but
things are vague. Aws is still working on it.

Piece by piece, we learned that although Sheik Aws had influence as
the highest-ranking Sadr cleric in Nasiriyah, he was having trouble with
the negotiations. The kidnappers were angry about many things. They
had found an American they believed to be a spy, and had taken him directly to the Sadr office. Sheik Aws had not been there at the time, and a
junior cleric had told them, Everyone is in Najaf, why are you bringing us
a hostage? What do we care? The kidnappers felt they had not been
shown respect. Whether they were trying, like a gang initiation, to do
something spectacular to impress the Mahdi Army or they hoped to extract money from the Sadr office or they thought they could single-
handedly affect the outcome in Najaf, at the very least they believed that
Micah's abduction would help the Sadr cause.

That initial rebuff made the negotiations harder. Then the negotiations took a turn for the absurd. First, the governor insisted that Micah be
turned over to the Iraqi police, who would then drive him to Baghdad to
deliver him to the Interior Ministry, as a political gift of sorts. Because of
the fighting in Najaf, because militants controlled many roads, and because the Iraqi police were themselves targets, this plan was more dangerous for Micah than staying where he was. An argument ensued. Then
it was the Sadr office's turn. Sheik Aws wanted the governor to provide a
physical receipt upon delivery of the captive, saying that no ransom had
been paid and that the captive had been delivered unharmed. The governor would not provide such a receipt. Another argument ensued. The
discussions stalled.

A faction of the kidnappers, led by one of the brothers, tired of the
whole thing and wanting it to end, met with Sheik Aws. They demanded
a reimbursement for their expenses. We caught a spy and brought him to
you, the faction told Sheik Aws, and you did not want him. Now he has
eaten twelve dollars worth of food and water and who is going to reim-
burse us? At twelve dollars, Micah would probably have been the lowest-
ransomed hostage in history. You don't get anything, Sheik Aws replied.

No one told you to kidnap him and you don't get anything. Osama was ready to pay twelve dollars out of his own pocket, but Sheik Aws refused.

The other brother then approached Osama with a different plan. He would rekidnap Micah and sell him to Osama and the Iraqi police for several thousand dollars. While others were away, he would run out with Micah from the house and into the road, where Osama would be waiting. No, that would not work, Osama told him. Too dangerous.

The brothers' father was brought in to help negotiate. And then something unexpected occurred.

On Saturday evening, someone leaked to Al Arabiya the news that Micah and Amir had been released; another group was taking credit. The kidnappers and Sheik Aws were livid. The media moment had been ruined. There would be no press conference, no platform, no political benefit to the release. Negotiations were over.

Osama called Mitch, who called Joel. You've got to do something, he said. Joel reached his contacts at Al Arabiya. Explaining that the report had killed the negotiations, he insisted, "You have to take this off the air, immediately." The producers were sympathetic, and said they would do what they could to correct the story. Joel anxiously watched the next broadcast. With a few minutes to go at the end of the news segment, just as he was losing hope, the last story aired, clarifying that Micah and Amir had not been released. Joel quickly called Mitch, who called Osama to relay the news, hoping it would help.

By Saturday evening in New York, the middle of the night in Iraq, there were no more calls, no updates, no news.

We had to wait another day.

I awoke Sunday feeling relaxed and hopeful. Three guards were watching us. They never revealed their faces, hidden behind well-wrapped keffiyehs, a clue I took to mean we would soon be free.

After black tea and *khubz*, they offered us a shower and took our clothes to wash and iron. It had been ten days since I had had a shower and clean clothes. As I emptied my pockets, a guard picked up my shiv and examined it. "Mosquito bite scratcher," I said, showing him my feet, still raw from the bites. He didn't look impressed or intimidated, and handed my small weapon back to me.

I stood under the trickle of warm water for fifteen minutes as a young man in a dishdasha and keffiyeh with an AK on his lap sat outside. The small window in the shower stall framed a picture of a bright yellow cement complex, a few palm trees—nothing recognizable.

After our showers, the guards led us from the communal room to the bedroom, which had a king-sized bed, armoire, mirror, and nightstand in matching wood veneer. A large television rested on a table near the back wall. Behind it, a mattress was propped up vertically, covering the only window. The guards would occasionally stand up and peer out from behind the mattress when they heard a car pass.

At a computer resting on a small desk to the right of the television, the young guards would sit for hours with their keffiyehs wrapped tightly around their heads, AKs resting on the ground, blasting digital tanks and shooting imaginary combatants.

A guard switched on the television and handed me the remote. It was satellite TV from Europe. Amir and I flipped through the channels, switching from BBC to Al Arabiya to Al Jazeera until we had caught up on the news. Having satiated ourselves with current events, we settled on a BBC call-in show. The subject was the situation in Iraq. I turned to Amir and commented, using one of his favorite words, "It would be quite a postmodern moment if we could call in from here." He laughed.

They wouldn't release us during the day: too much of a risk of being seen. As the day wore on, my energy level dropped dramatically and I became depressed. I realized how much more difficult it was to be confined indoors.

In the early afternoon, they brought us a full meal of *d'jaj wa timann*, rice and chicken, and watermelon. They wanted us to be well fed. *D'jaj wa timann* was the regular meal Marie-Hélène and I had eaten with Amir every afternoon in his translation bureau in Nasiriyah. After more than a month I had grown sick of it. But after nine days in the marshes, I devoured it until I felt bloated, then fell asleep on the bed.

I awoke an hour later to the vision of a naked woman dancing around in front of me with a home appliance. I squinted, one eye peering over the blanket, trying to focus. Some kind of strange soft-core porn was on the television, a cross between pornography and a home shopping channel. I lay motionless on my side with my back to the guard, so he wouldn't know I was awake. He had muted the sound so we wouldn't wake up as he peered at the Western perversions that paraded across the screen. After a while he flipped through the channels, then returned to the woman and her appliance. He turned it off when he heard another guard approaching.

The phone rang early on Sunday morning. "We've got to talk to you," Tom and Kim said from their room, asking that only Eva and I go up.

"What is it?"

"Just come upstairs, please."

Eva led the way to the elevator, past a slow-moving tableau of blissful tourists in the fountained courtyard below. We tried not to run, the carpeted hallway absorbing the sound of our quickening steps.

Their door was ajar. We pushed it open as we knocked.

Kim looked at our faces. "First, don't worry. This is the deal. They've said they would release him, but until now, nothing has happened. We want to get this resolved. The Special Forces are on the ground. They are assessing the situation and will decide whether to go in and get him."

Eva and I looked at each other. Were the negotiations over? Was military action our last hope? What if Micah got killed during a rescue attempt?

"It could be dangerous," Eva said. "There could be a firefight, things could go wrong. He could get shot."

"Look, our Special Forces know what they're doing," Tom said. "These guys are loaded with weapons. They're highly trained. They've been on call, waiting to bring him out."

Tom's face was slightly red and his eyes watered. "You've got to imagine who they are—big, tough guys, the best trained we've got, knives in their teeth, paint on their faces, ready to go and get Micah out."

"Of course, it's not that we don't trust them—if anyone were to go out, we'd want it to be them," I said. "We're just wondering if now is a good time. Osama said that Sheik Aws has gone out to keep talking to them."

"Listen, this time, it's not up to you, okay? You've been involved all along and made many decisions," Tom said. He looked at us as we sat opposite him and Kim. "This is a decision that only they can make. They are going to spend the next couple of hours surveying the situation and going through various scenarios. Believe me, there won't be a situation that they won't have planned for."

"Are they going to storm the place?" I asked.

We imagined a hail of bullets in a small room, confusion, darkness.

"One of the brothers, the brother that wants to see Micah released, will help him escape," Tom said. "One scenario is that he might run out with him, and then Micah would be picked up."

"But someone could see them leave."

I imagined the Special Forces in full training for a rescue. They were probably at the base, waiting for a signal, or for information that would indicate where Micah and Amir were being held. I saw their determined faces in my mind, and wondered if they thought of their involvement as a last resort. At this point, they probably thought that the negotiations were almost as dangerous as storming wherever Micah was being held.

All Eva and I could imagine was a huge gun battle. We did not know much about the motivations of these kidnappers. They might be willing to die. A final, glorious battle could mean that many people would be killed. Storming the house could create a backlash. For all we knew, the plan to run out with Micah could be a trap. We could not understand the motivation for one brother to want to release Micah against his brother's wishes.

"Don't worry, because there is nothing you can do on this one," Kim continued. "Have faith in the Special Forces. They'll do what is best."

"What they've got to know, though, is that the negotiations are happening, and that things are looking good," I said. "We just don't want that jeopardized. Please tell them. Can you just relay that?"

"Of course, we already have," Kim answered. "Don't worry. We'll let you know as soon as we hear back."

"Listen here," Go-To Pete said. "I don't know what you're worried about. Me? If I heard they were going in, I'd just pack up right now. Case done. Case closed. They'd be gettin' him out. All right?" He looked at me, nodding, comforting me in his own way.

Kim urged us not to tell anyone about the possible raid. "We don't want it getting out," she said. "If it does, it could endanger the operation, and they might have to call it off."

"As long as it's a last resort," I said.

"Of course."

We were losing control. The negotiations could drag on, which was dangerous for Micah. Though the window was quickly closing, I still believed that the delicate and difficult work the blob had done—the connections, the appeals, the negotiations—could achieve Micah and Amir's release. A raid would force a conclusion, but it was all or nothing, and so many things could go wrong.

The possibilities of peril for Micah and Amir seemed to be increasing, not decreasing. In the back of my head other concerns whirled about: a soldier could get shot. I did not want anyone killed trying to rescue them. A kidnapper could get shot. I did not want that either, afraid of the repercussions it could have, with future retaliations against others. An innocent person could get shot, a family member, a bystander. The cycle of violence would extend into never-ending and unimaginable rings of possibilities.

For several hours, there was no news. Then Kim and Tom called us back.

"Please come upstairs." Eva and I ran.

The raid was off. No explanation why. We didn't know what would happen next.

Together, we sat and waited. Waited. Sat. The TV muted, we took turns holding the remote, too anxious to hear other news, waiting for an image of Micah. "Hang in there. Things are looking good," we heard from Mitch and Joel.

Chantal decided to go chant at the Buddhist center. She hadn't been out of the hotel for days. Aparna left with her on "Operation Underwear" to pick up clean clothes. Zeugma sat at my feet.

• • •

In Nasiriyah, the deputy governor of Nasiriyah, Adnan al-Sharifi, continued to apply pressure, telling Sheik Aws that the kidnapping of an American was bad for everyone. The American army would storm the city and a lot of people would be killed, he threatened. And people would blame the deaths on the Mahdi Army.

Osama was on his way to meet with the kidnappers when he heard that Sheik Aws had completely lost patience with them. Sheik Aws understood that the delays were bad for Sadr and dangerous for Micah, and decided to take action. With Mahdi Army militia as backup, Sheik Aws showed up where Micah was suspected to be held.

"We're here to take the American," he said.

By five P.M. I couldn't sleep anymore and sat up in bed. I looked at my watch. Just a few more hours.

"They will take us out at nine P.M.," I said to Amir, convincing myself that they would probably come one hour after sunset. Any later would be difficult. As it got close to nine, I started getting nervous.

Sure enough, at nine P.M., they came.

The guards looked for cloth to blindfold us. I had made sure to keep the same piece of cloth the entire ten days, the same banner from the Sadr office, the one used to bind my hands in the enclosure. Though it was dirty, the Sadr slogan painted in blue was still clearly legible. Amir's bindings had disappeared, perhaps left behind in the washing. The guard took the cloth from me and paused to read it slowly before tearing it in half, using the two halves to blindfold each of us. To see that cloth torn in half in our last hour of captivity was defeating. I wanted to maintain my memory of what had happened, and the few artifacts I could hang on to were key to doing so. I still had my shiv in my pants pocket and the small Roseman cigarette box cover that said MH, ZEUG, LOVE.

They bound our hands tightly and double-tied the blindfolds, then led us out through a hidden metal revolving door leading out from the room.

I could tell from the cloth seats, the sound the doors made when they closed, and the quiet engine that we were riding in the back of a modern car as we set off down the road.

"Mike, do you recognize me?" a voice asked. It was the kidnapper with the bullet hole in his knee who had wanted to come to America, sitting between Amir and me in the back. I told him I recognized his voice.

"How can I stay in contact with you when you are free? Can you give me your phone or address in America?"

"Email is best," I replied.

"What is your email?"

"I can write it for you, but you need to remove my blindfold."

He carefully lifted my blindfold up and handed me a notepad and a pen. The journalist in me wanted to give him my real email, but I didn't think it would be a good idea to maintain email contact with my kidnappers and gave him a fake Yahoo address. He thanked me and lowered my blindfold again.

They were criminals, but I felt pity for them: dirt poor, brutalized under Saddam, with no job prospects, losing friends and relatives every day, driven to do things they might not do living in a normal society. Asking their American captive for French perfume, a chance to go to the United States, or simply an email address—it was a pathetic and twisted situation, because they were fully capable of killing me if they had to.

In the car I tried to form mental pictures from the sounds I heard. For a while we were the only car on the road. Then I began to hear other cars pass, and I could see regular flashes from what must have been streetlights. The car stopped by a house with a barking dog. We heard voices; then we were taken out and put in another car.

"Good-bye, Mike," the kidnapper with the hole in his knee said as the car pulled out. After an hour in that car, we stopped and were led to a third car. That trip took less than ten minutes.

The men in the front seat explained to Amir that they were taking us to the Sadr office. One of the two was Amir's former student, who had not returned since the first night.

"Sadr's office? Tell them to drop us off at the museum," I said.

Amir relayed their words: there was going to be a press conference and we should thank Sheik Aws al-Khafaji and Sayed Muqtada al-Sadr, who had helped secure our release.

"Amir, what do you mean? Sadr's office is where this all started."

"Yes, yes, I know, but there will be a press conference. Thank him, and that is all. It is over." This was the way things were done.

"Fine, but I don't want to answer questions." Speaking at a press conference was the last thing I wanted, but I didn't see any way out of it.

I could tell we had entered Nasiriyah from the city sounds and the smooth paved street. The car picked up speed.

"Remove your blindfold."

We reached up with our hands and removed the blindfolds. The two men in the front looked back at us with big smiles, sharing in the excitement of the moment.

"You are free," they announced as we pulled up to Sadr's office.

Kim came down a while later, and quietly opened our door. "How far is Tallil Air Base from Nasiriyah?" she asked casually, poking her head into our room.

"*Why?*" I jumped up.

"Is there anything?" Eva asked.

"Nothing definite yet. We just need to know."

My mind whirled. All the trips Micah and I had taken down that dusty broken road flashed through my memory, jumbling together: the large power plant, the ziggurat of Ur in the distance, the Bedouin with their sheep, a long thin convoy of semitrucks along the horizon, stalls with names like *Indiana* selling Saddam relics to soldiers, and the slow dust-choked approach to the American checkpoint. Though half a world apart, Micah and I were both heading down that same road again.

"About twenty minutes, maybe half an hour," I answered.

"I'll check back in a bit," Kim said, returning to the FBI room.

I grabbed the phone and dialed Chantal's cell phone.

"Come back now," I told her. I did not want to say anything on the phone. "We have news about the package."

"What? What is it?" she asked.

"It's good, just come back."

"I'm on my way."

Chantal ran to Barnes & Noble to find Aparna. Scanning the crowd and not seeing her, she ran to the front desk.

"You need to make an announcement!"

"What's this concerning?" the clerk asked Chantal.

Not wanting to reveal anything, she grabbed the intercom. "Aparna Mohan to the front desk!"

People were gathered outside Sadr's office as we pulled up. Opening the car door, we were immediately surrounded by Arab cameramen and photographers.

It was like stepping out on a red carpet as Amir and I were led into the small white building, then into the room to the left, where we had originally been taken ten days earlier. The cameras were rolling. Sheik Aws al-Khafaji met us with outstretched arms and a big smile. I was directed to sit in a large plush, floral chair, while Amir sat to my left on a matching couch. Sheik Aws al-Khafaji took his seat behind a wooden desk. He welcomed us, offering cold water, then made a speech, which the Arab news crews filmed. Amir, translating, told me it was my turn to talk. All the cameramen and reporters turned to me.

"Thank him," Amir said.

I was conflicted; we were being set free where we had been blindfolded and led away ten days earlier. I still didn't know who had kidnapped us and who had liberated us, but I knew Sheik Aws had publicly called for our release. With many cameras trained on me, I thanked Sheik Aws for his help, and then repeated a quote that Amir had taught me.

"A revered man in Islam, Imam Ali, once said, 'Truth has left no friend to me.' But today we have many friends here in Nasiriyah." Amir translated and Sheik Aws al-Khafaji grinned a huge grin.

"Why did you come to Iraq?" a reporter on his knees in front of the group asked, holding a microphone up to my face.

I explained that I was here to bring attention to the tragic destruction of Iraq's culture and history.

"Do you plan to stay in Nasiriyah?" another reporter asked.

Certain that our friends in Nasiriyah—Mr. Hamdani, the governor, the deputy governor, and others—had done everything they could to help free us, I wanted to send a message of solidarity to them. Nasiriyah belonged to them, not the kidnappers, and they could not scare me away. "This experience has not made me want to leave at all. My plans are to continue on with this project."

"You can stay here. I will build you a house," Sheik Aws said, still smiling.

We stood up and a man came over and gave Amir a warm embrace. He was a friend who ran a humanitarian agency in Nasiriyah. Amir grabbed my hand, introducing me as we sat down with him on the opposite couch. Amir beamed, holding both our hands as he recounted our long journey.

A man with a small digital camera came up and said with a broad smile, "Micah, I am from the AP. Jeff says hi." Jeff was the Associated Press office manager in Baghdad. Marie-Hélène and I had met him a month before at a party. I was touched that Jeff had sent someone down. But where was someone who could help me? I looked around for a familiar face.

"Can we do an interview?" he continued.

"Sure," I replied. Still disoriented, I began to feel uncomfortable by the media spectacle, but caught up in the joy of being out of captivity, I forgot about my previous idea not to answer any questions.

"Can you hold this can of Pepsi?" he asked, handing me a can. Pepsi was a sign of success in Iraq. Holding a Pepsi at that moment was probably a visual clue that I was indeed free and okay.

"Sure," I laughed, holding it up. "This is *not* a product endorsement."

I thanked the American people; my sister, who had appeared on television; my family, my fiancée, who had been in Iraq working with me for three months; and, of course, Zeugma.

"Who's Zeugma?" a man to my left asked. I thought it was better to ignore the question.

Another man entered and asked me to come out to the courtyard to speak to Al Jazeera by satellite phone. In the courtyard, Sheik Aws handed me the phone.

"Tell us how you were kidnapped?" the voice on the other end asked.

"We were walking through the souk spending some time before going to work. I had a small camera with me and I was taking some pictures. People misunderstood what I was doing. So that was a misunderstanding by some people." I carefully navigated around the question, still not knowing who was responsible for the kidnapping and what role the Sadr office had played in my release. I didn't want to say anything that would create controversy, or anger the kidnappers if they happened to be standing right next to me. I was free; that was enough. Calling it a misunderstanding was my way of saying, Let's just forget about it, and let me go home.

There was a long pause.

"By who?"

"I think they felt that we were taking pictures and they didn't want me to take those pictures. There were many people on the street. I cannot specify who they were. They saw me while I was taking pictures with my camera. They knew I was a stranger and hence the misunderstanding, as I told you."

I gave a message of thanks to my family, friends in Nasiriyah, fiancée, and Sadr, then handed the phone back to Sheik Aws.

Mitch's driver and fixer, Osama, suddenly appeared, putting his hand on my shoulder. "Micah, man, we've been looking all over for you. Man, it's great to see you."

A familiar face! I hugged him. I knew Osama only through Mitch and wondered what he was doing in Nasiriyah.

"Who's looking for me?" I asked, still trying to put the pieces together.

"Your family. Everyone."

Everyone?

"Why did you come down?" I asked Osama.

"I am working for Mitch, for CPJ. Come on, I've got a car, I will take you over to the American base," he said, looking around nervously. He wanted to get me out of there right away.

"Hang on, let me tell Amir." .

Back inside, Amir was talking with the stout man from the Sadr office who had hit him with the cane. The stout man apologized to Amir, saying that he knew that Amir was a good man.

I told Amir I was heading over to the American base and asked him to wait for me while I went back to the courtyard to look for Osama. The crowd was thinning and Osama was nowhere to be found. I realized I would soon be standing alone at night in Sadr's office, where it had all started.

I thought quickly about where I should go: the Al-Janoub? The museum? Amir's house? I figured I should get to the American base, but would they let me in? I still didn't know if the American army had any knowledge of my kidnapping. I thought of what it would be like showing up late at night at the main checkpoint and trying to explain to the soldiers that I had been kidnapped. Would they believe me? They would radio it in, the public affairs officer would be off duty, and after a half hour they would say politely, "Sorry, sir, anyone else you want us to try?" I would sit out there on the darkened road, watching the insects swarm around in the bright spotlight until morning. It was the best option I could think of.

"Amir, can you take me to the American base?"

"Yes, certainly."

Amir's friend, the one from the humanitarian organization, was waiting in a car double-parked outside. As we left the Sadr office I realized I didn't have any shoes.

There were dozens of pairs of sandals outside the door.

"Take any one," Amir said. I slipped my feet into the first pair of sandals I saw. A man standing behind me suddenly became agitated. They were his sandals.

"Take them, take them," Amir urged, as he said something to the man in Arabic, trying to calm him down.

I took one last look around for Osama, then left with the man's sandals. As we drove by the river, I looked through the back window and noticed that a car was following us. We turned north and then immediately south over the bridge across the Euphrates. The car was still behind us. We pulled over just before the road that led out past the power plant toward Ur and the American base. A large, heavyset Iraqi man was waiting by the side of the road. Amir opened the back door and the man started to get in.

"Who is he, Amir?" I said, stopping him.

"Welcome back," the man getting in said cheerfully in English.

"Don't worry," Amir assured me. "He is a former student of mine and a translator for the Italian military."

The car that was following us had pulled over as well, about fifty feet back. I told our new companion about the car. He told us to wait and walked over, leaned in the window, and spoke to the driver. Soon he returned.

"Don't worry, they won't follow us."

"Who is it?" I asked.

"I don't know, but he says he knows you."

"If it's Osama, I am supposed to go with him to the American base." I looked back out the window again, but the car was pulling away.

"Don't worry," Amir said. "He will meet you at the American base."

The translator spoke to Amir in Arabic. Amir turned to me.

"He says the Italians have planned a surprise for you. There is a reception and the ambassador is there."

"Amir," I said quietly, "I don't want to go to the Italian base. Just take me to the Americans."

"No, believe me, it's fine. He says they have planned a big reception and then they will take you straight to the Americans. You will be on the American base anyway. You can just walk from the Italian base."

Halfway along the dark, empty road to the base our car pulled over. An Italian army GMC was parked on the opposite side with its lights off. The truck immediately swung around beside our car. The translator opened the door.

"Amir, listen to me, I don't want to go with the Italians," I protested.

"Don't worry, they have prepared a reception."

"Where are you going?"

"To see my family."

My ride ended there. We were separating after ten days together, and I was reluctant to part.

"Are you going to be okay?" I asked, worried about Amir's jaw and his safety.

"Yes, yes."

"Let's meet tomorrow."

"Not tomorrow, I will be with my family. The day after tomorrow."

"Okay. Take care, Amir." We both hugged, sad to be parting so quickly.

I climbed into the back of the GMC, and it took off toward the base.

"Welcome back. How are you?" one of the soldiers I recognized asked, concerned.

"I'm fine," I said cautiously.

"We have been looking for you. Are you feeling okay? Do you need to see a doctor?"

"No, thanks, I'm fine."

"Your fiancée was very concerned. Would you like to call her?" He handed me a satellite phone. I tried calling but could not get through.

"Don't worry, you can make a call at the base."

The GMC drove quickly past the American checkpoint and onto the Italian base. Within minutes we were parked outside General Dalzini's office. The Italian soldiers led me in past rows of eyes, an apparition dragged in from the desert night. I passed Captain Sarli, who smiled and said, "How are you? I'm happy you are back."

They brought me into a small, empty room next to the general's office and asked me to have a seat. There was no reception, no ambassador.

"Would you like some water?" an Italian soldier asked.

"Thanks," I said, trying to smile while getting my bearings. He handed me a cold bottle of clear, clean water, which I drank in fast gulps, followed by several more.

"Are you okay? Must have been a terrible experience. Let me get a doctor to look at you."

"Okay," I agreed. I wasn't sure what was going on, but a doctor seemed like a good start. I had lost about fifteen pounds in ten days and was dehydrated. As the empty moments wore on, waiting alone in General Dalzini's headquarters, I began to feel anxious. A doctor arrived and looked at me briefly.

"How are you feeling?"

"Fine," I said.

"Quite an ordeal," he continued, sitting in a chair across from me.

"Yeah. I'm okay, except for the mosquito bites." I pulled up my pants and showed him my raw feet covered in bites and scabs. He looked down for a moment, then back at me.

"There are no mosquitoes in Nasiriyah."

No mosquitoes in Nasiriyah? What was he talking about? I hadn't noticed many at the base, but malaria from mosquitoes and leishmanias, a parasite transmitted by sand flies, were both major health concerns for the troops.

"Well, there are lots of mosquitoes in the marshes," I said, but saw no point in arguing.

He appeared doubtful. "Well, you look okay," he said, and then went out, leaving me alone in the room.

I could tell something was going on, but they didn't seem to know how to approach me. Finally a soldier came in. I asked him if I could leave.

"Yes, of course, but we would like you to write a statement, if you don't mind," he said nervously, looking back at the door.

"What do you mean, a statement?"

"Well, there have been a lot of journalists saying that you were kid-napped because we made you leave the base. As you know, we did not kick you off the base, so we just would like you to write that and sign it."

"Wait a minute," I said, getting angry. "It was my decision to leave the base, but I am not going to sign anything right now."

"Just a simple statement," he said, pushing a blank piece of paper and a pen in front of me—my second coerced statement in three days.

He was growing agitated, as if under pressure to get this done quickly. I didn't know what to do. I didn't think they would let me leave without the statement. If writing some simple statement would allow me to get out of there, I decided I would do it. My only thought was regaining my freedom and contacting my family.

"Something simple," he said, clearly in a hurry for me to do it.

I wrote a short, purely factual two-sentence paragraph, but not saying that they did not ask me to leave. "I left Nasiriyah on . . . ," I wrote and signed the paper.

"I want a copy," I said, which he made and handed me, thanking me for the statement.

"We would like to take a picture of you with the general, if you don't mind," he said, escorting me to the door.

General Dalzini was in his office next door. Checking first, a soldier led me in. The general stood up and walked over to where I was standing by the door. He stood stiffly beside me and reached out his hand to shake mine, breaking into a smile as Captain Sarli started taking pictures.

As I stood there awkwardly shaking hands with General Dalzini, an American soldier appeared, rifle in hand, pistol strapped to his leg. He pushed past the Italian soldiers, looking displeased.

"You okay? We're going to get you out of here," he said, leading me away, looking in both directions. He turned and led me out the door quickly, parting the Italian soldiers as we went, several other American soldiers following us out.

"Thanks," I said as we emerged into the warm desert night.

"We are so glad to see you," he said. "How did you end up at the Ital-ian base?"

"I don't know," I replied, trying to remember the sequence of events that had led me to General Dalzini's office, explaining it as best I could. He shook his head in disbelief.

"We've been looking for you for two days. I am really glad to see you," he said again, beaming.

"How did you know I was here?"

"The Italians called and told us you were here. We'd been trying to get in for fifteen minutes."

"They wouldn't let you in?"

"No. We were getting pretty pissed. We finally pushed our way in. Welcome home," he added, handing me a folded American flag neatly tucked in a clear plastic bag.

The packed hotel room filled with our energy and anticipation, our hope unfurling.

The CNN report was the same one that had been looping all morning: release imminent.

Chantal and Aparna burst in, arms extended. "What, what is it?"

We all looked at one another, at the screen, at the phones, at the door, back at one another.

The door opened, and I saw Agent Tom's face as he leaned in. He gave us a thumbs-up.

"He's home," he said, smiling. Tears filled his eyes.

The words, spoken so simply and quietly, reverberated. Our joy exploded out of us, through the walls, spilling outside, everywhere. Micah was coming back to life, to us, to me.

We hugged each other, family, friends, and FBI. I couldn't stop hugging everyone. "Thank you, thank you for all your support," I repeated over and over.

"Don't thank us," Go-To Pete said. "It's our job. Any American citizen can expect our help."

As soon as the celebrations were over, the FBI quickly disappeared out the door, and were gone.

"I am an Army psychologist and I'm going to help you get through this. It is probably pretty confusing right now, but anything you need, just ask me. I am going to be your buffer, so no one gets to talk to you unless you want to. I'll make sure of that. You won't have any more of what just happened to you back at the Italian compound. Kidnapping is about losing control. You may have thought you were in control, but you weren't. You weren't in control in the Sadr office and you were not in control at the Italian camp. I am going to help you get control of your life back. From now on, you make the decisions. Everything is your call. Just let me know what you need."

It was after midnight. The helicopter that was supposed to whisk me away had left, and we had to wait until three A.M. for another.

"You don't mind, do you?" the army psychologist asked.

"No problem," I replied.

He was still grinning. "Man, it's just great to see you."

"I need to call my family."

"Let me get you a phone," he said and went off to find one.

Still holding the flag neatly folded in the clear plastic bag, my blindfold wrapped around my hand, I began to feel numb. I patted my shirt pocket to make sure the cover of the packet of cigarettes that said MH, ZEUG, LOVE was still there. My shiv was still in my pants pocket. I put the shiv and the blindfold in the bag with the folded flag and stood alone waiting, the other soldiers giving me space.

The army psychologist returned with a satellite phone. I was afraid to call, worried that I would hear bad news—that my parents had died of heartbreak.

Mitch signed on to instant messaging at 2:31 P.M. with Joel.

> *Mitch:* tequila shot being done.
> *Joel:* you and Osama are rock stars.
> *Mitch:* he's at the base.
> *Joel:* excellent. the eagle has landed. Mitch, can't thank you and Osama enough, you guys have been simply amazing.
> *Mitch:* the kebab is on the plate.
> *Joel:* nice!
> *Mitch:* just doing my job.

I closed my eyes and, in my heart, embraced everyone who had worked for Micah and Amir's safe return. Family members who had rallied together, friends, the journalistic community, no effort too small, constant and unflagging, amplified over time, each pressure point merging into a swell, carrying them finally to safety.

"They took the wrong guy," Sheryl laughed on the phone. "Don't mess with a photographer."

The tight-knit group of journalists working around the world had put everything on the line to look out for one of their own.

The emails began to pour in, and the calls, as Amanda returned with champagne. Amir's was one of the first, subject line "Set Free":

```
We are free after 12 days of brutal trip. I will
write more in the coming days of this everlasting
journey.
     Amir
```

Then my cell phone rang.

Standing alone in the desert night by the helicopter landing pad, the Special Forces team waiting inside, I nervously dialed my apartment in New York on the satellite phone. No one there. My mom's house. No one there. My dad's house. No one there. My anxiety increased with the growing emptiness on the other end of the line.

When I called Marie-Hélène's cell phone, a voice on the other end started screaming: "Micah? MICAH! MICAH! How are you, are you okay? Oh my God! Are you okay?"

The intensity of love I felt coming through the receiver over the stalled, crackling connection was overwhelming. I had to speak slowly, breathing deeply so I wouldn't cry.

"Micah, we love and we miss you!" Marie-Hélène? Eva? Chantal? I felt bad that I couldn't tell their voices apart as the phone was passed around; they all sounded like one voice.

Everyone was fine, they promised me when I asked about my parents; I shouldn't worry. I was so relieved we had all made it through alive.

My brother came on the line, his voice grounding for me.

"Wassup?" he said warmly.

"They got me," I said, joking as well, trying to assure him I was okay. If I still had my sense of humor, all was well. We were both reserved and not used to openly expressing our emotions, but I could clearly hear joy and relief in his voice—"Wow, oh man, I'm so happy," he repeated—as he made sure I was all right. He gave me the number to their "secret undisclosed location," and with my finger I traced the numbers in the dirt.

"Who was I just talking to?" I asked him. He told me Chantal had answered the phone, then Marie-Hélène, then Eva, then my mom.

Marie-Hélène came on the phone again; this time I recognized her voice. "Micah, Micah," she repeated over and over. My dream of returning to my life with Marie-Hélène and Zeugma was becoming real.

"I have a funny story to tell you," she continued, and related what An-drea Koppel at CNN had asked: "Does Marie-Hélène live on Christopher Street with her fiancé?"

It was her gentle way of telling me that the world thought we were en-gaged. I understood immediately, having learned about our "engage-ment" from the guard in the enclosure.

I had taken a shower, and this was the time.

"Well, you can tell Andrea Koppel that Marie-Hélène *does* live on Christopher Street with her fiancé," I said, smiling and nervous at my most unusual and unexpected satellite-phone proposal.

There was a pause.

"Really?" she said excitedly.

Really.

The Black Hawk arrived at three A.M. The seats had been removed, so I sat on a cooler and attached a clamp to my belt to tether me to the heli-copter, which lifted off slowly from the tarmac, and soon we were racing across a darkened landscape fifty feet above the ground. The helicopter flew low to avoid enemy gunfire, rising at the last minute over power lines, then gently sinking back down. Two soldiers and the army psy-chologist sat opposite me on the floor with their feet outstretched, Osama across from me by the other door.

The magnitude of what had just happened was beginning to sink in as I watched the dark ground unfold beneath me. I held my head in my hands for a while, then sat up and stared out the window.

America had not eaten its children, as the guard in the enclosure had bluntly suggested. I looked around the helicopter at the faces of a dozen soldiers lit by a faint green light. Did they understand what had hap-pened to me? Did I understand? Did I understand what they had been through? What my family had been through? I was standing at the precipice of something so large and profound, I could only sense its dark-ened edges.

I was beginning to see glimpses of how the shock waves of my jour-ney had reverberated out from the marshes—my family gathered to-gether in New York, my sister on international television, the Special

Forces team, my engagement. The immensity of it was dizzying, and humbling.

For ten days it had been our shared journey, Amir's and mine, a personal experience that we had endured together through patience and perseverance. But it was not just our experience; it was a shared experience that I would come to learn everyone was emotionally invested in. Amir and I owed our lives and our freedom to the love and hard work of our families, friends, and colleagues around the world.

EPILOGUE

I spent another week in Iraq in the Green Zone, where, with the help of the army psychologist and a very concerned Captain Duck, a member of the Hostage Working Group, my transition was smoothed back to reality.

"Was I in the news?" I asked the psychologist, still not knowing what had happened outside the enclosure.

"Well, we'll have to talk about that," he answered, carefully detailing just a few of the hundreds and hundreds of media stories about the kidnapping. In one week, the number of Google hits on my name had gone from 80 to more than 55,000.

An army optometrist gave me a new pair of glasses, the 1950s standard-issue large, brown plastic frames handed out to army recruits.

"They gave you BCGs?" Captain Duck laughed, using military shorthand for "birth control glasses" because their wearers never get dates. "No, no, those won't do."

Captain Duck and the army psychologist brought me back to the optometrist and tried to get a new pair, but the cool, silver aviator frames were only for aviators, not former hostages.

Days of drinking marsh water caught up with me during my stay in the Green Zone VIP quarters. Finding me sprawled on the bathroom floor, an even more concerned Captain Duck called in an army medic, who, equipped with a field kit, got me back on my feet with an IV and a bag of Cipro.

I had a brief, emotional reunion with Mr. Hamdani, Munawar, and Amir—who also had new glasses. Amir and Mr. Hamdani had made the dangerous four-hour ride from Nasiriyah to see me off. "I was afraid I had lost two friends," Mr. Hamdani said, shaking his head and hugging me. Amir held my hand, squeezing it tightly. "The road to Ur has been long. We will understand its meaning in the coming days." Looking over at my army escort, Munawar added with his deep-bellied laugh, "You're still not free, habibi!"

With two hundred dollars pocket money from Captain Duck and my Iraqi friend Suha, the trip home went smoothly, except for getting the plane ticket. I already had a return ticket, but the State Department travel agent noted that I had missed my flight. My only option was to purchase a new business-class ticket for twenty-two hundred dollars, but they didn't take credit cards. At the last minute, the State Department purchased the ticket for me, after I signed an IOU to the U.S. government for the cost of my flight home.

I returned to New York on August 27, met on the tarmac by Agents Tom and Pete, who drove me to a joyous reunion with Marie-Hélène, my family, and Zeugma. "You should have seen your family in action," Tom said with a huge smile. "Man, they're going to be happy to see you."

I stepped out of the van, fifteen pounds lighter, tucking my BCGs in my pocket, to many hugs, kisses, and licks. Eva, waiting by the window, rushed to the van and threw her arms around me, then Tom. I embraced my mom, Jon, and Dad, for the first time in a long time.

In a quiet moment with Marie-Hélène, I pulled out the Roseman cigarette cover that read MH, ZEUG, LOVE, and handed it to her myself.

Amir returned home to a great feast and celebration—three sheep slaughtered to honor his homecoming. Friends and neighbors came to the house to congratulate Amir's father on his son's safe return. Amir's jaw fully healed and he returned to work at his translation bureau. He is now happily married.

A week after Amir and I were released, the new civil guards began protecting Umma, and for two thousand dollars a month the looting at Umma was brought under control. Three months later, the trucks John Russell had requisitioned were finally brought from Baghdad to Nasiriyah, along with a new mobile Iraqi Archaeological Protection Force. Though an important first step, the looting of archaeological sites continues in southern Iraq.

In November, my twenty-two-hundred-dollar debt to the U.S. government was forgiven by the State Department because of my ordeal.

I formally proposed to Marie-Hélène by the water—this time a real surprise, with Zeugma at my side on a beautiful day in early September.

GLOSSARY

abaya: A long, usually black, garment worn in public by women in traditional Muslim society.

abudiyya: A type of lament sung in southern Iraq: a quatrain in local dialect using a classical poem with a rhyme scheme a-a-a-b, and the fourth line ending with the sound "iyya."

AK: A Russian-style assault riffle used widely around the world, also know as a Kalashnikov. The model AK-47 is the most popular variety.

Akkadian: The Akkadian empire ruled Mesopotamia in 2300 B.C. The Akkadian language, also known as Babylonian-Assyrian, was the spoken language in Mesopotamia in the third millennium B.C.

Al Arabiya: An Arabic language satellite news station based in Dubai founded in 2003.

Al Jazeera: A pan-Arab satellite television station based in Qatar founded in 1996 with twenty-four-hour news coverage.

Ana bisharbic: An Iraqi tribal saying used to ask for help that literally translates "I am in your mustache."

AP: The Associated Press: the oldest news gathering organization founded in 1848 serving thousands of newspaper, television, and radio stations around the world.

APTN: The Associated Press Television Network: the television arm of the Associated Press.

Babylon: The capital of the Babylonian empire in the 18th century B.C. located along the Euphrates river near Hillah, sixty miles south of Baghdad.

Carabinieri: An Italian paramilitary force with policing functions responsible for safeguarding cultural history in Italy.

CPJ: Committee to Protect Journalists: a nonprofit organization founded in 1981, based in New York City, established to promote press freedom and defend the rights of journalists.

cuneiform: The earliest form of writing invented in Mesopotamia in the third millennium B.C. using wedge shapes pressed in clay.

Dhi Qar: One of eighteen provinces in Iraq of which Nasiriyah is the capital.

dishdasha: A long robe frequently worn by men in rural Iraq.

diyya: Blood money. A concept in Iraq tribal society whereby an injury or death is settled through payment—usually cash or a female of the offending tribe.

dulaimi: An inexpensive hotel popular with journalists on a budget in the Karada district of central Baghdad.

Fajr: A small town between Nasiriyah and Kut known as a hub for the antiquities smuggling trade.

fixer: Someone with local connections who arranges meetings for journalists.

Freedom's Gate: A motif of a red door signifying freedom in the paintings of Kamal, a modern artist in Nasiriyah, and the name Micah gave to a possible escape route in the enclosure.

Green Zone: A heavily fortified four-square-mile compound in central Baghdad, the former Saddam palace and seat of government for the Baathist regime, now occupied by the Coalition, the interim Iraqi government, and the U.S. Embassy.

Hawza: A term that refers to a school of Islamic studies. The name, al-Hawza, refers both to the religious seminary in Najaf as well as the newspaper started by Muqtada al-Sadr in Baghdad. The "speaking hawza" is a school of Islamic thought that combines politics with religious practice. The "silent hawza" is a school of Islamic thought that maintains a separation between politics and religious practice.

hijab: A headscarf worn by women, often with an abaya. Also the practice of dressing modestly.

Husserl, Edmond: 1859–1938, Czech philosopher known as the father of phenomenology.

Inshah Allah: Arabic saying meaning "If God wills it."

Kalashnikov: A popular name for the AK assault rifle after the inventor Michael Kalashnikov.

keffiyeh: A headscarf that covers the head and face, often made of cotton with a black or red checkered pattern, worn throughout the Middle East, particularly in rural areas of Iraq.

Sheik Aws al-Khafaji: Head cleric for the Sadr office in Nasiriyah.

khubz: A traditional flat, round wheat bread made with yeast, popular in the Middle East.

madhif: A communal meeting hall traditionally built of reeds found in southern Iraq.

al-Mahdi: In Shi'ite tradition, al-Mahdi, the twelfth Imam born in A.D. 868, went into occultation at age five and is expected to return to earth one day to usher in an age of peace and justice.

Mahdi Army: A Shi'ite militia under the leadership of Muqtada al-Sadr.

Muqtada al-Sadr: A Shi'ite cleric opposed to the U.S. occupation of Iraq who hails from the "speaking school" of Islam, combining political rhetoric and spiritual teachings.

Najaf: Capital of Najaf province and a city of five hundred thousand people two hours south of Baghdad. Najaf is the location of the Shrine of Imam Ali, one of the holiest sites in Shi'a Islam.

Nasiriyah: Capital of Dhi Qar province and a city of five hundred thousand people along the Euphrates River in southern Iraq founded in 1870.

phenomenology: A school of philosophy that looks at the phenomena of subjective experience as a way to understand objective reality.

RSF: Reporters Sans Frontières, Reporters Without Borders, an international organization based in Paris focused on defending press freedom.

SAIS: Johns Hopkins School of Advanced International Studies in Washington, D.C.

SCIRI: The Supreme Council on Islamic Revolution: a Shi'ite organization based in Iraq, led by Mohammed Baqir al-Hakim before his assassination in Iraq on August 29, 2003.

Shi'a: A minority branch of Islam founded in A.D. 680. The term *Shi'ite* comes from Shiat Ali, meaning the followers of Ali, the Prophet Mohammed's cousin, whom Shi'ites believe was the rightful successor to the prophet. Unlike Sunni Muslims, who follow locally appointed Imams, Shi'ites have a hierarchical religious structure and follow just a few senior clerics, grand ayatollahs, educated at the Hawza in Najaf or the Hawza in Qum, Iran.

Shrine of Imam Ali: Located in Najaf, the site of the tomb of Imam Ali, cousin of the Prophet Mohammed, and, for Shi'ites, his successor.

Grand Ayatollah Ali al-Sistani: Born in 1930, the most revered Shi'ite spiritual leader in Iraq and based in Najaf.

Sumerian: One of the earliest known civilizations, based in southern Iraq in the fourth millennium B.C. The Sumerians invented writing.

Sunni: The largest branch of Islam comprising 90 percent of the world's Muslim population. The Sunnis ruled the Muslim world through the end of the Ottoman Empire.

Umma: An important Sumerian archaeological site in the desert two hours north of Nasiriyah. Under Lugalzagesi, Umma conquered Lagash in 2360 B.C., uniting Sumer for the first time before falling to Sargon of Akkad in 2334 B.C.

Ur: An ancient Sumerian city twenty minutes southwest of Nasiriyah famous as the site of the Ziggurat of Ur built by Ur Namu in the third millennium B.C. Also popularly known as Ur of the Chaldees from the biblical reference to the Chaldean settlement in 900 B.C., and as the birthplace of the Prophet Abraham.

Zakat: The third pillar of Islam—the purification of wealth through charitable giving.

ACKNOWLEDGMENTS

So pleased that your journalist has now been freed.
Get him back home.

—Just an old lady in the desert who is respectful
and concerned about all the journalists of the
planet.

It would take another book just to thank all the people who helped ensure Micah's and Amir's safe return home. We are forever grateful for your astounding work, fierce support, and unwavering faith. There are many people we would like to thank—those whom we know and those whom we are still learning about—who, because of modesty or circumstance, wish to remain anonymous. There are many people whose efforts we will never know about. To those "friends of friends," we honor your quiet concern and your selflessness.

We are grateful to everyone who prayed for Micah and Amir, individually, in prayer groups, monasteries, mosques, churches, Buddhist centers, especially the SGI Centers in New York and Bloomington, and other centers of worship, and the many relatives, neighbors, friends, and strangers who expressed their love and concern.

We extend our love and respect to our friends in Iraq. Amir Doshi, the poet-philosopher of Nasiriyah, who understands the meaning of friendship as much as he does Foucault. Abdul-Amir Hamdani, the bravest archaeologist we know. Munawar, with your wise words, you are invited to the wedding, habibi!

Thank you to Mr. Hamdani's and Amir's family, who saw us as part of their family, and to our friends in Nasiriyah, especially Governor Salah Rumaiaith and Deputy Governor Adnan al-Sharifi. Thank you to Sheik Ayad Jamal Uddin, as well as Imam al-Husainy. To those in Iraq who

spoke out on Micah's and Amir's behalf, and to all those in Iraq who con-
demn kidnapping.

A great many thanks to the Carr Foundation, Greg Carr, and Noble
Smith for caring about culture and believing in our vision, and for their
tremendous work during the kidnapping. To our many friends in Iraq
who helped with our documentary work, Amer, Sami, Fared, Kais, Abu
Fetah, Sheik Saleem, the wolf with the glasses, as well as Donny George,
shokran jazeelan. Warm thanks also to John Russell, Zaineb Bahrani, and
Kristi Clemens.

To the organizations who promote press freedom and step up to the
plate when a journalist is in trouble. Our immeasurable thanks to the
Committee to Protect Journalists, under the leadership of Ann Cooper
and Joel Simon. Never-ending thanks to Joel Campagna, Mitch Prothero,
and Osama Monsour, whose insights, connections, patience, and ability
to go without sleep for a week prove that you are indeed rock stars.
Thanks to Reporters Without Borders, especially Raphael Botiveau,
Lucie Morillon, and Tala Dowlatshashi; the Overseas Press Club; and
Sarah de Jong at the International News Safety Institute.

The journalist community, especially the freelance journalist community, whose commitment to their work and strong camaraderie we owe a
debt of gratitude. To those who dropped what they were doing and put
everything on the line without asking for anything in return—their contacts, their reputations, and in some cases even their lives—for one of
their own, we send our deepest, most heartfelt thanks.

Special thanks to John Burns for your immediate concern, support,
and well-written articles. James Longley, for the most efficient use of a
Thuraya. Sheryl Mendez, who burned up the phone lines. Rita Leistner
for taking the initiative. Gaith Abdul-Ahad for your persistence in Najaf.
And to Justin Adler, Chris Albritton, Jon Lee Anderson, Eric Bageot,
Francesco Battistini, Andrew Berends, Jane Burns, Massimo Calabresi,
Jill Caroll, Alina Cho, Francis DeBlauwe, Patrick Dillon, Dave Enders,
Gio Fazio, Rick Gladstone, Mark Gordon-James, Julia Guest, Talal and
Anita al-Haj, Scott Heidler, Katja Heinemann, Sara Khorshid, Katherine
Kiviat, M'hamed Krichene, Justin Lane, David Lewis, Natasha Lunn,
Matthew MacAllister, Agostino Mauriello, Hafez al-Mirazi, Jeff Purzan,
Tracy Purzan, Daniel Rosario, Elizabeth Rubin, Lauren Sandler, Paul
Shin, Joao Silva, Wendell Steavenson, Bob Sullivan, Dan Woo, Stefan
Zacklin. And to Andrea Koppel for asking the right question.

And to the media organizations, especially *The New York Times* and the New York Times office in Baghdad for providing so much help, CNN, the Associated Press, and the *Daily News,* and Al Arabiya for your kindness and compassion when we needed it most. Thank you to the media who respected our privacy, knowing that two lives were at risk

Our sincere gratitude to the humanitarian and relief organizations, including Medea Benjamin at Global Exchange, Mark Bartolini at the International Rescue Committee, Human Rights Watch, International Committee for the Red Cross, Médecins Sans Frontières, OXFAM, and Barbara Ayotte at Physicians for Human Rights. Many thanks to Alison Gardy and the 92nd Street YWHA. Sincere thanks to Alison Levy, who coordinated among all these groups.

To the Johns Hopkins School of Advanced International Studies (SAIS) graduate school network, who looked out for one of their own, even by extension, relentlessly putting their well-placed contacts at our disposal. We are grateful for your love and dedication: Maria Arwitz, Heather Bourbeau, Ruslan Chilov, Chris Chivvis, Britta Crandall, Russell Crandall, Jeff Dawson, Dean Engle, Daniel Ginsberg, Sumona Guha, Jennifer Haefeli, Michelle Jeong, Lisa Laudico, Sheri Levy, Alexis Martin, Aparna Mohan, Lawrence Petroni, Louise Schneider, Rob Sohn, Ned Steiner, Christine Stevens.

To the Pearl family, the depth of your compassion is beyond compare. Thank you for standing by us in so difficult a time. Special thanks to Terry Anderson for your advice and your honesty.

To the many friends and colleagues whose constant presence and countless acts of kindness were a tremendous support for our families, including: Isobel Allen-Floyd, Jennifer Anderson, Murat Armbruster, Carol Atwood, Andy Avillo, Giovanni Battistini, Adam Behrens, Kirsten Busch, Garrett Byrnes, E. Eugene Carter and Rita M. Rodriguez, Lynn Chu, Andria Coletta, David Corson and Lisa Trent, Shelby Denenberg, Kirk Dornbush, Jenny Einhorn, Amy Eldon, Dave Ellum, Lissa Engle and the Engle family, friends at Environmental Defense, Luba Evans and Howard Margulis, Alex Finkral, David Gochfeld, David Gurfein, Akiko Hagiwara, Lisa Handy, Jack Hidary, Derek Johnson, Jasmine Jopling, Liz Kalies, Patricia Klosky, David Konisky, Bill and Paulette Koningsberg, Schuyler Kraus, Philippe Lagadec, Tia Lessin, Chibli Mallat, Karen Manasfi, Massimo Marengo, Heather McCarthy, Melissa and Jonas McCray, Denis and Kari McDonough, Glenn McGinnis and Irene Schindler

McGinnis, Corey McIntosh, John McKenna, Sandy and Norman Methot, Piotr Michalowski, Cyrus Miller, the Mohan Family, Michael Moore, Kiernon Murphy, Corrine Nunley, Sigrid Peterson, Alexia Prichard and Michael Prichard, Courtney Pyle, Halla Qaddumi, Emily Record, Kristin Reed, Samantha Rothman, Mark Santo, Stefan Schmitz, Dan Senor, Cathy Sohn, Elizabeth and Jonas Svedlund, Rafael Torres, John Jr., Bonnie, and John III Van Slyke, Guido Wollmann.

Special thanks to the many organizations, institutions, and companies who helped, including: the Social Venture Network, especially Deborah Nelson and Pamela Chalout; Yale University, especially President Richard Levin; the Yale School of Forestry and Environmental Studies, especially Thilippe Amstislavskie, Mark Ashton, Elisabeth Barsa, Carol Carpenter, Tim Clark, Michael Dove, Emly McDiarmid, and Dean Speth; the Carnegie Council on Ethics and International Affairs; Shawn Panepinto and members of the Harvard Ceramics studio; and companies who gave time off to their employees so they could help us.

Our considerable thanks to the many individuals and offices of the U.S. government who helped: the FBI team in New York, who withstood our emotional assaults with grace and humor and didn't have to be told that Zeugma was part of the team; the U.S. Embassy in Baghdad, especially Bob Callahan and the Hostage Working Group. For the U.S. Special Forces ready to "bring Micah out" and the army psychologist who helped ease the transition. To strangers who became quick friends and advocates in the Green Zone, especially Captain Duck, who gave Micah a new pair of shoes and enough money to get home, and Suha Yacoub for her concern. Members of Congress, particularly Senator Joseph Lieberman and Senator Christopher Dodd and their offices, and local leaders including Mayor Cohen of Newton, Massachusetts. The Office of Former President Bill Clinton, especially Jim Kennedy; and to the French government for your understanding and support.

Our friends in the Italian forces in Nasiriyah for hosting us warmly, especially Air Force Lt. Col Angelo Gurrado, Major Frascinetto of the Carabinieri for his hard work to protect Iraq's history and efforts to win Micah and Amir's release. Corp. Marco Briganti, killed in Iraq on May 31, 2005, an Italian air force pilot whose love of flying was surpassed only by his love of culture and Mesopotamia history.

To the heart of "the blob," our ever-growing network of friends and family: Eva, whose first worldwide public television appearance was a true act of love. Chantal, whose response to that early morning call was a great source of strength, we could not have made it through without you. Suzanne for her calm, quiet strength and constant loving support. Jonathan, who along with Nieves and Tomas provided emotional support for our family. Alan for so eloquently expressing his belief in our work, and working so hard for Micah's safe return. Aparna Mohan for her energy that kept the blob together at all hours and her "spot on" media advice. Loren Nunley for his positive outlook and unshakeable belief in seeing Micah again. Nabila for embodying Iraqi friendship; when a friend asks for your help you cannot refuse. Sally Levy for her tremendous efforts day and night. Leslie Bakke for her generous spirit that was a refuge. Amanda Harmon for showing Zeugma as much love as we do. Tom Carpenter for being calm under pressure. David Bloom for loyal friendship. Glenna Park for tapping her broad spectrum of helpful contacts and liaising with our extended family. Giovanni Fazio for his efforts and support. Marie-Claire for teaching Marie-Hélène how to be strong and how to love. Tante Olivia for always looking on the bright side. Everrett Carleton, Marie-Hélène's father, much love. Sally Garen-Chapman and Heather Chapman for being with us. And our extended family: cousins, aunts, uncles, nephews, and nieces from Kansas to Rhode Island to Florida to California.

And to those who made telling this story possible, as much a journey for them as it was for us: ICM; Marvin Josephson for having the courage to travel to Iraq and his concern for archaeology; Richard Abate, our agent, who steered us, with empathy and aplomb, through the emotional waters; and Kate Lee.

To Simon & Schuster for helping us tell our story, especially David Rosenthal and Geoff Kloske, our editor, whose Job-like patience and gifted use of the blue pencil was a creative companion, Laura Perciasepe, and production editor Tricia Wygal.

Our many editors and readers: Mitch Zuckoff, Chantal Carleton, Lisa Cornelio, Suzanne Garen-Fazio, Aparna Mohan, Rory Stewart, Eva Garen, Marie-Claire Carleton, Jon Garen, Nieves Jamart-Garen, and Alan Garen. Thanks to the dozens of people who spent hours recollecting with us, to help our memory and understanding of those ten days. And to Jim Laakso for transcribing those emotional memories with speed and discretion.

The MacDowell Colony; John and Bonnie Van Slyke; Lisa Cornelio, Leslie Bakke, Giovanni Fazio, and Suzanne Garen-Fazio for providing us the mental and physical space to write this book. No one hears you scream in the woods.

And finally, to our families for rising up to face such a difficult ordeal with love, strength, and dignity. We owe you a debt of gratitude for your continued kindness, understanding, and support.

Our thoughts go out to those hostages still held in Iraq, and the families of hostages who never returned home.

ABOUT THE AUTHORS

Marie-Hélène and Micah are writers, photographers, and filmmakers. They live in New York City with their dog, Zeugma.

To learn more about Micah and Marie-Hélène, visit their website at fourcornersmedia.net.

Printed in the United States
By Bookmasters